Administrative Excellence

Revolutionizing Our Value in the Workplace

By
Erin O'Hara Meyer, PHR

Beaver's Pond Press, Inc.

ISBN 1-59298-105-4
Printed in the United States of America
Library of Congress Control Number: 2005923055

Book Design by Ronna Hammer, Design53, St. Paul, MN
Cover photograph old: Property of AT&T Archives, reprinted with
permission of AT&T.
Cover photograph contemporary: © Image Source/Alamy

First Printing: April 2005
09 08 07 06   6 5 4 3

Beaver's Pond Press, Inc.

7104 Ohms Lane, Suite 216
Edina, MN 55439
(952) 829-8818
www.beaverspondpress.com

To order, visit www.BookHouseFulfillment.com
or call 1-800-901-3480. Reseller discounts available.

This book is dedicated to:

My Father
Thomas J. O'Hara
1928-2004
A Successful Businessman
A Quiet Leader

My Mother
Betty Y. O'Hara
A Strong and Determined Woman
A Visionary Thinker

My Husband
Steve Meyer
A Calm and Stable Force
An Encouraging and Dedicated Partner

Table of Contents

Forward vii
Historical Perspectives ix
Message to Administrative Professionals xi
Introduction xv
Defining Administrative Excellence xxv

Part I
Administrative Excellence

Chapter I   Perception 3
Chapter II   Purpose 21
Chapter III   Progress 33
Chapter IV   Partnership 51
Chapter V   Professionalism 63
Chapter VI   The **Five Ps**: A Model of Administrative Excellence 77

Part II
Revolutionizing Our Value in the Workplace

Chapter VII   Leadership 85
Chapter VIII   Empowerment 95
Chapter IX   Growth 113
Chapter X   A LEG to Stand On 137

Part III
Conclusion

Chapter XI   New Beginnings 141

Bibliography 147
Acknowledgments 149
About the Author 151

Forward

When I first met Erin O'Hara Meyer in 2001, she was accepting the International Association of Administrative Professionals' Award for Excellence on behalf of her employer, Ryan Companies, for their outstanding administrative professional development plan. I knew that Erin was not only a champion for the administrative profession, but a person with rare and probative insight. I'm sure that having been an administrative professional for 15 years, in the early part of her career, provided valuable first-hand observations. Moving into a Human Resources position and overseeing the organization's administrative area added to her understanding of the partnerships that are necessary for "admins" and managers to empower each other. Her ability to focus on the issues underlying day-by-day team productivity in the workplace, the achievement of ultimate professionalism over the course of one's career, and the progression of the administrative profession over time and into the future is indeed far-reaching and inspirational. I can't think of a better individual whose life has vortexed into the "perfect storm" to discuss the role and revolution of today's administrative assistant.

Over the last 20 years, serving as the Manager of Education and Professional Development for the International Association for Administrative Professionals® (IAAP®), I've watched the role of support staff move from clerks to secretaries to administrative assistants to project managers to technology specialists who coordinate the flow of communication and information. What used to be one-on-one focus has turned into global interactions, in synchronous and asynchronous time, in three-dimensional and virtual space. And along with these phenomenal changes, I've watched many administrative professionals achieve recognition and compensation that is in direct proportion to their contributions. I've seen what can happen when a group of dedicated individuals take control over their professional destinies and expand their responsibilities and increase their value to the organizations that employ them.

I laud Erin's direct and engaging style in *Administrative Excellence: Revolutionizing Our Value in the Workplace*. She relies on her experience with human nature and workplace hierarchies. She forges workable, dynamic plans that use the administrative professional's repertoire of skills, including the honing of new skills, as technology and business economies continue to reshape the landscape.

With the administrative profession encompassing one of the largest segments of the workforce, by focusing on their training, development, and inclusion, individuals and companies will reap the benefits of a highly competent and evolving staff. Administrative professionals who apply the suggestions and follow the vision presented within these pages are sure to achieve the respect and personal satisfaction they desire. Organizations that incorporate these tenets and processes are guaranteed to enhance their productivity, increase employee satisfaction, and gain the admiration and distinct positioning they deserve.

Susan Fenner PhD
Education and Professional Development Manager
International Association of Administrative Professionals
www.iaap-hq.org

Historical Perspectives

"A teacher of stenography told me he believes nineteen out of twenty study stenography with an eye single to broadening their field for husband hunting."

> Pauline Pry, "The Earth is Theirs,"
> *Daily Globe*, St. Paul, Minnesota, 1888

"We make no requirements. If they can handle the work, we don't care about their education. If they cannot, we make a change."

> M.C. Elmer, quoting a supervisor of clerical and secretarial staff, *A Study of Women in Clerical and Secretarial Work in Minneapolis, Minnesota*, Minneapolis, MN: Women's Occupational Bureau, 1925, p. 29

"Experienced girl for clerical work. Must be good at figures."

> An employment advertisement, *Star Tribune*, Minneapolis, Minnesota, 1940

"Many secretaries achieve their executive secretarial status by working for a man who moves ahead."

> Esther R. Becker, *How to be an Effective Executive Secretary*, New York, NY: Harper & Row Publishers, 1962, p. 9

"An office should always have the appearance of being thoroughly clean. Never permit it to become dusty or cluttered up. Such a condition looks old-fashioned. Modern desks are clean, files clean, rooms clean. Every desk should be dusted every morning. If necessary, desks should be dusted again at noon. Do not resent dusting—it's a part of the job."

> Lois Hutchinson, *Standard Secretarial Handbook*, New York, NY: McGraw-Hill, Inc., 1979, p. 472

"If you're planning to use an entry-level position as a springboard for higher aspirations, take care where you start. In some companies, an assistant is still dimly viewed as a coffee-fetching robot who is unqualified to be promoted or simply uninterested in advancement."

> Fawn Fitter, "Why Not be a Secretary?"
> *Cosmopolitan*, August 1995, pgs. 121-122

"I believe that many times administrative professionals are not given the credit we deserve and that in turn limits the opportunities for us to shine. If I had one wish, it would be to elevate the position of administrative assistant and associated support staff so that we can have greater opportunity for growth and, as a result, experience greater personal satisfaction and increased job satisfaction."

> Lisa Oliver, Administrative Professional,
> e-mail correspondence to author, 2003

TO: AdminProfessionals.com

FROM: erin@adminexcellence.com

RE: Administrative Work – A Valued Profession?

DATE: April, 2005

"There are two ways of meeting difficulties. You alter the difficulties or you alter yourself to meet them."

Phyllis Bottome

I write this book for you, administrative professionals who strive for excellence and seek greater appreciation of your work. Perhaps you are called an administrative assistant, executive assistant, secretary, receptionist, or office manager. Your title is less important than the work you do. Your role as an administrative professional is crucial to the success of your organization. You are a vital contributor to your team, department, or manager. You are continually challenged to learn and expand your knowledge, to stay in control of chaotic office environments, and to keep abreast of the latest technology. Your ability to perform your job effectively takes skill, competence, and expertise.

So why then, with such demanding expectations, do many workplaces still marginalize the role of the administrative professional (AP)? I happen to know that the very people you support often overlook your value. Lack of communication, limited feedback, and little recognition are commonplace for many APs. Many managers only distantly see the connection between your contributions and their specific success. I am also aware that some of you devalue your own contributions by diminishing yourself, your responsibilities, and your importance to the organization. These are destructive thoughts that directly devalue the profession and sabotage your personal success as an AP.

You see, like you, I am an administrative professional. I understand the significance of what you do in support of corporate goals and objectives. Although I no longer perform "hands-on" administrative work, I worked as an AP for fifteen years. Through hard work and continued growth, I became for several years a Human Resources (HR) manager dedicated to the administrative area of an organization. A significant part of my daily responsibilities included staffing, coaching, maintaining employee relations, and managing performance of APs. As an HR manager, I helped to create an award-winning professional development plan for administrative associates. With over twenty years of relevant experience, I chose to leave my corporate career to become a trainer and consultant with an expertise in administrative staff development. I now work with APs around the world to help them unearth their potential and learn the required skills to manage their careers more effectively.

My interest in the administrative profession began early. I can remember as a six year old being fascinated with the organizational ability of my grade school nurse. Like many grade school kids, each year we would go single file to the nurse's office for our annual vaccines. I wasn't interested in the medical supplies that surrounded me or apprehensive about the impending shot in the arm. I was intrigued with the systematic and controlled approach the nurse used to manage this task. As the students would enter her office, she would select their respective file from the color-coded, alphabetized assortment of files on her desk and administer their shots accordingly. She made it look easy. She was quick and efficient, but more impressive was the power she wielded through her coordinated effort. There was no doubt that she was in charge. I knew then that when I grew up, I too wanted to be in control of a system and exhibit the same sense of power in performing my responsibilities. I wanted to handle paperwork as seamlessly and as confidently as she did. I wanted to be a secretary, as we were all called in the late 1960s.

I did exactly that. I pursued my career interest through the applicable high school classes and then completed my formal education with a two-year secretarial degree. I began my career as a typist in a typing pool. Twenty-three years later I was an Assistant Director of Human Resources. Over the course of my career, I held a number of administrative positions: secretary, executive assistant, office manager, and director of administrative employment.

I have hired, managed, coached, and mentored hundreds of administrative employees during my career. I have networked with many more through professional associations and educational forums. I have trained and developed even more. I have a passion to help APs grow.

I know this profession, the roles, and the responsibilities. Regardless of your title, I know your situation and can relate to the rewards and frustrations you experience as an AP. I know personally how to succeed as an AP, but most importantly I know what has made others succeed in these challenging positions.

Why, however, do many others perceive so little value in our profession? Why are APs overlooked and undervalued in several organizations? Why do many APs belittle their own jobs and their own organizational value? Why do "secretarial stereotypes" from the past century still invade the thinking in twenty-first century workplaces? What is clear is that these limiting attitudes, whether they belong to our employers or to us, stifle our growth and potential.

Social anthropologist Margaret Mead once said, "Never doubt that a small group of thoughtful, committed citizens can change the world; indeed, it is the only thing that ever has." Change always starts somewhere. Why not with you?

You understand the importance of what we do. You understand the need for our training and education and the need for greater respect of the profession. Each day you have opportunities to make a difference within your own working environment.

It doesn't matter if we work in small offices or internationally recognized corporations. All APs bear responsibilities and enjoy opportunities to work towards a better personal and professional future. No one else can or will do it for us.

If you are willing to take some risks and push yourself to new heights, you can make a difference in your workplace and in your life. As the epigram at the beginning of the chapter suggests, you either alter the difficulty or you alter yourself to meet the difficulty. Our difficulty is the perception of our profession and the value placed on it. As APs in the forefront of a new century, we can challenge this difficulty with new thoughts, behaviors, and actions, thereby altering ourselves to meet our difficulty.

This book will tell you what you need to know to make a difference. I assure you that nothing in it is extreme or will jeopardize your job. The changes that need to happen are subtle. The risks are personal and you decide which risks you are willing to take. Small changes can reap big benefits. The opportunities are abundant.

This book is based on my experiences. I have written it to help you discover your strengths, build your confidence, and gain the skills and knowledge necessary to achieve three goals:
1. To succeed as an AP by achieving administrative excellence.
2. To earn the personal and professional respect of those you support.
3. To change impressions in your workplace so that your value and professional contributions are better appreciated.

These three things will have an impact on our profession and how, as APs, we are perceived in today's office environment.

As you embark on a journey to *Administrative Excellence,* I wish you well. If you embrace the ideas suggested in this book, I wish you success in *Revolutionizing Our Value in the Workplace.*

Introduction

> *"If society will not admit of women's free development, then society must be remodeled."*
>
> Elizabeth Blackwell

For over one hundred years, the administrative professional has been the steadfast, silent business partner to busy executives, successful company owners, productive manufacturers, and complex governmental entities. Our contributions keep the processes flowing and the communication current. We are essential. Organizations and managers cannot move their products and services out the door without us. We have tirelessly taken on ever-greater responsibilities. Downsizing demands even more of us. However, our efforts remain largely invisible to organizations. The reason for this can be traced to our professional past.

Our Administrative Roots

APs entered the American workforce in the late 1870s with the invention of the typewriter. Middle-class women, having nimble fingers and good dexterity from years of piano lessons, were thought to be the ideal candidates for typist positions.

The 1880s brought to the workplace a need for switchboard operators, the pioneers of today's receptionists. These operators were often referred to as "hello girls" by 19th century businesses and their customers. Although this was an innocent, deferential expression, it also clearly indicated early administrative stereotypes.

Prior to the invention of the typewriter and switchboard, office work was performed by young men eager to move up the organizational ladder to career success. The industrial revolution in the 1870s-1880s expanded technology and provided the opportunity for many of these men to fulfill their career aspirations as business managers. As a result, women replaced men in performing day-to-day office functions.

Many people thought these office tasks were good job opportunities for women. In post-civil war times, office work was considered a prestigious alternative to the domestic service or manufacturing work readily available to females. However, most women sought these job opportunities because they faced unfortunate personal circumstances. In Victorian-era society, the majority of women that worked, worked as a means to survive, not to satisfy career aspirations. These distressed women were willing to work for less money than their male counterparts. In this transitional period, administrative work became a "job" for women rather than a "career" for men.

It was at this time that business schools sprang up to prepare women for the demands of modern-day office work. Once employed, their working conditions were often crude and challenging. Not only did they experience poor lighting and ventilation; unsafe, rudimentary office equipment; low wages and long hours; they also had to contend with the biases of male supervisors. A journalist from the *St. Paul Globe* (St. Paul, MN) researching women in the workplace in 1888 found that "one girl – mighty pretty she is – told me that she often has nothing to do for three days at a time, and when she suggested to her employer that she was a superfluity, he assured her it was worth double her wages to see her about the office. So she continues to draw her little $50 a month and look pretty."

Office work, perceived as viable work for men in the mid-19th century, was quickly demeaned as trivial "women's work" by the 1880s. The introduction of the time clock in 1910 reduced the status of the female office worker even further and paralleled her value to that of a semi-skilled factory worker.

By 1930 stenographers and typists were 91.8% female. Today, of the four million people employed as APs in the United States, 98% are women.* This dramatic gender change created assumptions.

The manager in the mid-1800s who worked hard to find a management opportunity for his promising male assistant evolved to a manager in the mid-1900s who assumed that his female assistant had no career aspirations other than to perform her role in support of his ambitions. This manager saw his assistant as the dutiful secretary, interested only in doing her job. The successful secretary of the 1950s knew her place and performed her responsibilities accordingly. Her personal power was defined by the positional power of her "boss."

The following excerpt, describing the time management expectations of an accomplished assistant, appears in the 1960s executive secretarial handbook, *How to be an Effective Executive Secretary,* Esther R. Becker, (Harper & Row Publishers, New York, 1962).

> "PROTECTS executive from unnecessary interruptions: PREVENTS conflicting engagements; ANTICIPATES his needs and PROVIDES him with maximum opportunity for creative work and the exercise of his functions.
>
> Conserves superior's time by assuming as much of the detail as is practicable.
>
> Will be under constant pressure meeting deadlines; but will be able to keep caught up; will be allowed to hire part-time help as needed.
>
> Must have ability to organize a large volume of correspondence, coupled with a large number of telephone calls, in such a way that the Chief Executive receives only those things that he should personally deal with.
>
> It is within the power of the executive secretary occupying this position to save the time and energy of the President. The extent to which she can do this depends very largely on her sensitivity and intelligence."

---

*For this reason this book references the AP as "she" or "her." This is not intended to overlook or diminish the valuable contributions of male APs, but to speak to the majority of readers.

This excerpt shows a well-defined hierarchical relationship between the male manager and the female assistant, emphasizing the assistant's subordinate role in supporting the manager's career goals. At this point in history the term "corporate wife" was occasionally used "tongue-in-cheek" to describe the role of the executive secretary. By the early 1970s lower-level administrative employees working in the "steno pools" were derogatorily referred to as being part of the "secretarial or pink collar ghetto." The later expression used to refer to a working environment or profession that was female-oriented with no upward mobility.

These are the underlying societal attitudes that perpetuate a bias of the profession and impact our perceived value in today's workplace.

I realize some organizations do value their APs. I also realize some managers view their assistant as a business partner rather than as a subordinate. However, I suspect that many more organizations and managers take for granted the contributions of the administrative support staff.

I once had an AP share a painful story. She approached her Human Resources manager with a request to implement a training program for the administrative staff within her organization. The HR manager replied, "We're not doing that. You're just secretaries." This conversation sent an unforgettable message about the small value her organization placed on APs.

Are APs Appreciated at Your Office?

The argument that APs are undervalued and overlooked is reinforced by an April, 2004 survey conducted on the website of Monster.com. The site posted a survey asking the question, "Are administrative professionals appreciated at your office?" Results from the 7,137 people who responded were disappointing:

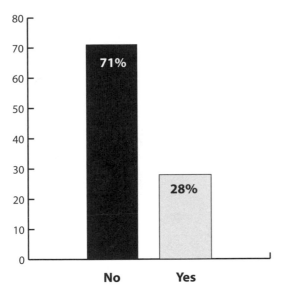

Fig. Intro-1 Monster.com Survey

Seventy-one percent said, "No, they're a vital but *overlooked* part of our organization."

Twenty-eight percent said, "Yes, we *value* their hard work every day." The same survey question from April, 2002 showed similar results. As an administrative professional, I find these results inexcusable and view them as a call to action.

Whether we work in large corporations or small companies, public agencies or private industry, we can influence the perceptions that exist and begin to eliminate the residual stereotypes of the past. We can accomplish this change by sparking a mindset shift in our organizations.

The Encumbered AP Staff

Figure Intro-2 below visually represents organizations that overlook their administrative support staff. This model may reflect the 71% of organizations identified by the Monster.com survey.

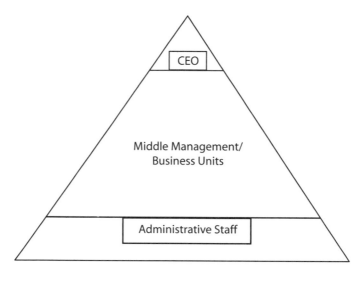

Fig. Intro-2
The "Encumbered" AP Staff

I refer to this model as the "encumbered" AP staff. To encumber means to hinder or impede the action or performance of something or someone. This model suggests that the organization views the administrative support staff as foundational, behind-the-scenes employees. Organizational charts typically follow this top-down format, keeping the hierarchical approach to business ingrained in our corporate cultures and entrenched in our psyches. Most of us have adjusted and adapted to the hierarchical, organizational structure in our work lives.

In the encumbered model the company leadership sits at the top of the organization. Decisions flow downward. In the middle of the organization sit all of the core operational units and support departments.

These groups produce the product or provide the services that generate revenue for the company or support the organization by adding value to customers. At the foundation of this model is the reliable, unfaltering administrative support staff.

This model instills in managers' minds the assumption that we will always be there, waiting to pick up the pieces, to get the work done, and to handle whatever falls our way. This model also suggests that we are a detached member of the team, perhaps not as important as our associates because of the status or functions of our jobs. This model clearly places our value at the bottom of the organization, as an afterthought to achieving corporate goals. The overriding principle of this model is *"Here's what we, the managers, need you to do,"* and it puts APs in the position of waiting for direction.

Such thinking by management causes many APs to believe "we're just secretaries, we're not important, we just work here, no one listens to us." These disparaging thoughts often become self-fulfilling prophecies. This kind of thinking also attacks self-esteem, negatively affects performance, and diminishes any hopes APs might have for personal growth and professional development.

Some of you may be asking, "What's wrong with being the foundational employee? It's an important role. We hold the organization together." I couldn't agree more. Yet we should not remain forgotten, overlooked, undervalued employees because of outdated and uninformed beliefs.

The Empowered AP Staff

Now let's look at the same administrative staff and shift our thoughts to an empowered model. This model may reflect the 28% of organizations in the Monster.com survey that value administrative staff. In this model CEOs and top management remain at the helm. They direct and lead our organizations. Their vision drives the success of the organization. The core functions of the business remain intact as well.

Yet, here's the significant change: Instead of seeing APs as the foundational behind-the-scenes employees, we are now seen as front-line employees. This simple adjustment in thinking produces vastly different results *(see Figure Intro-3).*

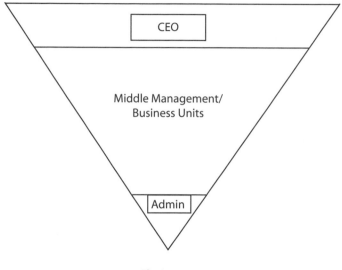

Fig. Intro-3
The "Empowered" AP Staff

In this model the AP is viewed as the conduit, the crucial link, between the internal operations of the organization and external customers or clients. This model recognizes that APs perform the tasks that keep the wheels of the operation rolling and touch the vast majority of projects before they go out the door. The AP is seen as central to the flow of work. Our perceived value increases tremendously as managers recognize our vital contributions to projects. Such recognition positions us for partnership, alignment, influence, and increased productivity. Such a model underscores our direct impact on customer service, corporate image, deadlines, and profitability. The guiding principle of this model is, *"What can we, the managers, do to help you do your job better? How can we help you help us?"* In this way we become empowered, integrated, and valued team members.

We explore both of these corporate cultures in more detail in later chapters. I share them with you now to ignite your thinking. Consider your current situation: Which corporate culture more accurately reflects your working environment?

If you find yourself performing your responsibilities as an "encumbered" AP, then you can choose to live with your circumstances and accept that "it's just the way it is," or you can decide to take a stand to make a difference. If you are fortunate enough to be part of an "empowered" AP culture, then I encourage you to maximize your good fortune by sharing new thoughts and ideas learned in the book with your manager to gain even greater professional respect.

Regardless of your circumstance, you can help your manager see your value by taking thoughtful and purposeful action. After all, they need you. That need places you in a very important and influential position. You can't leave this recognition to chance. You greatly influence how this value gets communicated to your manager.

John D. Rockefeller said it best when he acknowledged the importance of the employer-employee partnership:

"I have long been profoundly convinced that in the very nature of things,

employers and employees are partners, not enemies;

that their interests are common not opposed;

that in the long run the success of each is

dependent upon the success of the other."

No longer should we place blame on stereotypes and biases, or the limiting attitudes of managers or APs. The cycle of AP devaluation needs to be interrupted and realigned in partnership with our managers. This book emphasizes the importance of the management-administrative relationship in achieving success.

You are the Spark for Change

Change begins with you and your dedication to your administrative career. You will find this book beneficial if you are:
1. Interested in personal and professional development.
2. Eager for job enrichment and expanded responsibility.
3. Seeking respect and value in the workplace.
4. Willing to take calculated risks and push comfort zones to affect change.

This book will help you whether your primary interest is personal and professional development or increasing the value of the profession in your workplace. This book shares new skills and ideas. It includes numerous exercises and opportunities to stimulate your thinking. You will become more confident and more effective as you challenge yourself and work through potential obstacles of achievement. As you continue to learn and take on new responsibilities, you become more valuable to your manager and more indispensable to your organization.

Together, as a profession, we can position ourselves to promote our intrinsic value and gain visibility in today's corporate environments. In the next chapter you will learn how administrative excellence is the catalyst to your career success and the basis of a better future for our profession.

Defining Administrative Excellence

> *"The secret of joy in work is contained in one word –*
> *excellence. To know how to do something well is to enjoy it!"*
>
> Pearl S. Buck

A s APs our job functions can be divided into two primary skill sets: technical skills and people skills. Technical skills refer to things like the knowledge and understanding of office equipment, the proficient use of software programs, and the ability to organize data or effectively proofread documents. These skills are also referred to as hard skills and, as such, include tasks that are easily measurable or quantifiable. People skills, on the other hand, refer to our ability to get along with others, effective communication, teamwork, and establishing strong relationships. These skills are called soft skills and include such things as initiative, attitude, and flexibility. Soft skills are more observable than measurable.

When people ask me how I define administrative excellence I say, "It is the seamless blend of the hard skills and the soft skills that are required of all APs to perform their jobs effectively." We achieve maximum performance when we become adept at balancing and simultaneously applying these two sets of skills to produce results. This may sound simplistic, but it is far from simple. Research shows that 75% of derailed careers went off track because of poor soft skills. Soft skills are harder for people to grasp and apply because they require introspection and ownership of personal behaviors. Lack of hard skills, however, can often be remedied with specific training or instruction. Roger Enrico, former vice chairman of Pepsico, once said, "The soft stuff is always harder than the hard stuff."

In my experience as a manager, I too recognized that many people struggle with the soft skills required by their jobs more often than the technical skills. This book focuses on improving the soft skills necessary to achieve administrative excellence.

The "Five Ps" of Administrative Excellence

In my management role, I came to realize that competent APs combine solid technical skills with excellence in five specific areas:

1. **P**erception – self-awareness of behaviors and skills that maximize strengths and minimize weaknesses.

2. **P**urpose – understanding the importance of job responsibilities and identifying with the overall objectives of the team, department, and organization.

3. **P**rogress – ability to think progressively for continuous personal and professional improvement.

4. **P**artnership – willingness and ability to foster good relationships and teamwork with co-workers, managers, and customers.

5. **P**rofessionalism – high standards of appearance, personal conduct, work product, and expertise.

These are the **"Five Ps"** of administrative excellence. Practicing and exhibiting them will strengthen your performance, earn you respect, and formulate a *Model of Administrative Excellence, (Figure AE-1).*

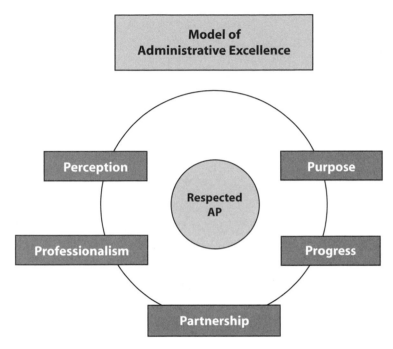

Fig. AE-1

I find that if any one of these five areas is weak or out of balance, then your overall performance will suffer. As an example, I once knew an AP who was very technically proficient, but also a chronic complainer. This complaining affected how co-workers regarded her and her role. They tended to avoid her and dismiss her opinions and concerns, thus preventing her from forming effective partnerships. This one shortcoming held her back and prohibited her from achieving a reputation of excellence and from earning respect as an AP.

Chapters I-V offer insight to each of the **"Five Ps."** Each of these chapters will help you learn the necessary skills to manage your own career most effectively.

The Path to Success

"You get out of it what you put into it." We've all heard the claim. The expression applies to administrative careers. Our performance (input) determines the level of excellence we achieve. Our level of excellence determines our value (output) to our manager. As we create and add value, we become more important to our manager and our organization. This professional success ignites our personal success.

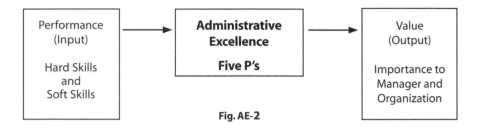

Fig. AE-2

You will likely gain leadership, empowerment, and growth from following this path to success:

1. **Leadership** skills that enhance performance and firmly establish your reputation of administrative excellence.

2. **Empowerment** as a valued team member and recognized contributor to organizational success.

3. **Growth** and job enrichment opportunities that elevate job satisfaction.

Leadership, empowerment, and growth are the result of top-notch performance and are the essence of changing the perception of the administrative profession.

The Cycle of Administrative Success

When combined, leadership, empowerment, and growth form a *Cycle of Administrative Success (Figure AE-3)*. Each gains momentum and builds off of the other to create professional stamina. As you exhibit leadership skills, you gain empowerment and you grow professionally. As you continue to grow, you become a stronger, more influential leader with increased empowerment. Thus, the cycle continues and you revolutionize not only your value in the workplace, but our value as a profession.

Fig. AE-3

An Administrative Role Model

This cycle of success is nicely demonstrated by an executive assistant at an international technology company. At a strategic planning initiative, her organization was identifying "key employees" in the company. Key employees were considered those individuals that were instrumental to the long-term success of the organization. A list of key employees was compiled, and as the assistant to the president, it was her responsibility to prepare and distribute this document. She was disheartened to find that she had not been identified as a key employee. She felt this was unfair in that she had several years of progressive experience with the company and played a crucial role in helping the president achieve organizational results. As uncomfortable as it was for her, she took the initiative (**leadership**) to speak directly to her manager, the president, about her concern. In their discussions, he agreed that she was right. He determined she did play an integral role in the organization and should be viewed as "key" to organizational success. He then asked her to take a lead role (**empowerment**) in another new corporate initiative, Six Sigma. In this role, she needed to spearhead **(growth)** a joint-training program with their Asian office. As an additional responsibility, this training initiative would require a trip to Thailand to coordinate and participate in the training activities.

This one event—speaking to her manager about a concern—created a cycle of administrative success. By addressing the situation, she achieved "key employee" status and became more confident and assured in her role as an AP. As she takes on new challenges, she experiences increasing job satisfaction through expanded responsibilities and job growth. These are mutual rewards beneficial both to her and her manager. Her leadership, empowerment, and growth revolutionized her value in the workplace.

All of that happened because this AP took a risk. Her deliberate action affected change by provoking a mindset shift for her manager. Beyond her own success, however, is a victory for the administrative profession because an AP is now viewed as a key employee in this particular organization. *Her* increased value increases the value of *our* profession in her workplace. No longer are her contributions as an AP overlooked, undervalued, or invisible to her manager. When the key employees meet, she attends.

You can manage your own administrative career by employing these same tactics for professional respect, job enrichment, and personal accomplishment. Leadership, empowerment, and growth offer a formula for your success. Part II of this book will focus on these important elements of success.

Why Should I Aspire to Administrative Excellence?

It is important to understand that leadership, empowerment, and growth are not entitlements that come with seniority or longevity. To achieve them you must aspire to excellence and learn to apply the skills and abilities that engage them. You obtain them through initiative and decisive action. These are choices. Choose them and you choose to make a difference in your worklife.

I expect some of you to have underlying suspicions about the value of these efforts. You may think, "Why should I put this much effort into my job?" Others may think:

"This sounds like too much work."

"I'm not sure my manager would notice excellent performance."

"My company is just as likely to outsource my department as recognize my worth."

I can understand your resistance or reluctance. Perhaps you lost loyalty to all managers and organizations. Maybe you were a casualty of downsizing or unethical business practices. If so, I understand your skepticism—and your anger. It's enraging and discouraging to be a victim. Your morale suffers. But almost every book of advice on adversity encourages you to move from victim to survivor by taking charge of your reactions and decisions. That's what I am encouraging you to do here.

I am not encouraging you to become single-mindedly devoted to your job. You have a life filled with other demands, priorities, and interests after all. Rather, I'm suggesting that you become more single-mindedly devoted to *your* career, *your* professional role, and *your* talents. Take control by taking charge of yourself. Everything you read and learn in this book is a transferable skill or behavior. In other words, you can pack them up and take them with you to another employer, one who notices excellence and who encourages corporate success by encouraging your success. No one wants to work for someone or some company that promotes corporate success at the expense of staff and morale. Think of yourself like a flight attendant wheeling your belongings and skills through the terminal toward the next flight. Maybe you'll "fly" with your current work crew, maybe you won't. No matter, you'll be soaring.

I'm making you a win-win, you-can't-lose proposition. You only have something to gain from performing in the ways I outline in this book. Embracing the **Five Ps** of administrative excellence, **Perception, Purpose, Progress, Partnership,** and **Professionalism,** will make you much more marketable. You cannot be a victim when you are in control of performance and can sell yourself as someone that understands and practices excellence. You cannot be a victim when you have the skills to assess your performance and the insight to make the necessary adjustments to keep your contributions positive and productive.

It is time to make a statement as APs, to revolutionize our thoughts, behaviors, and actions. It's time to get the respect and recognition that we deserve. To accomplish such a lofty vision, we need to band together and demand higher expectations of ourselves, our managers, and our organizations. It begins by taking control of our careers, as individuals, one by one. As each of us strives for administrative excellence, we will collectively raise the bar. Leaders will emerge. Empowerment and growth will be the reward.

Understanding and applying the **Five Ps** of administrative excellence is the first step towards our goal. These five strengths are central to revolutionizing our value in the workplace.

Part I

Administrative Excellence

Chapter I – Perception

AP Strength #1
Perception

Perception is self-awareness. It is the ability to understand yourself, how you relate to other people, and how you react to other people's behaviors. Perception is realizing how others see you. A self-aware person not only understands her or his behavior, but also the strengths and weaknesses of that behavior. With this kind of insight, self-aware people can skillfully manage their careers. The capacity to know yourself gives you confidence and a healthy self-image. These attributes will help you achieve your goals.

The Value of Self-Awareness

Successful APs know their strengths and how to maximize those strengths to broaden their job responsibilities. They also understand how to use their strengths to work more effectively with others. And, more importantly, successful APs understand and take ownership of their weaknesses. They find ways to minimize or eliminate personal obstacles to success. Successful APs are firm in their resolve to become their best.

What is your level of self-awareness? To discover your true self and latent potential you need to know your inner strengths. You need to have a realistic picture of how you react, interact, and socialize with co-workers and perform on teams. You need to know what to focus on to ensure your on-going growth and development. Time spent in personal reflection can go a long way in identifying your strong suits and empowering yourself to take control of your career. When you know yourself, it makes your path to job satisfaction much more apparent.

Workplace Behavioral Styles

So let's get to know ourselves better by looking at four specific types of behavioral styles. These are the behavioral styles we encounter in the workplace every day. One of these behaviors is your type. You'll recognize the other styles of behavior to be those of your co-workers, managers, and customers. In this section we learn the strengths and weaknesses of each style. We also learn how each style can adapt to the other styles to improve teamwork.

The behaviors are based on the principles of the DiSC® behavioral profile.* DiSC asserts that our behaviors combine four behavior preferences, but that one of the preferences dominates *(see Figure 1.1)*. The preferences reflect how we prefer to interact with our environment—people, ideas, things, and so on. No one style is better than another. As you read through the following descriptions of behaviors, you may see a little of yourself in each style, but try to isolate your style by identifying the description that **best** represents your dominant or preferred behavior in the workplace.

---

*When people take the DiSC® profile as part of a training session, the assessment determines primary and secondary (back-up) behavioral styles. The assessment also measures the level of intensity of each of these styles as "high," "medium," or "low." The information in this chapter is a broad overview intended to help you identify your strengths and contributions in the workplace.

DiSC– Dimensions of Behavior

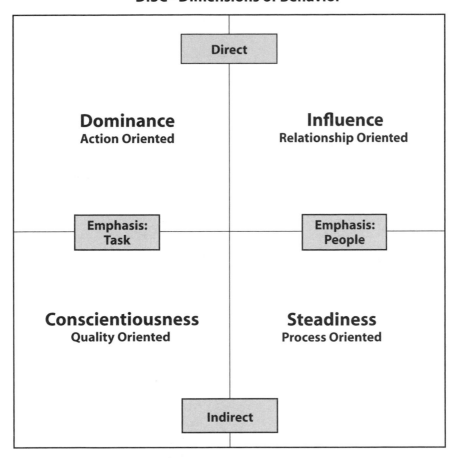

Fig. 1-1 DiSC Overview

The Dominance Style ("Ds")

Those who prefer to interact with their environment by trying to dominate it are people who shape their environment by overcoming obstacles to accomplish results. These action-oriented and results-driven people—we call them Ds—like to challenge the status quo and manage trouble. Ds are very good problem solvers. They think broadly and operationally. Such people thrive on challenge and become restless with routine tasks. Ds are risk takers willing to take charge when others may seem reluctant. They are good at giving direction and setting goals. They stay on task and provide the direction and scope that others may need to get things done. Ds are fast-paced and have a need to keep things moving. They are motivated by environments that can keep pace with their energy and meet their needs for accomplishment. They like to be in charge and are inspired by power and control. Our "high D" co-workers are direct communicators who self-assuredly and confidently share opinions and make quick decisions.

As every style has strengths, it also has weaknesses. It is important for you to understand these limitations so you can manage them effectively, whether in yourself or by adapting to others with this behavioral style. If you possess the Dominance style, then you need to be aware of how your associates may perceive you. In your need to accomplish results, you may overlook personal feelings. Such behavior can look strong, aggressive, opinionated, and sometimes callous and rude to co-workers.

Perceived Strengths:	Perceived Weaknesses:
■ Orienting behavior toward action	■ Making hasty decisions
■ Controlling a situation; making decisive choices	■ Being inattentive to personal needs of others
■ Taking charge	■ Being too blunt and direct
■ Managing problems	■ Acting aggressively
■ Taking risks	■ Seeming overly confident

(**Note:** That strengths and weaknesses stand alone and are not "paired" as in a continuum of behavior.)

Fig. 1-2 Perceived Strengths and Weaknesses, Dominance

I have facilitated several DiSC training sessions for administrative support teams and I have found the Dominance style to be a minority style of APs. Ds typically represent about 10% of the attendees. However, APs that do possess the Dominance behavioral style are very good at stepping up to the plate and achieving results. Ds are not afraid to take on those ugly projects that no one else wants by rolling up their sleeves to get things done. They are also champions of pushing boundaries and supporting change.

If this is your style, how can you make it work to your benefit? Reflect on the strengths and weaknesses associated with this style. Consider those things that you could do to make further use of these strengths. Are there changes that you could make on your job to capitalize on these abilities? What adjustments will you make to lessen the impact of your weaknesses? How can you take control of these weaknesses to turn them into areas of growth?

How can Ds adapt to other behavioral styles? How can others adapt to Ds?

Adapting to Others:	Adapting to the Dominance Style:
■ Considering the personal implications of an action	■ Being direct and to the point
■ Respecting others' ideas	■ Keeping emotions in control
■ Taking time in making decisions	■ Sticking to the facts; limiting details and excessive information
■ Recognizing and appreciating others' contributions	■ Knowing your goals, objectives, and expected outcomes
■ Developing patience in working with others	■ Resisting efforts by others to overrule or intimidate you

Fig. 1-3 Styles of Adapting, Dominance

The Influence Style ("I's")

Now let's look at the second workplace behavioral style. This is the Influence style. These individuals shape their environment by influencing and motivating others. They are relationship-oriented and alliance builders. Influence-driven co-workers like to inspire and persuade others. They are creative and emotional, meaning there is much feeling behind their thoughts and actions. These associates thrive in environments that are team- and committee-oriented. They are idea generators eager to share their thoughts, concepts, and visions. They oftentimes, however, need to rely on others to carry out the details of these ideas. They are good at energizing people and creating momentum. They are gregarious and very good at using humor to defuse stressful situations. They are optimistic and intuitive in their decision-making style. They are motivated by public recognition of their accomplishments. Our "high I" associates are direct communicators who confidently and expressively share their ideas.

Influence personalities also need to be aware of how *we* might be perceived by *our* associates. Yes, I'm a "high-I" person. Because we are people-oriented, others can view us as too talkative and not focused on our other responsibilities. Our lack of detail can also be frustrating for others. Also, others may perceive the Influence style as insincere because we are so outgoing and establish relationships with many people. And because high-I people tend to rely on a "gut feel," we can sometimes seem illogical.

APs that possess Influence qualities are very good at establishing relationships throughout the organization. They become good liaisons and ambassadors because they know many people. They will connect well with most people because they have a strong need to be liked and respected.

As an Influence behavioral style, consider what you can do to make further use of these strengths. What changes can you make on your job to capitalize on these abilities? What adjustments will you make to lessen the impact of your weaknesses? How can you take control of these weaknesses to turn them into areas of growth?

Perceived Strengths:	Perceived Weaknesses:
■ Establishing relationships	■ Talking too much
■ Inspiring others	■ Overlooking details
■ Motivating and persuading others	■ Becoming overly emotional
■ Promoting ideas and concepts	■ Rushing to conclusions
■ Networking and socializing	■ Being unorganized at work

(**Note:** That strengths and weaknesses stand alone and are not "paired" as in a continuum of behavior.)

Fig. 1-4 Perceived Strengths and Weaknesses, Influence

Influential people communicate most effectively by understanding how to adapt to others. Others can benefit from learning how to adapt to us as well.

Adapting to Others:	Adapting to the Influence Style:
■ Respecting demands on other people's time	■ Being friendly and personable in your approach
■ Providing clear instruction	■ Keeping conversation on track and focused
■ Staying on track and focused in your approach to others	■ Providing details in writing
■ Keeping emotions in check and sticking to logical facts	■ Being clear in expectations and objectives
■ Being firm in having needs met or conveying expectations	■ Recognizing accomplishments and personal contributions

Fig. 1-5 Styles of Adapting, Influence

The Steadiness Style ("Ss")

The third behavioral style is the Steadiness style. These co-workers accomplish results through collaboration and proven methods. They are our process-oriented associates. Steadiness co-workers are loyal and dependable. These associates value environments that are harmonious and free of conflict. They value tried and true methods of accomplishing tasks and, as a result, will be inclined to resist change. They are stable, patient, tactful, and kind. They are good at organizing projects and can be counted on to get things done. They are motivated by environments that are inclusive of everyone and will oftentimes put the needs of others before their own. These particular traits make Ss similar to the Influence style because both styles place people before tasks. Our Steadiness associates are indirect communicators who prefer listening to speaking and group recognition to individual recognition.

Steadiness behavioral styles also need to be aware of the perceptions of others. Because they are process-oriented and prefer a more peaceful, controlled environment, others can view them as passive or timid. Because of this, Ss need to be careful not to get taken advantage of. It is not uncommon for the needs of Ss to be overlooked because of their desire to meet the needs of other people.

APs that possess Steadiness qualities are very good at wading through volumes of paperwork and accomplishing results. They remain calm in the face of demanding, crazy environments and they often become respected for their ability to de-escalate mounting pressures and interpersonal conflicts.

As a Steadiness behavioral style, consider those things that you could do to make further use of these strengths. What changes can you make on your job to capitalize on these abilities? What adjustments will you make to lessen the impact of your weaknesses? How can you take control of these weaknesses to turn them into areas of growth?

Perceived Strengths:	Perceived Weaknesses:
■ Following proven processes and procedures	■ Lacking assertiveness
■ Organizing cumbersome projects	■ Resisting chance
■ Being patient and repectful	■ Appearing timid or weak
■ Resolving conflict or tension	■ Being taken advantage of
■ Being dependable and loyal	■ Speaking up and sharing ideas

(**Note:** That strengths and weaknesses stand alone and are not "paired" as in a continuum of behavior.)

Fig. 1-6 Perceived Strengths and Weaknesses, Steadiness

In order for Ss to communicate effectively, they need to adapt to others. In partnership, other styles can benefit from learning how to adapt to them as well.

Adapting to Others:	Adapting to the Steadiness Style:
■ Telling others exactly what you need	■ Being warm and sincere
■ Being assertive and confident in your approach	■ Defining clear goals and objectives
■ Becoming open-minded to change and short-cut methods	■ Giving them time to absorb change
■ Becoming straightforward in your communications	■ Showing a sincere interest in them as people
■ Varying your routines and slowly expanding your comfort zones	■ Reminding them that they are important and central to plans

Fig. 1-7 Styles of Adapting, Steadiness

The Conscientiousness Style ("Cs")

And the fourth style is the Conscientiousness style. These co-workers achieve results through quality and accuracy. They are our analytical and logical associates. Conscientiousness co-workers are diplomatic and thoughtful. They thrive in environments that value quality and precision. Cs hold themselves to extremely high standards and prefer rules and written procedures to ensure compliance. They prefer emotionally controlled environments and business-like interactions. They are exacting and very good at evaluation and assessment because of their orientation to detail. Our Conscientiousness associates communicate indirectly and prefer working independently to meet their high level of achievement. They are similar to Ds because they place emphasis on tasks before people.

Cs also need to be aware of the perceptions of others. Because Cs are more reserved, they may appear aloof, unfeeling, or distant. Additionally, Cs have a tendency to impose their own high standards on others, often times creating unrealistic expectations.

APs that possess Conscientiousness qualities are very good at complex projects and technical or procedural work. Their strong need for accuracy makes them exceptionally good at delivering a quality, comprehensive product.

As a Conscientiousness behavioral style, consider those things that you could do to make further use of these strengths. What changes can you make on your job to capitalize on these abilities? What adjustments will you make to lessen the impact of your weaknesses? How can you take control of these weaknesses to turn them into areas of growth?

Perceived Strengths:	Perceived Weaknesses:
■ Seeking detail and accuracy	■ Appearing rigid and inflexible
■ Analyzing and researching	■ Hindering creative thought
■ Acting diplomatically and logically	■ Slowing down a process
■ Understanding policy and protocol	■ Seeking perfection
■ Exacting and meticulous methods	■ Withholding concerns, thoughts

(**Note:** That strengths and weaknesses stand alone and are not "paired" as in a continuum of behavior.)

Fig. 1-8 Perceived Strengths and Weaknesses, Conscientiousness

Conscientiousness people need to understand how to adapt to others. Other styles can benefit from learning how to adapt to Cs as well.

Adapting to Others:	Adapting to the Conscientiousness Style:
■ Adjusting standards to meet the needs of the environment or person	■ Providing facts and logical information
■ Confronting concerns directly rather than indirectly	■ Ensuring they understand why you want or need to change something
■ Valuing informal interactions with others	■ Keeping interaction business-like and focused on results
■ Realizing that changes are part of the work experience	■ Respecting quality and accuracy
■ Developing tolerance for emotionally charged situations	■ Respecting need for personal space

Fig. 1-9 Styles of Adapting, Conscientiousness

All behavioral styles have a role in our workplace. What would be the result of a team that was made up only of Ds or Is? As you can imagine, homogeneous teams are ineffective. Think about a team of all Ds. This team would probably spin its wheels as everyone clamors for control. A team of all high-I people would probably get off on too many tangents to accomplish the goals at hand, and so on. We need each of these styles to become functional teams and to accomplish our objectives. Each style brings a unique perspective and provides for a well-balanced approach to solving problems or completing projects.

Have you identified your style? Does one style jump out at you? You now have insight into your own style, the style of others, and specific ways you can adapt to the behaviors of others. This single ability maximizes your communication potential and gives you the opportunity to establish better relationships with those that are important to your career success.

Through my observations and experience, I estimate that 75% of the APs I have trained in DiSC possess either the Steadiness or the Conscientiousness style. This makes sense because the natural abilities of Ss and Cs contribute directly and effectively to fulfilling the many responsibilities of APs. I doubt it's coincidental that individuals with these behavioral styles seek careers that require these specific talents. Does that mean that high-D and high-I people are less effective in performing these roles? No. It just means that they bring a different dynamic to their positions.

Recognizing Strengths and Partnering Differences

My style is Influence. I took the DiSC profile for the first time about 10 years ago when I was working as an executive assistant at Ryan Companies, a national design and build construction company in Minneapolis, MN. DiSC was enlightening for me because it was the first time that I really understood myself. After taking the profile, I knew that I established strong relationships because it came naturally to me. I also understood why I had to work harder than some of my administrative colleagues to make sure I thought about the details and coordination of projects. It was because detail and coordination are secondary behaviors for me—that is, they are not my preferred or dominant behavior. For me, the people-oriented soft skills come most naturally. So hard skills, such as details and project coordination, do not come as easily for me. By understanding my limits, I could focus on improving these secondary skills in my personal and professional life. To be a well-rounded AP, an assistant that could balance the soft skills and the hard skills for peak performance, I needed to concentrate on my weaknesses, the hard skills.

I want to illustrate how effective this personal knowledge can be in partnering with your manager. I worked with my manager at Ryan Companies, the vice president of construction, for eight years as his executive assistant. Before we took DiSC as a company-wide training initiative, we didn't fully understand each other. We only knew we were different from one another, especially in the mornings. My manager would come into the office each day ready to hit the ground running, work in hand, expecting me to share his enthusiasm for immediate results. I, on the other hand, liked to come into the office in the morning and take a few minutes to ease into my day. I would like to turn my computer on, check voice mails, get a cup of coffee, and talk to a few co-workers. It was important to me to see how they were doing, what they did the night before, etc. I wanted to connect with people before I tackled the work on my desk. My manager and I would look at each other like we were from different planets. I know he was thinking "Come on, we've got things to do," while I was thinking, "Relax, I'm going to get to it in a minute."

We were educated, however, after we took DiSC. We then fully understood each other's style. He was a D, the action-oriented, results-driven behavioral style. I was an I, the people-oriented, relationship-driven behavioral style. Aha! Different approaches. We now understood each other and respected our differences. As a matter of fact, we were able to use this insight more broadly by utilizing my people skills to act as a liaison throughout the organization. Since my manager knew that my approach in working with other managers or staff would be different from his, he would often encourage me to act on his behalf in gathering information or attending a meeting. This was career growth for me because it provided visibility and the opportunity to work with people in the organization that I otherwise would not have had the occasion to interact with.

Benefits of Knowing Yourself and Others

Having insight to my strengths and behavior paid off in further career growth. Knowing I was strong in people-oriented skills, I expressed an interest in HR responsibilities should Ryan ever centralize those functions. As the company grew and this need materialized, I was offered the opportunity to move into an HR role. I was then able to further develop these skills and abilities by taking on greater responsibility in the most people-oriented department in the company. I tapped into my potential. I became deeply involved in employee training and development and employee-focused initiatives, such as directing leadership groups, assessing employee surveys, and spearheading a professional development initiative for our APs. For the next six years I grew and thrived in this environment.

Understanding DiSC strengths and styles can benefit you and your career as much as it aided me and my career. Think about the possibilities that exist in your organization for putting your talents to use.

Maximizing Your Behavioral Style

What have you learned about yourself? Take a minute to complete the following thoughts to help you identify areas of growth for yourself.

I believe my strongest, preferred DiSC behavior style is the _____ behavioral style.

My strengths are:

I can further use these strengths by:

My limitations are:

I will diminish the effect of these limitations by:

I believe my manager's DiSC behavior style is:

We can enhance our working partnership by:

All of us possess some mix of each of these styles as part of our own complex, unique behaviors. Should you ever take a DiSC assessment in a training or classroom setting, you will see to what degree you possess each behavioral style. Your goal should be to understand these four basic human behaviors and then use the strengths of each of these styles as you need them in your working environment.

Engaging All Styles for Personal Effectiveness

The ability to do this is an admirable skill of a friend of mine. Nancy is an executive assistant to the president of a large dairy distributor in the Midwest. We have co-chaired several committees through our involvement in the professional organization, International Association of Administrative Professionals. I have watched her many times skillfully use all four styles to her advantage. She is gifted at adjusting and flexing to meet the needs of the moment or of another individual. She is poised and confident and asserts herself when she feels strongly about an idea or a situation (D behavior). Nancy is also someone that has very good people skills and is friendly and persuasive in her manner (I Behavior). She is very detail-oriented and thinks about the big picture (C Behavior), while valuing the opinion of others and considering the needs of the team or the committee (S behavior). She balances these four behavioral styles effectively and appears comfortable and in control of her objectives at all times.

Not only is DiSC insight beneficial in determining your strengths and weaknesses, it allows you to be a better communicator by adapting to the behavioral styles of those around you, as Nancy does so effectively. This ability sets you apart and identifies you as having highly developed interpersonal skills.

Perception: A Step Towards Administrative Excellence

Understanding these dimensions of behavior provides you with:

- ❧ Knowledge of yourself, your strengths, and your weaknesses.

- ❧ Knowledge of others and a strategic approach to dealing and working with them more effectively.

This is powerful knowledge. Understanding these two things gives you the opportunity to release your untapped potential and transform relationships. When you manage this knowledge adeptly, you have the potential to improve your worklife significantly.

Chapter II – Purpose

"I'm doing what I think I was put on this earth to do. And I'm really grateful to have something that I'm passionate about and that I think is profoundly important."

Marian Wright Edelman

AP Strength #2
Purpose

Many years ago I was a typist in a typing pool. Some people thought that an insignificant job. It didn't matter to me. I saw the connection to the bigger picture and understood that returning reports quickly and accurately was important. I was satisfied to know I did my part.

Purpose focuses your efforts. Purpose is a compass for moving forward, a wide-angle lens for seeing your job within the larger context. When you are validated in your work and proud of your accomplishments, then you enjoy a sense of purpose and feel satisfied and fulfilled. As an AP, this means that you appreciate *how* and *why* you are important to your manager and to your organization.

Not long ago, an insightful AP clearly defined purpose for me. This AP has worked as an administrative assistant for five years. She received her technical degree after high school and then joined the administrative profession. Her first job was as an office assistant, performing a variety of responsibilities, and backing up several senior APs. Over time she took on additional responsibility and became an AP supporting a corporate services manager. She saw this as a turning point for her administrative career. As an AP she felt *ownership* of her work. She performed her tasks and felt responsible for results. With this pride and responsibility came a sense of importance and a feeling of being needed. In her own words, *"I realized I had a purpose."*

She recognized that she grew dramatically as a professional at that point. She met with her manager and determined goals and set expectations. She soon found that when her manager wasn't in, she was the go-to person. Her manager empowered her as well and gave her authority and responsibility to act on her behalf in her absence. This AP understands her value to the success of her manager and the organization.

Know Your Purpose

To enjoy your work as an AP you must know your purpose. For example, in the spring of 2003, I read a newspaper article about a young sailor in the United States Navy who stocked his ship's vending machines. Each morning he conscientiously performed his task. He felt it was an important job because he knew others counted on him to have the machines filled. He knew others wouldn't think that it was a very important job, but he took pride in knowing that it would make another sailor's day to have a cold beverage and snack available when he or she wanted it. This American sailor understood his purpose, and found satisfaction in his duties, by connecting his responsibilities to the greater needs of his shipmates. His efforts did not go unnoticed. The United States Navy recognized this sailor's efforts in a national press release.

While reading this article, I recognized the similarities between this sailor's responsibilities and the routine aspects of an AP position. This sailor's story, combined with my own experiences, helped me to put our roles as APs in proper perspective. *It is not our tasks and responsibilities that define our level of success; rather it is our attitude towards these tasks and how we choose to perform them that contributes to our level of success.*

To identify your purpose, ask yourself these important questions:

- What is the purpose of my manager or my team?

- How does the purpose of my manager or team connect with the overall purpose of my organization?

- What are our team goals? How do these goals relate to strategic plans or organizational expectations?

- What is the vision or mission of my organization?

- How do my personal values relate to organizational values?

- Do I respect the purpose of my manager, team, department, and organization? Why or why not?

- What is my purpose in helping my manager, team, department or organization achieve results?

To be an effective AP you must be in sync with the goals and objectives of your manager and organization. This is *how* you become a strategic business partner to your manager and *why* you are a necessary, valuable contributor to organizational success. If you don't know the answer to some of these questions, specifically the questions regarding the goals and objectives of managers, departments, or organizations, then you need to ask your manager to clarify these issues.

If you don't personally share or value the firm's goals and objectives, then you need to decide whether you are a good fit for your organization. I once managed a receptionist who resigned her position because she did not respect the purpose of our organization, a construction company. She valued the history of all old buildings and didn't respect the fact that we many times demolished these existing structures to erect new, modern buildings. I admired her for recognizing her values and their effect on her comfort and success as an AP.

Achieving Personal Satisfaction

Identifying your purpose is important. Achieving personal satisfaction from performing your responsibilities is essential. Let's see where you stand.

Reflect on your past accomplishments. Whether you realized these accomplishments in your current workplace or at an earlier job is unimportant for the moment. Consider these questions.

- When did/do you feel the most job satisfaction?
- What tasks were/are you performing when you feel this way?
- What personal accomplishments make you most proud of yourself?
- When have you felt the strongest and most focused in your administrative career?
- What excites you on the job and makes you "jump into" a project?
- What specific job responsibilities make you feel most valuable to your manager or organization?

Such questions help you determine exactly what inspires you. They also help you see your unique value and contributions as an AP.

Now ask yourself three more important questions.

- In my current work environment can I do more of the things that I like to do?
- Does my job support or expand my talents?
- How can I (or my manager and I) adjust my current situation to help me enjoy greater personal satisfaction from my work and add value to my role as an AP?

Whatever your thoughts, addressing them with your manager may provide additional avenues for enriching your job and achieving personal satisfaction. Taking on new, interesting responsibilities may create a win/win situation for you and your manager.

Finding the Connection

Identifying with your purpose by personally connecting with your responsibilities is essential to your success and satisfaction as an AP. However, many APs lose sight of their purpose. Heavy workloads and tedious, routine tasks can distort our view of the bigger picture and can cause us to question the value of our daily efforts. Although effective managers communicate strategic goals and corporate objectives so that we understand the direction of the company, we bear the burden of linking our day-to-day responsibilities to the bigger picture of our corporate environments.

For eight years, as an executive assistant at Ryan Companies I was responsible for ordering and picking up bagels and rolls for our Friday morning department meetings. This task could have made me feel insignificant. After all, how important can I be if this is one of my responsibilities? Well, I placed that task in its proper context. Insignificant? Yes. Important? Yes, because a little goes a long way. I looked at bringing snacks as a way to build the culture of our department. Our staff looked forward to Fridays and their "treats" at the Friday morning meetings. This is an example of a small responsibility that can make a tangible difference in the larger context of our work environments. Remember the sailor and the vending machines?

So let's concentrate for a moment on a routine, non-challenging aspect of your job. Is there something that you are required to do that frustrates you or makes you question your value to the organization? Write down some of the details to the questions below.

I don't like it when I have to:

This responsibility frustrates me because:

Now think about the sailor and his attitude toward his responsibilities. How can you find value in your responsibility? Look at it from a different perspective. Take a minute to identify the value of this task and how and why it is important to the bigger picture of your working environment. Now answer the following question:

This task has value because:

Could you see this task differently when you thought about it differently? Thinking about your tasks in this way can help you connect your smaller, daily activities to a larger importance. This perspective may help you overcome feelings of insignificance or frustration.

The Purposeful Roadmap

Think about your "admin" career and what you want to accomplish. It doesn't matter if you have a full career ahead or if retirement is on the horizon. Use the steps on page 27 to express your vision and discover your path to professional fulfillment. The steps are easy: A-D-M-I-N. Following them will help you set personal goals and answer three significant questions:

1. What do you want for yourself as an AP?

2. What do you need to do to achieve it?

3. How will you know when you have achieved it?

How does "the purposeful roadmap"— activation, determination, motivation, innovation, and navigation—help you answer the three "A-D-M-I-N" questions above? I encourage you to sit down, ponder, and spend time answering those questions. Your answers sketch a personal mission statement to help guide your career.

ACTIVATION

Activate your strengths to achieve your goals. Chapter I helps identify your strengths. What does the DiSC information tell you about your abilities? Take action with these skills and behaviors, the source of your potential. Opportunities surround you and most organizations welcome employees that take on additional responsibility. Taking initiative shows managers that you are serious about your career and that you have drive and ambition.

DETERMINATION

Determination comes from personal strength borne of a belief in yourself and a clear sense of what you want to accomplish. Obstacles do not mean failure. Obstacles are opportunities to take different approaches, try different methods, and look with different perspectives. Obstacles are valuable stepping stones to growth because they force you to look at yourself and what you need to do differently or better to achieve results. If you strongly believe in something, then you will not let an obstacle deter you. Determination inspires the confidence that you need to realize your goals.

MOTIVATION

Motivation drives your accomplishments. Motivation is energy, the energy to stick to your plans, stay the course, and achieve your goals. You cannot succeed without motivation. Some people unenthusiastically approach their work. They wait for direction and do no more than what is expected of them. They perceive their job as a means to an end, not an avenue for growth and development. These individuals perform a job. They do not manage a career. They show no motivation. You can, and in turn, you will succeed.

INNOVATION

Innovative APs, the employees most closely attuned to the processes, products, and clients of an organization, bear a responsibility to offer insight on how to perform tasks more efficiently. This is one way in which APs can add value to their roles and to an organization. You improve others' perceptions of you and of APs in general when you can suggest new and better ways of doing things that save the organization time and money.

NAVIGATION

No one steers your career for you. To chart a course for success requires personal reflection, vision, and accomplishment. It matters less how you accomplish your goals than that you have goals and you work to achieve them. Striving to improve turns good companies into great companies and turns average APs into committed, excellent APs. Navigating toward your goals makes the difference between *knowing what you want* and *getting what you expect*.

Career Reflection

As you read this chapter, you may experience doubts about your role as an AP. Perhaps you discovered that you are not fulfilled or satisfied with the responsibilities of being an AP. If so, then you must determine your commitment to this profession. Performing AP responsibilities is not for everyone.

A hiring manager once asked me, "Why is it that I go through the interview process, explain the necessary job functions, receive positive feedback and a 'can-do' attitude from the AP candidate, but once hired, the AP is dissatisfied and irritated by her responsibilities?" I don't believe that this is an experience unique to one manager. This situation is common and may be related to the reasons an individual chooses an AP career.

While many of us followed a traditional path to our AP roles, many more of us perform these responsibilities without passion or desire. These situations may include:

1. Individuals that perform AP responsibilities to supplement another personal interest such as acting, writing, teaching, or other creative ventures that may not provide the steady income or health-related benefits that an AP position offers.

2. Individuals on an administrative track because they were uninterested or denied an opportunity to attend a four-year college. They became APs to earn a living until deciding what to do with their lives. Or perhaps such people fell into an AP role after college because they were unable to secure a job in their field of study.

3. Individuals that use AP jobs as a stepping stone to future job opportunities within a corporate structure, a "foot in the door" so to speak.

If you chose AP work for any of the above reasons, I am not assuming that you are ineffective in your role. I have known many individuals that have taken AP jobs for these exact reasons and are very good, very effective, and personally fulfilled by the work they do. However, many APs "go through the motions" because of their choices. Their lack of commitment and passion about their job responsibilities leave them unfulfilled by the role and its expectations. This dissatisfaction affects their work and their attitude. These attitudes often damage perceptions of the profession and perpetuate many demeaning professional stereotypes.

Seriously consider your talents and abilities and how they might better contribute to your choice of career. You spend 60% of your time working. Are you devoting this time to something meaningful to you?

Take advantage of the exercises and questions that are in this book. Use them to guide you toward your goals. To achieve career success as an AP, you have to enjoy what you do and respect the role you play. Otherwise, you will be unhappy, frustrated, and resentful.

Another reason you may doubt the value of your work is because your work environment may not support you. Perhaps it could be adjusted to better suit your abilities. Or maybe you need to establish boundaries for the types of work you are willing to do.

As an example, several years ago, one of the managers I supported would occasionally ask me to take some of his clothing to the dry cleaner that was located in the lobby of our office building. I had no problem doing that for him. We had a respectful relationship and I was happy to help him out. However, he crossed boundaries when I found some of his girlfriend's clothes on my desk with a note to please take them to the cleaners. I felt that was outside the scope of my responsibilities and I promptly told him so.

You will want to talk with your manager about the work you are performing or your need for more meaningful work. Perhaps you work in an environment where you feel you perform insignificant, routine tasks and do not have a balance of challenging work to offset these frustrating assignments. If that is the case, then take control of that situation and bring it to someone's attention. Follow the A-D-M-I-N steps to address your situation and determine the opportunities for more challenging and meaningful work.

Every job involves less interesting and less challenging tasks. Routine, mundane tasks are not exclusive to AP positions. Even managers, politicians, and celebrities do some monotonous work. Remember, it's not necessarily how you do the big things, but how you do the small things that get noticed and make you stand out as someone different and special. Small, symbolic-but-essential tasks are often deeply appreciated in the workplace. Think of presidential candidates shaking hands for hours on the campaign trail. Think of the co-worker who willing cleans up after office celebrations or the co-worker who volunteers to work late and stuff envelopes for a large mailing. Think again of the sailor and his vending machines. Your attitude toward routine responsibilities often leads to job growth. Managers often give more responsibility and respect to employees with a positive attitude and an eagerness to get the job done.

Beyond the Walls of Our Workplace

Our jobs do not complete us as a person. We are more than the work that we do. Outside activities such as family, friends, hobbies, interests, and involvement in personal and professional organizations often meet our greater need for purpose.

I can personally relate to this as I reflect on my career at Ryan Companies. There came a time when I started to feel like something was missing. I didn't know what it was, nor did I think it was important. I was employed by a great company, had wonderful co-workers, and loved my job and responsibilities. However, on a deeper level there was something that I couldn't put my finger on. An inner voice occasionally encouraged me to do something different. I decided to become more involved in my community, so I joined a local volunteer organization to expand my horizons and meet new people. Although it was a rewarding experience and I met many nice people, it didn't seem to fulfill me.

These feelings of want and need coincided with Ryan Companies winning the 2001 IAAP Award for Excellence for implementing a successful AP development plan. As a result, we were scheduled to present our accomplishments at the IAAP 2002 International Convention in Nashville, Tennessee. I co-presented the Ryan plan to 250 APs. The reaction to our plan was overwhelming. The energy was palpable. These APs were excited, interested, and motivated to make changes in their working environments. Many APs approached us wanting more information *(Chapter IX details this plan)*. Many others asked if we consulted or would help them establish plans. The interest continued for months via e-mail and phone calls.

The enthusiasm generated at the IAAP convention for administrative development was my motivation for leaving Ryan Companies and following my passion for AP staff development. Standing on that stage in Nashville, I knew immediately my new purpose. I wanted to help APs find their strengths, pursue their own ambitions for administrative excellence, and promote change in their organizations. I knew that these things would give voice to our profession. For me, this seemed a logical next step in my administrative career. This epiphany has since met my need for purpose on a deep, personal level.

Use your imagination to consider new heights of administrative achievement. I have known several APs who have directed their talents and rerouted their administrative careers to specialized positions in property management, human resources, event planning, specification writing, marketing, and information technology (IT). These avenues are extensions of their skills and interests and meet their needs for purpose in the workplace.

Purpose: A Step Towards Administrative Excellence

When your purpose is clear and when it complements your inner desires, then you will perform at a higher level because:

    ❧ You will understand your value to your organization's success.

    ❧ You will find satisfaction in your role.

When these two needs are met, they generate a positive attitude. Katherine Graham, the late publisher of *The Washington Post,* proclaimed, "To love what you do and feel that it matters – what could be more fun!" When you enjoy what you do it shows. Your attitude conveys enthusiasm and confidence and announces that you are capable. You become an admirable force for personal and professional momentum when you can confidently say, *"I know my purpose."*

Chapter III – Progress

"The most damaging phrase in the language is "it's always been done that way."

Rear Admiral Grace Hopper

<table>
<tr><td>AP Strength #3
Progress</td></tr>
</table>

Erin Brockovich, an AP made famous in the 2000 Universal Studios movie of the same name, was a file clerk at the California law firm of Masry & Vititoe. Erin applied critical thinking skills to routine responsibilities. For example, her interest was piqued when she discovered that medical records were included in several real estate files. With the approval of law partner, Ed Masry, Erin began to research this mystery further. Her investigation discovered that over several decades, poisonous gases from a neighboring utility plant had devastated the health of over 600 residents of a small California town. Erin's efforts resulted in the largest direct action lawsuit of its kind, forcing the utility to pay the largest toxic tort injury settlement in U.S. history.

This injustice may have gone unnoticed if Erin had not been actively involved in her work. She could have worked like a robot, simply done her job, and filed the case files accordingly. With $333 million dollars in damages paid to the 600 residents of this small California town, there is little doubt these citizens are grateful for Erin's dedication and tenacity in performing her job responsibilities. With her law firm entitled to a percentage of the damages, there is little doubt about their satisfaction with Erin's contributions. Erin is now the Director of Research at her law firm.

Think Progressively

You may not affect your organization's bottom line or your community's health to the extent that Erin Brockovich did, but you can engage in the work that you do. Engaging is a choice that requires a concentrated effort. Heavy workloads and the heavy expectation of quick results often cause people to rely on standard, standby principles: "That's the way it's always been done" or "I just do what I'm told to do." While these responses may make your job easier or faster to do, they ultimately prevent you from adding value to your responsibilities. An alternative is to think progressively. That is, think about the tasks you are performing and use your intellect and judgment to question what you are doing, why you are doing it, and if you are doing it correctly. Such critical thinking skills helped Erin Brockovich progress in her job at Masry & Vititoe. And the rest is legal and Hollywood history!

Some of you are still thinking, "I don't have time to think progressively because I need to do my job and get the work out the door." That kind of detrimental thinking causes you to perform your responsibilities as if on "auto pilot," and it can be costly to your performance and to your organization's success.

A manager once shared such a costly experience with me. In cleaning out her files, she gave several notebooks of outdated financial material to an AP to destroy. The AP did what she was told and shredded the contents of the notebooks. The manager soon realized that she had mistakenly included with the financial information a notebook of handwritten speeches, important to prepare for future speaking engagements. When she asked about it, the AP replied, "Oh yes, I noticed that the notebook was different from the other materials, but I shredded it anyway."

If this AP had questioned this unusual notebook, she would have saved the manager hours of rework in recreating the notebook's content. A proactive response would have also earned the manager's trust and confidence, necessary for increased responsibility. More importantly, the manager would have formed this new trust and confidence whether the notebook needed shredding or not, because the manager would recognize the AP's initiative and concern. This experience emphasizes a need: for the benefit of APs and their organizations, APs must challenge the work they are given.

The Link to the Bottom Line

Progress is improvement. No one is better positioned to help organizations improve than APs. AP responsibilities are largely defined by processes and procedures, the systems that make the organization function. Systems are not always effective. Opportunities are plentiful to streamline, enhance, or eliminate processes and procedures in many organizations. These changes can significantly improve an organization's efficiency and profitability. Such changes occur because people think progressively, examine their responsibilities, and propose ideas for new and better ways of doing things. By thinking progressively, APs add immediate value to an organization's bottom line. Thinking progressively and suggesting change, however, may require you to challenge your normal thinking style and to push the boundaries of your comfort zones.

Think Big and Broadly

Learning to think more broadly is a skill honed by asking yourself probing questions:

- Is there a better way to do this?

- Is this what he meant to say in these instructions?

- Is this the message that she wants to convey in this letter?

- Is this to be mailed to Albany, Georgia or Albany, New York?

- How can I do this more cost-effectively?"

Such questions may seem time consuming, but the answers save time, money, or potential embarrassment. Eventually, big and broad thinking becomes a natural way to challenge yourself, your abilities, and the work you are given.

Below is a good exercise to help you think this way. Here's the task: Connect **all** of the dots by drawing four straight lines without lifting your pen. The solution appears at the end of the chapter.

Pushing Your Comfort Zone

Learning to think broadly helps your *organization* progress. Taking risks and pushing your comfort zone helps *you* to progress.

I was not always a progressive thinker when it came to my job or the administrative profession. For many years, I went about my business, doing my job to the best of my abilities, and failing to recognize my untapped potential or the potential of the APs that I managed. I carried out my tasks without giving much thought to doing things differently or challenging existing processes, procedures, or cultural norms.

Two events, both requiring me to step out of my comfort zone, significantly jump-started my thinking. Both helped me advance my career and, ultimately, support the growth of fellow APs. In hindsight, these events profoundly influenced where I am today personally and professionally.

The first occurred as part of a team-building event at an outside orienteering course. One challenge involved harnessing ourselves to a wire about 12 feet off the ground. Together with a partner, we were to climb a tree, grab the wire, and shimmy out on this wire as far as we could go. The purpose was to take a personal risk and establish trust with another person in helping to complete this task. I was one of the last ones in line, intentionally. As I watched others complete this heroic feat, my stomach churned, my nerves kicked in, and I thought, "I can't do this. No way." One by one the teams proudly and excitedly fulfilled their missions. I was still not convinced that I could go up that tree. When my turn came, I gave it a try. Not until that moment in time had I ever been an adventurous risk taker. But with my partner I did it! My achievement exhilarated me because I discovered I could push my limits and do things I never thought possible. It was a turning point. I expanded the walls of my comfort zone. That attitude transferred to my job and my personal life and to this day has made a difference in my self-confidence. I am thankful I took a chance and realize what I would have sacrificed by not participating.

The second event was my decision to join Toastmasters International, a professional organization dedicated to increasing an individual's self-confidence in public speaking. My employer established an in-house club, and I knew that professionally I needed to take advantage of the benefit. However, it was outside of my comfort zone because I was uncomfortable speaking in front of large groups.

Toastmasters eases you into public speaking by requiring you to perform ten speeches throughout your membership. The first speech is a two-minute icebreaker. Subsequent speeches increase in length and have a specific topic. The goal of my fourth speech was to "sell something" to my audience. After nothing else came to mind, I settled on Tupperware® products. Let me clarify: I do not sell Tupperware as a side line. I had never tried to sell it or anything else before. For my speech I brought in several Tupperware pieces and began to "sell" my audience on their value. My audience was interested, excited, and attentive. I think that if I had really been selling Tupperware, I may have had buyers. This was a major accomplishment for me because I realized I can be confident and persuasive. It was also a major accomplishment since men made up most of the audience! This event was another professional turning point because it revealed personal abilities that I was unaware I had.

After my successful orienteering climb and sales pitch, I began to think differently on the job. I realized I can accomplish much if I put my mind to it. I developed strengths that I never before saw in myself, and I started to take more risks on the job. I became comfortable with speaking up and sharing my ideas. I became comfortable taking on responsibilities that I previously would not have considered. I began to facilitate employee training courses, I began to think about creative ideas for administrative staff development, and I volunteered for opportunities to speak in front of managers and employees. I gained confidence as an employee.

Most people do not have to take extreme measures to find their confidence and ability. But we do have to step out of our comfort zones to maximize who we are as individuals and as APs. The role of APs is to support organizations. However, the supportive aspect of these roles can hide our individual abilities and hinder our contributions. Remedy this by thinking progressively, thinking big, and thinking confidently about expanding your comfort zone. You don't have to climb a tree to do it.

Fear, An Ingredient of Growth

If you've never felt fear from taking on a project, from speaking up, or from joining a committee, then you are not asserting yourself enough. Think about these words by Julia Soul: "If you are never scared, embarrassed, or hurt, it means you never take chances." If you don't take chances, you won't grow.

If you are comfortable in your routines, then you are sheltered by your responsibilities and environment. This shelter protects you from failure, humiliation, and vulnerability. You will never grow if you are not willing to extend the boundaries that define your comfort and self-confidence. To grow is to be willing to fail and to risk criticism. Yes, failure and criticism temporarily bruise your self-confidence, but your ability to look at yourself and learn from any experience will distinguish you from others. If you do that, then you will flourish rather than fail. Real failure is the decision not to try or to take a different direction because you are afraid to fail.

Failing Forward

Mary Kay Ash, founder of Mary Kay Cosmetics, believed that "people fail forward to success." No one knows about "failing forward" better than Katie Couric, co-host of NBC's *Today Show,* and Oprah Winfrey, the popular syndicated talk show host. Katie Couric and Oprah Winfrey are proof that failure can breed success.

One of Katie's first "on the air" jobs was at CNN. After the president of CNN saw her broadcast, he told the assignment desk, "I never want to see her on the air again." Most of us would probably have given up, determined that we don't have what it takes to succeed in broadcast journalism. Katie could have looked at this feedback and turned her back on her chosen career. She didn't. She learned what she could from the situation and moved on to greater things. Katie said of this experience, "I'm part of a generation of women who don't take no for an answer, and I was willing to work doubly hard to get where I wanted to go." If Katie had believed the opinion of the president of CNN, then she wouldn't be a recognized face in American homes each day.

Oprah Winfrey was fired from a Baltimore television station before moving to Chicago. I think that turned out pretty well for her and for her legions of fans. Oprah often tells her audience that she doesn't believe in failure. Rather, what some people call failure, she believes is simply a sign from the universe to try again, try a new approach, or try something else. Success is there, but you might have to look for it.

Nobody knows you better than you know yourself. Nobody knows better than you do what you can achieve. Believe in your abilities, dreams, and desires. This belief will move you forward toward progress. As you take risks and gain confidence in yourself, others will gain confidence in you.

Think Extraordinary, Not Ordinary

You decide the risks you are willing to take on the job. Perhaps you will take on a larger project, have a difficult conversation with a manager or co-worker, present information to a group, take a class, learn new skills, propose an innovative idea, ask a question, or seek a new AP position. The possibilities are endless. You decide what's appropriate for you in your working environment. However, let's first think about why you would want to take risks on your job.

The danger of staying in your comfort zone is the risk of boredom, monotony, and ordinary experiences. Comfortable behavior will cause you to repeat your responsibilities over and over again. From this standpoint it is easy to fall into a rut. Do you remember the movie *Groundhog Day?* Do you remember how frustrated and cynical Bill Murray's character became when he realized he was waking up to the same day—the same routines, the same details, the same people—everyday?

- Do you want to look back on your career to realize that you stopped growing several years ago?

- Do you want to feel stuck because you are afraid to take risks and assert yourself?

- Do you want to sit idly by and watch administrative peers surpass you with increasing levels of responsibility?

These situations terribly waste your potential and limit your value to an employer.

You define and measure your comfort zone which is as large or small as you want it to be *(see Figure 3-1)*. Your career success is likely to be in direct proportion to the size of your self-imposed boundaries. Tight boundaries may comfort you and protect you from potential risk, but they may also smother you and hinder your growth and development. Or you can push the limits and open yourself up to endless, extraordinary possibility. I encourage you to open up and let a little fresh air and light in there!

Starting my own business was a risk. The discomfort, anxiety, and uncertainty sure felt like a risk. But I pushed my comfort zone, took chances, and learned new things, and I am deeply thankful that I did.

Fig. 3-1 Comfort Zone

It has been the hardest but most rewarding thing I've ever done. Less than two years after starting this business, a large international organization offered me the opportunity to present to a regional audience of APs in Istanbul, Turkey. This was a location and experience that I never imagined for myself. In recent months I have been contacted with additional opportunities that I could only dream of two years ago: more international travel, large and prestigious corporate and governmental clients, and teaching opportunities in the academic arena. This is what I mean about opening yourself up to new, extraordinary possibilities.

Take advantage of the opportunities that surround you to push yourself, expand your personal boundaries, and increase our knowledge. You never know what possibilities exist that will require your skills and abilities unless you take some chances, ask some questions, and present yourself as someone interested in personal and professional development.

I remember an AP who was asked to chair a corporate United Way campaign. She was initially apprehensive because this responsibility would require her to speak to large employee groups, organize and run committee meetings, and make decisions regarding fund-raising and campaign goals. Yet she took the opportunity, and it transformed her confidence. She became comfortable with speaking publicly and developed self-esteem by running a highly profitable campaign. Her comfort zone expanded dramatically because she took a risk and proved her abilities. Increased confidence shifts your thinking in numerous ways.

Think Value-Added

In the book's Introduction we looked at the difference between an encumbered and an empowered staff. Let's now look at performance differences between an *encumbered* and an *empowered* AP. These opposing mindsets influence your value to an organization.

An encumbered AP detracts from her value by performing traditionally. An empowered AP adds to her value by performing in a progressive manner. *(See Figure 3-2).* Figure 3-3 explains the difference.

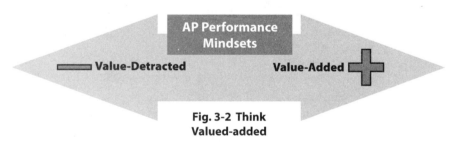

Fig. 3-2 Think
Valued-added

As discussed earlier, the culture of the organization may impose these behaviors, roles, and values upon you, *or* perhaps you impose them upon yourself. I share the following experience to help you understand this point.

I once asked an AP for a business card in order to follow-up with additional information. Her response was, "They don't give us cards.

Traditional, Encumbered AP	Progressive, Empowered AP
■ **Cautious** Yields to surroundings and hesitates to take action.	■ **Confident** Sure of self and willing to share thoughts and ideas.
■ **Unassuming** Blends into environment, overlooks personal needs and desires. Does what is asked.	■ **Undeterred** Committed to personal principles and convictions in carrying out responsibilities. Does what is right.
■ **Knows Place** Accepts role as subservient to organizational results.	■ **Knows Value** Understands role and contributions to overall organizational success.
■ **Comfortable** Satisfied with level of knowledge and responsibility.	■ **Curious** Eager to learn and broaden knowledge and responsibility.
■ **Pays Respect** Demure and retiring in interaction with others limiting opportunities to absorb information or knowledge.	■ **Pays Attention** Assertive and attentive in interaction with others to gain knowledge and insight.
■ **Reactive** Waits for direction and produces results accordingly. Holds others accountable for end result.	■ **Proactive** Takes initiative and inserts self into project to produce results. Holds self accountable for end result.
■ **Follower** Follows the thoughts and actions of others. Resists problems or challenges.	■ **Leader** Encourages others through thoughts, behaviors, and action. Tackles problems or challenges.
■ **Doer** Takes on projects and responsibilities without question or comprehension.	■ **Delegator** Considers alternatives and finds solutions for excessive workloads or complex projects.
■ **Risk Avoider** Intentionally removes self from situations that push comfort zone.	■ **Risk Taker** Takes calculated risks to push boundaries of comfort zone.
■ **Subordinate** Sees self as a minor player in achieving team results.	■ **Partner** Sees self as an integral player in achieving team results.

Fig. 3-3 Performance Mindsets

We're just peons." This was unsettling to me because it shows how APs diminish themselves in organizations that are prone to cultural biases towards APs. It implies an "us versus them" mentality and accepts that "it's just the way that it is." On the other hand, this same AP could have taken an opportunity to discuss the value of business cards for APs with her manager. A conversation such as this may have prompted a shift in the manager's thinking and caused a change in the organization's protocol. You will never effect change unless you move toward progressive, empowered behavior.

Job Versus Career, You Decide

An AP's mindset generally corresponds to her assumptions about APs' roles. Encumbered APs typically perform jobs. Empowered APs work in a career. *(See Figure 3-4).*

Whether you view your role as a job or a career depends on what you want and need from your work life. A "job" or a "career" is merely an attitude about the work that you perform. Your attitude, however, may mean the difference between a stagnant, oppressive job and a soaring, uplifting career.

Consider the career success of Helen Gurley Brown. After attending the Texas State College for Women and the Woodbury Business College, Ms. Brown started as a secretary at an advertising agency in the 1950s. Her strong writing skills helped her advance quickly to a position in the copywriting department. By the early 1960s, she was one of the nation's highest paid ad copywriters. Her career did not end there. In 1965 she was named editor-in-chief of *Cosmopolitan* magazine, a position she capably and successfully held for 32 years. With such career achievement, it is unlikely that Ms. Brown ever thought of herself as performing a job. Helen Gurley Brown is known for saying, "Beauty can't amuse you, but brainwork—reading, writing, thinking —can."

Encumbered AP Job	Empowered AP Career
■ Punches mental time clock and focuses on completion of assignment – waits for end of day.	■ Unaware of time and focuses on results – enthusiastic for next day and next project.
■ Perceives responsibilities as tasks and checks them off a list of things "to do."	■ Perceives responsibilities as learning opportunities and checks them off a list of goals and objectives.
■ Takes initiative as a result of direction.	■ Takes initiative as a result of motivation.
■ Relies on "that's the way it's always been" thinking to carry out responsibilities.	■ Relies on "innovative, progressive" thinking to carry out responsibilities.
■ Knows how to perform a task.	■ Knows why to perform a task.
■ Consistently responds to requests and follows through on them.	■ Consistently anticipates needs and takes action to complete them.
■ Committed to maintenance and status quo.	■ Committed to education, growth, and increased responsibility.
■ Invests in self, asks "How does this affect me?"	■ Invests in others, asks "How can I help my team achieve results?"
■ Believes in "getting by."	■ Believes in "getting ahead."
■ Sees obstacles, becomes overwhelmed.	■ Sees opportunities, becomes energized.

Fig. 3-4 Job versus Career

Performing a SOFT Analysis

A SOFT analysis identifies **Strengths, Opportunities, Faults,** and **Threats** that surround you each day. You may be familiar with a SOFT analysis. Several companies use this approach to analyze their position in the marketplace. It also works nicely for individuals to analyze their role in the workplace. The grid on page 48 will help you see yourself in your workplace.

Strengths

"How do I contribute to the success of my manager and organization?" This leadership-oriented question positions you to add value to your job each day.

Opportunities

"What opportunities exist for me to learn, grow, and expand my abilities in my current job? How do these opportunities support the goals of my manager and organization?" To think about opportunities is to think about the untapped potential in you and your job rather than the evident obstacles.

Faults

"What am I personally responsible for that limits my ability to achieve peak performance?" This question asks you to identify those features that are within your control to fix, change, or improve.

Threats

"What things are out of my control and cause frustration or low productivity?" This question asks you to identify those features out of your control that you would need to resolve with the input of your manager.

The SOFT grid *(Figure 3-5)* on page 47 describes a typical AP. Complete a SOFT analysis for yourself by using the chart *(Figure 3-6)* on page 48 and refering to the SOFT example.

The SOFT approach helps you analyze yourself in the workplace and define areas for improvement. Correct or implement those things within your scope, and address the more complex or broader issues with a manager.

Strengths

Those things you do that add value to your job, your team, and your organization.

Example:

- Coordinate department team events to contribute to a healthy working environment.
- Prepare timely and accurate monthly financial reports.
- Offer feedback to manager on departmental issues that he may be unaware of.
- Create and maintain corporate client database.
- Promote corporate culture and mission statement with both internal and external customers.

Opportunities

Those things available to you to help you maximize your skills and contributions.

Example:

- Mentor a less-experienced AP to promote growth and development and to share department knowedge.
- Take advantage of in-house educational opportunities to increase knowledge.
- Work with manager to expand level of responsibility and create avenues for increased delegation of responsibilities.
- Generate list of departmental processes to be reviewed for streamlining, reengineering, or elimination.

Faults

Those things that hold you back from peak performance.

Example:

- Tendency to withhold frustrations and not deal with them directly.
- Too many people asking for advice and input on personal matters.
- Inability to say no; taking on too many responsibilities at one time.
- Reluctance to ask clarifying questions in departmental meetings.

Threats

Those things that restrict performance and limit productivity.

Example:

- Supporting too many people without time to meet their needs.
- Ineffective software and outdated procedures.
- On-going, poor communication from new team member.
- Unclear team goals and departmental direction.

Fig. 3-5 A SOFT Example

Strengths	Opportunities
Faults	Threats

Fig. 3-6 Your SOFT Analysis

Focus on your Strengths and let your manager know what and how you are contributing. You may see this as self-promotion and feel that "tooting our own horn" is a boastful or arrogant attempt to gain recognition for your efforts. When done appropriately, in an annual review or another goal-oriented discussion for example, such promotion helps managers identify and build on your strengths. As a progressive, empowered AP, take responsibility and make things happen *for you,* not *to you.*

Thinking Out of the Box

Here is the promised solution to the connect-the-dots exercise on page 36.

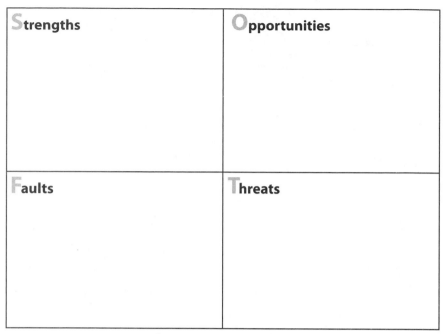

The only way to accomplish this exercise is literally to "think outside of the box." Those of you that could see only boundaries were not able to do that. Think back to the instructions. I did not tell you to stay within the lines created by the dots. But I'm sure many of you put those restrictions on yourself. You assumed it. To learn to "think outside of the box" frees you from long-held notions of thinking the "right way," the "expected way," or the "obvious way." Thinking outside of the box is a tool for seeing things differently and expanding possibilities.

Progress: A Step Towards Administrative Excellence

In 1899, Charles H. Duell, director of the United States Patent Office, declared, "Everything that can be invented has been invented." We can now laugh at his declaration, but thankfully progressive thinkers ignored his assertion and continued to move the world forward. Katie Couric and Oprah Winfrey would be proud.

Thinking progressively helps you:

- ✐ Move your organization forward by working more effectively.

- ✐ Move yourself forward by expanding the boundaries of your comfort zone.

Progressive thinking demonstrates your desire for continuous personal and professional improvement. This thinking and improvement distinguishes you as a progressive, empowered AP.

Chapter IV – Partnership

"In organizations, real power and energy is generated through relationships. The patterns of relationships and the capacity to form them are more important than tasks, functions, roles and positions."

Margaret Wheatly

**AP Strength #4
Partnership**

Partnerships help organizations prosper. Partnerships are relationships inside and outside an organization. These relationships extend from internal customers, such as co-workers and managers, to external customers, such as clients, vendors, suppliers, and other business-related associates. To *partner* is to establish trust, share information, and work in tandem to solve problems and achieve results. When partnerships are successful, both parties recognize the value of the relationship and want to continue it to promote mutual reward.

Valuing Those Around Us

We easily recognize the importance of our external customers. The organization exists to serve them, and they may pay us to do so. Therefore, we serve our best interests by keeping customers satisfied. As a matter of fact, most of you are familiar with the expression, "The customer is always right," right?

Many people find it more difficult to imagine a co-worker as an internal customer. If an organization is a network of people, and if all of the people in the network perform specific functions, then all job functions intricately link and combine to meet the needs of external customers. As such, employees must depend and rely on each other to satisfy external customers' demands. By thinking this way you become internal customers to one another.

Your effectiveness at meeting the needs of internal or external customers depends largely on your ability to form internal and external relationships.

Respecting Our Customers

For you to establish solid relationships with your work colleagues, you must value them as individuals and must take the necessary steps to develop productive partnerships. The core of every successful partnership is respect *(Figure 4-1)*.

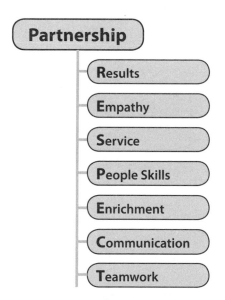

Fig. 4-1 R-E-S-P-E-C-T

R-E-S-P-E-C-T, offers the vital components of effective partnerships:

Results

Your first priority as an AP is to achieve results. To fulfill most of your responsibilities requires information or input from other people. Working effectively with others helps you complete your task quickly and efficiently. In turn, others will need to rely on you to be productive, thus establishing the need for an ongoing partnership.

Empathy

"Never judge another person until you've walked a mile in their shoes." To build relationships you must understand the perspectives, needs, and situations of the colleagues you work with and the customers you support. As you focus on your own priorities and responsibilities, it becomes easy to ignore or dismiss the needs of others. What you may think is a trivial or non-urgent request may be a critical or vital concern to the person who asked you. You enhance relationships by clarifying requests and showing you care.

Service

Service to internal and external customers is fundamental to every organization. Offering good customer service means that you please people with your concern and support. You gain credibility by producing a consistent, quality product. When working with you becomes a satisfying and beneficial experience, people will want to work with you again.

People Skills

People deserve to be treated with consideration. Body language is as important as the words we speak. How do you acknowledge people that approach your work area? Are you glad to help them out? Do you greet them with a smile and strong eye contact? Do you say hello and establish a comfortable atmosphere? Do you make them feel good about needing your help? Do you leave them wanting to work with you again? If you are friendly and approachable, then others will want to partner with you.

Enrichment

To enrich a partnership is to add value to the relationship. Most people are appreciative when others show a personal interest in them. This doesn't mean you need to become best friends or compromise professional boundaries. Relating to each other on a personal level brings a certain satisfaction to workplace relationships and tells others you care about them as individuals.

Communication

Listening is a valuable communication tool for working together effectively. Listening carefully helps you understand what people are saying and asking you to do. It then becomes your responsibility to verify what you've heard and to ask the questions that fill in remaining blanks. Your partners in the workplace also rely on your communication to them. Effective communication is a two-way street.

Teamwork

Every business shares the same goals: to meet the needs of customers, to produce a quality product, and to make money in the process. This can't be done without employees working together to achieve results. Such collaboration creates a sense of community in the workplace and uses the skills of each person.

What specifics, in addition to the R-E-S-P-E-C-T principles of partnership, can ensure a strong relationship with co-workers, managers, and customers?

- Be polite and courteous, but firm when necessary, to achieve results.

- Show enthusiasm and energy for the task or project at hand.

- Make sure clear expectations and instructions accompany each task.

- Take responsibility to update, report progress, and check in as needed.

- Be responsive by returning phone calls and e-mails promptly.

- Alert others when something is amiss or a deadline is in jeopardy.

- Have fun and use appropriate humor to reduce stressful situations.

Our ability to interact effectively with people is so essential that President Theodore Roosevelt acknowledged, "The most important single ingredient in the formula of success is knowing how to get along with people."

Transactional or Relationship-Based Service

As you practice R-E-S-P-E-C-T and responsibility, you build rapport. As you develop rapport, you move naturally from providing customer service via a transactional approach to a relationship approach.

Let me distinguish these approaches. A transactional approach to work is detached and distant. A relationship approach is involved and inviting.

Transactional

This approach focuses on the transactions, not the relationships, between individuals. This is a let's-stick-to-business approach. You pass information, paperwork, skill, or products to me, and I send some to you. People call this "quid pro quo," or "this for that." For example, if you need a report from the accounting department, then you call the accounting assistant and tell her what you need. Later, the accounting assistant walks up to your desk and hands you the report. You thank her and she walks away. Some other time she'll request information, whether unique or routine, from you. Note how little personal interaction or warmth accompanies this "interaction" or "exchange." Two cogs temporarily and briefly mesh to move the machine forward. Will you need to rely on her again? Is this an "over and done" interaction?

Relationship

Relationships are different. They focus on people dealing with one another to produce results. Imagine playing out the scenario above as a relationship. You need a report from accounting. You call the accounting assistant, tell her what you need, tell her you appreciate her time, and tell her you will certainly do her a favor if she needs it. Later, the accounting assistant walks up to your desk, says hello and lets you know that she has the report that you need. She then encourages you to call her if you need further information. You thank her and she walks away.

In this second version the co-workers exchange a bit of personal information. They are warm and friendly rather than cold and automated. The second version requires very little extra time from you or the accounting assistant, but it sets the tone for "ongoing" support and interaction, a relationship.

Keeping these style differences in mind, which accounting assistant would you prefer to work with in the future? Which one do you think provides better customer service?

A few years ago, I personally experienced these opposing service philosophies at a local department store. On a Christmas Eve I was buying clothes for my husband. A very nice, polite young man rang up my purchases, but there was no price tag on the final item. He explained that it was his first week on the job, and he wasn't quite certain what to do. He asked if I could be patient as he sought help from a co-worker. I told him, "No problem." He couldn't get anyone to help as everyone else was very busy, so he tried to phone a manager. No answer. He approached another salesperson, who was finishing with a customer. She came over and told him that, "Yes, I know where you can find the price." He asked her to please tell him so he could complete the sale. She then said that she would "only tell him if he gave her part of the commission." He was shocked. I was shocked. Yet she held firm. His body language said he couldn't agree, and I understood. She threw the pants on the counter and walked away!

What happened here? The young salesman wanted to meet my needs. I was his priority, and he was friendly and focused on me, his customer. He was clearly relationship-oriented in his approach to meeting my needs. His attempt to make me feel comfortable during this situation showed that he wasn't viewing this as a transactional sale. He cared about what was happening and was disturbed by his co-worker's behaviors. His concern showed me that he respected me as a customer and the store he represented.

The female sales associate, on the other hand, was clearly focused on a transaction. She didn't care about me, her co-worker, or how she was representing herself or her department store. She didn't care that she had an opportunity to support a new associate. Nor did she view it as an opportunity to partner with him to meet an external customer's needs. She only cared about getting her share of the sale. It didn't matter to her if I returned to that store or not. She selfishly exhibited poor judgment.

This situation is the most egregious example of poor customer service I ever experienced. After the saleswoman walked away, I told the salesman that I wanted to talk to a manager. When the manager showed up, we walked away from the counter, and I explained to her what had happened. I told her how helpful the young man was and how offensive the behavior of the saleswoman had been. I told her that I had managed many people in my career and had she, as a manager, witnessed this behavior she probably would have terminated her sales associate on the spot. After I finished the conversation with the manager, I went back to the young salesman and told him that I thought he had handled himself professionally and that I had appreciated his courtesy and willingness to help me.

Word Travels Fast

You never forget poor customer service. You remember it, and you tell friends, family, and co-workers. They then remember it too. This kind of "publicity" severely damages the reputation of businesses. Bad customer service in the workplace receives the same kind of publicity. Co-workers share their stories and their frustrations about working with poor performers or difficult people. Word of mouth travels fast, and it is influential in establishing the reputation of a person. Your best defense against a damaged reputation is to influence the thoughts of others through peak performance and considerate behaviors. You will never be able to please everyone, but you will at least know you did your best in trying.

Identifying Your Customers

Think about the customers you serve each day. Who are your internal and external customers? Now let's take a look at *Figure 4.2* and identify your internal customers by writing their names in the ovals. These people rely on you to help them meet their objectives. Then identify your external customers on the lines at the bottom of the triangle. As you consider what you've learned about establishing partnerships, what things will you do to enhance your workplace relationship?

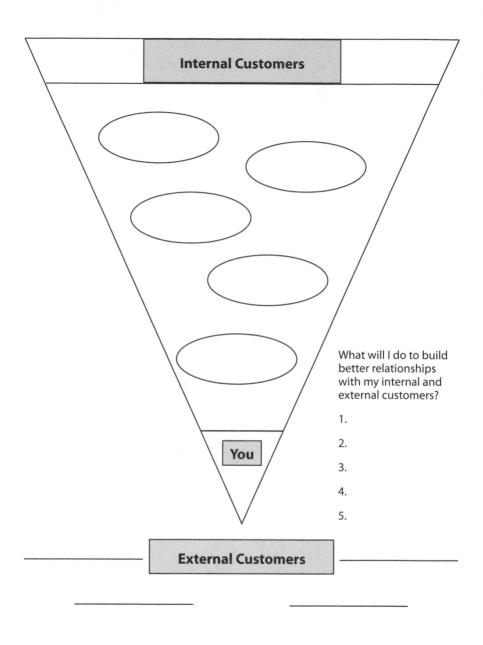

Internal Customers

What will I do to build better relationships with my internal and external customers?

1.

2.

3.

4.

5.

You

External Customers

Fig. 4.2 Internal and External Customers

Expanding Relationships

Now think about expanding your relationships. How might you develop new partnerships outside of your immediate team of internal and external customers? Consider establishing expanded relationships with peers or managers with whom you have little interaction. How might you increase your circle of influence within your organization?

The following ideas may help:

- Be the first to say hello in hallways and common areas.

- Introduce yourself to a new employee or an unknown colleague at every opportunity.

- Invite someone to lunch to learn about them and to get to know them as an individual.

- Defy your normal routine in the company lunch room and sit with a new group of people.

- Volunteer for company-wide teams or committees.

- Offer to assist someone who seems overloaded or frantic in meeting a deadline.

- Be friendly with lots of people, not tight with just a few.

- Buy someone a cup of coffee who looks like they could use a day brightener.

- Congratulate co-workers whom you may not know very well for their noted accomplishments.

- Send personal notes of appreciation to corporate leaders for new benefits or company functions/events that promote a healthy corporate culture and/or recognize the value of employees.

Think of opportunities specific to your organization. Whatever you can do to expand your personal network and establish relationships will benefit you in the long run. As you know more and more people within your organization, you will have a much larger pool of resources, knowledge, and experience at your disposal to do your job most effectively.

The Enormity of Partnership

APs who value relationships enrich their working environments and expand their personal knowledge because they respect other people for their:

- thoughts and ideas

- knowledge

- uniqueness

- cultural diversity

- strengths and weaknesses

- contributions

- skills

- experiences

Since we were kids, we've all heard that two heads are better than one. It's true, you know. And if two heads are better, then more heads are best. As you tap into the abilities of others, you contribute to your own effectiveness. Your own ideas are probably good, but when combined with the ideas of others, they may become great.

Partnership: A Step Towards Administrative Excellence

Partnership is the force behind solid business alliances. To value partnership is to recognize that:

- When you partner effectively with people inside your organization, then you become an integral part of the complex structure that keeps your organization strong and prosperous.

- When you partner effectively with people outside of your organization, then you become a positive, personal representative of your organization.

Successful APs are confident enough in their abilities to seek the input of others, and they are resourceful enough to build relationships that enhance their careers.

Chapter V – Professionalism

"There are no short cuts to any place worth going."

Sondra Thiederman

AP Strength #5 Professionalism

Professionalism is something you display and others judge. What images come to mind when you think of someone who displays professionalism?

The American Heritage Dictionary defines professionalism as "professional status, methods, character, or standards."

The International Association of Administrative Professionals describes the characteristics of an administrative professional as:

- mastery of office skills
- ability to assume responsibility without direct supervision
- ability to exercise initiative and judgment
- ability to make decisions within the scope of assigned authority

Admirable Qualities

Think about the impressive, capable, admirable people that surround you. How have these managers, administrative peers, and associates earned your respect? What qualities do you find most appealing? How do these colleagues exhibit professionalism? On the following page is a place to make a list.

As you look at the characteristics you've written down, I'm guessing you can categorize them in three ways:

1. Image and Appearance

2. Personal Conduct and Behavior

3. Technical Expertise and Proficiency

Professionalism in Action

I did not list the three categories in order of importance. Rather, the list is a sequence by which others judge your professionalism. Let's look at the categories more closely by imagining that you are witnessing an employment interview between an AP candidate and an HR manager.

#1 — Image and Appearance

The HR manager approaches the AP waiting in the organization's lobby and immediately notices the AP's clothing, accessories, and grooming. Based on the AP's appearance, the HR manager makes assumptions about the AP's competency. As they shake hands and make introductions, they form further opinions: "This person conveys confidence," or "This person seems unfriendly." They absorb and process these assumptions and conclusions within three to five seconds of their first eye contact or handshake. In that time, the HR manager has formed an initial opinion of this candidate's skill, knowledge, and ability. As they walk to the next location, the manager is again forming opinions. Is the candidate conversational or too uptight? Does the candidate keep pace walking with the HR manager? For example, more than once I needed to slow down and wait for a candidate to catch up. This always concerned me: Could the candidate keep pace in a hectic, busy work environment? We all know that first impressions are superficial and often inaccurate. But we also know that first impressions are absolutely critical.

A few months ago I ordered a sandwich "to-go" at a French bakery known for tasty sandwiches and good food. You can imagine my disappointment when the clerk handed me a poorly wrapped sandwich. The man behind the counter had quickly thrown paper around the sandwich, wadded up both ends, and secured it with a piece of masking tape. Some of the sandwich was exposed. The sloppy presentation made me wonder if the sandwich would be unappetizing. I was wrong, the sandwich was delicious.

First impressions are like sandwich wrappings. You judge quality based on exterior presentation. This may not be fair, but it is a natural way to form opinions. Conversely, an impeccable first impression is baseless without skill.

In the 1988 film *Working Girl*, Melanie Griffith plays determined secretary Tess McGill. Tess has drive, energy, ambition, and intelligence, but whatever she does, she does not get ahead. At the beginning of the movie she is a classic 1980s working girl with big hair and big jewelry. No one takes her seriously. She seizes an opportunity to get noticed and take on additional responsibility when her manager, played by Sigourney Weaver, is injured and unable to come into the office for several weeks. What Tess then does is entirely unethical. She pretends to be a peer of her manager and inserts herself into a business deal as the leading representative of her firm and "partners" with an outside firm to assist her in securing this deal. In her defense, she had earlier proposed this idea to her manager, who dismissed the idea. My point concerns how Tess "assumes" a management role and transforms herself to "look the part." Overnight she goes from the big-haired, big-jeweled, fast-talking secretary whom no one takes seriously to a polished, poised, stylish individual whom everyone outside of her company assumes *is* a managing partner in her firm. As she portrays a manager, no one questions her intelligence, personal power, or ability. She was still the same talented, smart, and ambitious person on the inside; but now her outward appearance and behavior validated all of those traits in the minds of others.

The Power of Immediate Presence. The importance of professional image hit home with me many years ago. In early 1981, right after starting my job in the typing pool of a Boston engineering firm, I decided that I wanted a better job. I arranged an appointment with a placement agency and confidently went in with resumé in hand, anxious to secure a top notch administrative job at the 60 State Street tower in the heart of Boston's financial district. My hopes were soon dashed when the placement coordinator told me, "If you want to *be* 60 State Street, you need to *look* 60 State Street." At the time, I was offended that the coordinator couldn't see beyond the fact that I didn't have enough money to invest in the right clothes to "*look* 60 State Street." Her message stays with me. There is a perceived correlation between image and ability, and I am thankful that she made me aware of that all those years ago. Whether you like it or not, your image is important in defining who you are and what you have to offer. I never did work at 60 State Street in Boston. I returned to my job in the typing pool and found my way to success in other ways, eventually earning enough money to invest in a professional wardrobe.

Branding Yourself. Tom Peters, author of *The Brand You 50*, declares that people can brand themselves much like products are branded. Products get branded and marketed so that consumers understand the quality of those products based on image and consistent value. Peters suggest that you can do the same thing by promoting yourself as a quality employee so that managers and organizations want to invest in your abilities and talents. Tess, the transformed secretary in *Working Girl* chose to re-brand herself as a confident, accomplished professional. In so doing she attracted success.

Your outward appearance makes an immediate statement about you. Your style needs to be your own and comfortable, but it must also convey proficiency. Here are three rules for appropriate workplace attire.

1. Make a good first impression and show self-respect.

2. Be consistent with the organization's business culture.

3. Convey skill, ability, confidence, and competence.

Adopting these three norms will give you the power of immediate presence. As a result, people will be inclined to treat you as a professional by considering your ideas and seeking your input. Image and appearance send lasting, powerful messages. Is your image and appearance sending the message you want to convey? The following checklist *(Figure 5-1)* will assure a polished first impression:

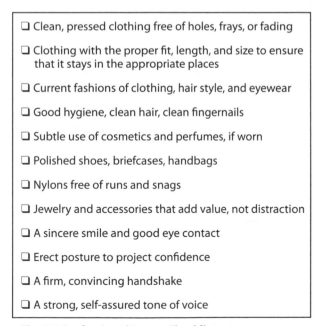

❑ Clean, pressed clothing free of holes, frays, or fading

❑ Clothing with the proper fit, length, and size to ensure that it stays in the appropriate places

❑ Current fashions of clothing, hair style, and eyewear

❑ Good hygiene, clean hair, clean fingernails

❑ Subtle use of cosmetics and perfumes, if worn

❑ Polished shoes, briefcases, handbags

❑ Nylons free of runs and snags

❑ Jewelry and accessories that add value, not distraction

❑ A sincere smile and good eye contact

❑ Erect posture to project confidence

❑ A firm, convincing handshake

❑ A strong, self-assured tone of voice

Fig. 5-1 Professional Image Checklist

Make personal attire choices that work for you, not against you. Don't let your skills, knowledge, and abilities be obstructed by misguided judgments or unnecessary distractions.

#2 – Personal Conduct and Behavior
The core of professionalism is found in personal conduct and behavior. This is the second way in which others will judge professionalism.

Let's return to the interview between the AP and the HR manager. They are now in the midst of the interview and the HR manager is trying to determine whether this individual is a "good fit" for the position and the organization. The HR manager is now assessing conduct and behavior based on the candidate's actions and responses. Is the candidate attentive and interested? Exhibiting good listening skills? Asking appropriate questions? Is the candidate considerate of the interviewer, allowing the interviewer to complete thoughts and questions? Is the candidate using appropriate grammar and language? Does the candidate appear prepared for the interview with notepad and writing instrument? Is the candidate organized and able to quickly locate additional copies of her or his resumé or references? Has the candidate turned off cell phones, pagers, and other electronic devices? Is the candidate making a positive impression on the interviewer?

Once hired, does the employee make a positive impression on the employer? Your conduct determines how far you will go in your worklife. It is an observable trait that administrative peers, co-workers, and managers subconsciously evaluate. Here are some ways to demonstrate professional conduct.

- Adhere to company business hours.

- Fulfill your employment obligations throughout the day.

- Be on time for meetings and scheduled events.

- Limit your absences from the workplace.

- Respect company policies and benefits.

- Interact tactfully and diplomatically with others.

- Use appropriate language and gestures.

- Practice ethical behaviors.

- Deal with conflicts or problems in a timely, constructive, positive way.

- Handle rejection or criticism in a mature manner.

- Take initiative to help others.

- Respect the property and work space of others.

- Respect the rights and privacy of others.

To conduct yourself in this manner displays good work habits and increases your value to an organization. These behaviors are your responsibility and within your control. If you don't hold yourself accountable for appropriate conduct, someone else will. Organizations would be remiss in ignoring the impact of recurring, irresponsible actions.

Professional Resolution. Don't gossip. I can't be any clearer than that. A reputation as a workplace gossip will significantly undermine your professional status. Gossip, rumors, and grapevines are prevalent and destructive in most companies. Because of that, it is worth talking about ways to curb the spread of half truths and misinformation.

I have seen rumor mills spin out of control. They damage everyone involved. When this happens, people become divided in their allegiance to co-workers, managers, or the organization. That environment undermines productivity and teamwork and creates a subculture of negativity. It is your responsibility, through your professionalism, to stop rumors and gossip. For example, as someone approaches you with grousing or "hear-say," deflect the conversation. Redirect these associates to someone who can help them resolve their concern. If you listen and contribute, you keep the rumor mill alive and you become part of the problem by your unwillingness to disengage from the conversation.

I am not talking about genuine, personal issues that someone wants to share with you as a friend or confidante. I am talking about gossip, hurtful comments, incomplete information, or speculation. As an AP you need to be part of the solution, not part of the problem.

When you fail to take proper action with your own workplace issues, you tend to become part of this cycle. In your frustration, you seek the opinions of others and, as a result, share personal information. This is how many grapevines get started. Unless you trust the people that you are confiding in, your personal matters are at risk of being repeated. Confronting your issues in a timely manner, with respect and maturity, will lessen your desire to air your frustrations with others. It is always best to deal with issues up front and on your own and to do your part in promoting a healthy working environment.

If you find yourself struggling with an issue or a concern, identify some options for resolving it. Should you decide that you want to address your concerns with a manager, a Human Resources representative, or a colleague, then the following steps will be helpful.

1. Be prepared. What do you want to accomplish in this conversation?

2. Outline your conversation. Consider the various responses you may get from the other party and determine how you would respond to these different avenues of feedback. Keep outlining until you've thought the conversation through and feel comfortable with the different paths the conversation may take.

3. Arrange a time and place to meet.

4. Project confidence by standing straight, establishing good eye contact, and taking a deep breath before speaking.

5. Offer "I" statements not "you" or "they" statements: "I think..., I want..., I believe..., I see..." Keep centered on yourself and your needs, observations, concerns, and take any ownership you may have in the conflict or situation.

6. Focus on solutions, not problems. Offer ideas to resolve or improve the issue or working conditions.

7. Give your listener time to consider your feedback.

8. Determine the next steps or actions for resolution.

9. Understand that the outcome may not be to your total satisfaction.

10. Decide what you can live with as a result of the conversation.

It can be hard to muster the courage to hold conversations that arise from conflict or frustration. To disregard them is to accept the situation and to feel helpless in your workplace or your relationships. Many times APs would come into my office frustrated by a manager or a co-worker and I would ask, "Have you talked to him or her about your concerns?" The answer was always the same, "No." Ignoring your issues prolongs your anxiety and stress. Few problems simply fix themselves or disappear. Addressing them will usually resolve the issue quickly and effectively.

Being prepared is the best way to address your concerns. It shows that you've given thought and consideration to the issue and that you want to take responsibility for resolution.

#3 – Technical Expertise and Proficiency
The third, and final, way in which others judge your professionalism is through your technical expertise and proficiency. Expertise defines a profession, whether you are an architect, doctor, teacher, pilot, or AP. Technical expertise is the critical knowledge that distinguishes professions. It is the foundation of any profession and, therefore, must be current and constantly improved to stay at the leading edge. As an airline passenger, how would you like to discover that your pilot has not been educated on the operation and safety of your aircraft? When you buy a ticket you probably assume, without consciously thinking about it, that the pilot's education is complete, ongoing, and inclusive of the latest technology. Your safety depends on it.

The need for AP training is not so dire, but it is nonetheless important and necessary to success. Learning is the avenue to new skills and proficiency. Let's conclude the AP-HR interview. The HR manager is now assessing the AP candidate's technical competencies. Would the HR manager be impressed to learn that the AP candidate has had no continued education or refresher courses to keep skills current? Or would this manager be more impressed by proven credentials and a candidate's interest in her profession demonstrated by additional classes, professional seminars, or advanced degrees or certifications?

Not only is your technical prowess determined by your educational achievements and by the number of software packages you know and skillfully maneuver. It is also determined by your ability to produce quality work. I recently saw an employment ad that required *"professional ownership of your work product."* This organization was clearly looking for an individual that takes pride in her or his output and values quality, accuracy, and superior presentation.

I remember receiving a resumé from an AP that immediately destroyed her technical credibility. It contained several typos. Some were blotted with "white-out" and corrected, others crossed-out and rewritten in pen. Needless to say, this person was not considered for the position.

Showcasing Professional Behaviors. As a strategy for achieving a reputation of excellence, find ways to showcase those things that set you apart and make you stand out. In exhibiting your talents for others to see, you provide opportunities for them to evaluate your abilities and assess your competence. This may sound like a performance review to you, and indeed it is. You gain value and visibility when others know what you are capable of achieving. Opportunities to exhibit professional sophistication surround you everyday. People notice you and judge your abilities in the following ways.

- How you answer your telephone or respond to e-mail.

- How you prepare correspondence and complete projects and documentation.

- How you interact with co-workers and associates.

- How you carry yourself, the image you project, and the level of self-confidence you possess.

- How you organize and personalize your workspace.

- How you share ideas and approach problem solving, interpersonal conflicts, and crisis situations.

- How you step up to the plate and take on additional responsibility.

- How you handle confidential, sensitive information.

- How you represent your manager and organization, inside and outside the organization.

- How you treat your internal and external customers.

- How you display your values, morals, and ethics.

Setting Professional Standards. Professionalism will be carried out differently by different people. Each AP will bring an individual sense of self to the workplace. But let's take a closer look at some vital elements of professionalism specific to the administrative profession. These elements form a composite of behaviors of many successful APs I have known.

Professionalism for the administrative professional involves:

- Performing your responsibilities with accuracy, adeptness, and a sense of urgency.

- Conveying an image that implies knowledge, confidence, and skill.

- Remaining cool, calm, and collected in the face of challenge, change, and chaos.

- Displaying values, morals, and ethics that are above reproach.

- Learning, expanding, growing, and holding yourself accountable and responsible.

- Making decisions and judgment calls based on insight and experience.

- Respecting yourself and others.

- Removing yourself from petty, inconsequential issues, and workplace gossip.

- Holding your work in high esteem and striving for a quality result.

- Working together with co-workers, managers, and customers to meet goals and objectives.

Committing to Professionalism

Professionalism is a tall order. It takes steady commitment. When you think of professionalism as a composite of these many traits, attributes, and abilities, you create a benchmark for the continued pursuit of professionalism. As you endure conflicts, problems, dilemmas, obstacles, and frustrations in the workplace, you can reflect on your actions and ask yourself if your behavior exhibits professionalism as outlined above. I invite you to use this definition of administrative professionalism but I encourage you to create your own list based on your environment and your beliefs about professionalism.

Take a minute to think about elements of professionalism from your perspective. What's important to you? What do you believe and value in performing your responsibilities as an AP? Jot some of these thoughts down and create your own definition of professionalism.

To me, professionalism as an AP means:

As your thoughts take shape, you create your own form of measurement. These thoughts allow you to follow your own distinctive path of professionalism.

Remember, becoming a "professional" and attaining professional standards is completely in your hands; you determine this for yourself. However, being recognized as a "professional" is only partially in your control. Others are more likely to perceive you and treat you as a professional when their observations, experiences, and interactions consistently tell them that you conduct yourself professionally. Creating your own definition of professionalism will clarify the action you want to take to become professional and to be treated by others as a *"professional."* If after your consistent and repeated efforts, neither your work environment nor your treatment changes very much, then perhaps you want to consider working elsewhere for colleagues who treat you respectfully. They need your talents and skills, and you deserve their respect and support.

Professionalism: A Step Towards Administrative Excellence

In the game show *Let's Make a Deal* the host enticed contestants to trade a known prize for an unknown and perhaps better prize located behind a mysterious door or within a beautifully wrapped package. The gamble was that the contestant didn't know what he would get by choosing a different prize. He may get something of more or less value than the original prize. The exterior presentation was not an indication of the quality of the prize inside the box or behind the door. The outcome was left to chance.

Skills, knowledge, and ability are internal attributes. These attributes can be hidden, suppressed, or understated by exterior presentation, or they can be enhanced by exterior presentation. Successful APs understand that professionalism is akin to the gift wrapping of a valuable prize. These successful individuals realize that:

- Equal displays of image, conduct, and expertise are necessary for others to view you as a professional.

- Professionalism must be consistently demonstrated to be respected and appreciated.

Successful APs do not leave their professionalism to chance. They act like professionals. They exhibit behaviors that confirm their professional status.

Chapter VI – The Five Ps:
A Model of Administrative Excellence

"Any transition serious enough to alter your definition of self will require not just small adjustments on your way of living and thinking but a full-on metamorphosis."

Martha Beck

Mark Twain once said, "Success is a journey, not a destination. It requires constant effort, vigilance and reevaluation." I agree, but let's take a further step. Let me tell you what to be vigilant about, how to apply your efforts, and how to evaluate your performance.

The first five chapters of this book describe a base of administrative excellence, the **"Five Ps"** of administrative performance: **Perception, Purpose, Progress, Partnership, and Professionalism.** If you improve in these five areas then you catapult yourself toward earning deserved respect as an excellent AP *(see Figure AE-1).*

Evaluating Your Performance

Saw blades wear with use. Worn blades need sharpening or replacement. Your skills and abilities are *your* professional saw blades. As you get comfortable in your work and workplace and with the people you support, then your skills and abilities can dull. Committed APs want to "cut it" as an AP and make the necessary adjustments to be "on the cutting edge" of performance.

Chapters I-V explain the importance of each of these five areas and how each contributes to administrative excellence. Take some time to reflect on each of these areas *(Figure 6-1).*

Perception: Recognizing personal strengths and weaknesses; respecting the behavior styles of others.

- I know my strengths and how to capitalize on them.
- I know my weaknesses, take ownership of them, and try to minimize them to the best of my abilities.
- I recognize the behavior styles of others, and I adapt to their style to meet their needs and work together most effectively.

Purpose: Understanding and respecting your role in meeting corporate goals and objectives.

- I understand the goals of my manager, team, and organization.
- I respect the role that I play in helping to meet these goals.
- I am challenged and fulfilled by my workplace responsibilities.

Progress: Thinking broadly to enhance your performance and challenging yourself to take personal risks.

- I try to find new, better, more efficient ways to do things.
- I challenge myself by taking smart, calculated risks to expand my comfort zone.
- I think in terms of continuous personal and professional improvement.

Partnership: Building strong relationships to achieve results.

- I respect the needs of other people.
- I value the opinions of other people.
- I apply equal importance to internal and external customers.

Professionalism: Displaying qualities that build character and ensure professional status.

- I project an appearance that validates my skills, knowledge, and abilities.
- I conduct myself with honesty and integrity.
- I educate myself, stay current with technical updates, and produce quality work.

Now rate yourself on a scale of 1 to 4 (1= low score, weakness and 4= high score, excellence). Be honest with yourself.

Perception
❏ 1   ❏ 2   ❏ 3   ❏ 4

Purpose
❏ 1   ❏ 2   ❏ 3   ❏ 4

Progress
❏ 1   ❏ 2   ❏ 3   ❏ 4

Partnership
❏ 1   ❏ 2   ❏ 3   ❏ 4

Professionalism
❏ 1   ❏ 2   ❏ 3   ❏ 4

Fig. 6-1 Evaluating Excellence

If you are less than satisfied with your administrative success up to this point, you may find the answer in one of these areas. Would you like to sharpen your skills and enhance your performance in one or more of these areas? If so, refer back to the corresponding chapters and create an action plan for yourself. Use the *Model of Administrative Excellence (Figure AE-1)* as a benchmark to manage your career. As you experience job frustrations or performance challenges, refer to the **Five Ps** of administrative excellence and identify your area of opportunity. Actively keep your skills sharp and your efforts focused. This will keep you "a cut above" in your performance.

Excellence Not Perfection

Strive for excellence, not perfection. Striving for excellence means you give your best at all times. Excellence, however, should not be confused with perfection. Perfection is unrealistic. Striving for perfection is unproductive.

I offer the following by an unknown author to help you see the difference:

Excellence is the willingness to be wrong
Perfection is being right

Excellence is risk
Perfection is fear

Excellence is powerful
Perfection is anger and frustration

Excellence is spontaneous
Perfection is conformity

Excellence is accepting
Perfection is judgmental

Excellence is giving
Perfection is taking

Excellence is confidence
Perfection is doubt

Excellence is flowing
Perfection is restriction

Excellence is surrender
Perfection is consuming

Excellence is trust
Perfection is selfishness

Excellence is a journey
Perfection is a destination

Excellence and You

How do you define administrative excellence? What does it look like to you? How does it feel to you? What do you accomplish when you achieve administrative excellence?

In the space below, write your own definition of administrative excellence:

Now based on your definition, what thoughts, behaviors, and actions will you take to demonstrate your administrative excellence and to help change perceptions in your workplace? In *Figure 6-2* are some examples and some blank spaces for you to express your own ideas.

Thoughts	Behaviors	Actions
How can I change some of my own encumbered, traditional thinking?	*What behaviors can I incorporate to enhance my performance?*	*What actions can I take to make a difference in my administrative career?*
Negative, unproductive thought: I am not as smart as my manager. **Positive**, affirming thought: I may not share his or her technical expertise and our formal education may vary, but I have other strengths and abilities and my own areas of expertise. I am well educated through my own life and work experiences.	Example: I am going to focus more attention on details so that I don't overlook some of the small things that are important to completing projects. I will become recognized for delivering a quality product.	Example: I am going to take a class in public speaking to improve my communication skills and to gain self-confidence. This will help me interact more effectively with my team members and develop the skills to speak up and participate in department meetings.
Your Thoughts	**Your Behaviors**	**Your Actions**
Fig. 6-2 New Thoughts, Behaviors, Actions		

To take control of your thoughts, behaviors, and actions is to invest in yourself and to take more control of your environment and those things that directly affect you. Don't let weak performance or negative self-talk hamper or confine you.

Professionalizing Our Profession

An early message of the 1990s Total Quality Management (TQM) movement was to "fix thyself first." That remains true. To influence others or to improve a workplace you must first be a model of administrative excellence, constantly reflecting on your own skills, abilities, and shortcomings. Your starting point—your performance—makes all the difference in influencing change in your organization and determining your end results.

The **Five Ps** of administrative excellence set a base of (excellent) operations and form a gateway to leadership, empowerment, and growth. Part II describes how these three factors benefit you, your organization, and the administrative profession.

Part II

Revolutionizing Our Value in the Workplace:

Leadership, Empowerment, and Growth

Chapter VII – Leadership

"We don't know who we are until we see what we can do."

Martha Grimes

Leadership is influence and influence is personal power. Hillary Clinton. Oprah Winfrey. Laura Bush. Condaleezza Rice. These women are recognized leaders. Each has personal power, although each has a different leadership style. Leadership—whether quiet strength, charismatic energy, or some other traits—is as unique as the individuals who have it. Think back to the DiSC behavioral differences we discuss in Chapter I. Each of the four DiSC behaviors brings forth a different approach to leadership.

There is no better time for administrative leaders to emerge. Economic forecasts show that jobs as office and administrative support staff will grow only half as fast as other occupations from 2004-2014. Simultaneously, the impending large-scale retirement of baby boomers will stress the workforce by leaving significant gaps in knowledge and job expertise. Organizations will need the contributions of each employee to remain competitive and will need leaders at every level to maintain efficiency and productivity. Vacancies will create opportunities for personal and professional growth. Vacancies will also create opportunities for workplace recognition of those people who develop new, necessary skills. The need for top talent will be crucial. A highly-skilled AP, willing and able to assume greater responsibility, will become invaluable in such a marketplace.

The Power of Personal Power

Many APs react negatively to the word *power*. You might think of authority, control, or criticism. Perhaps these words trigger feelings of autocratic work environments or aggressive personality types. Perhaps these words describe traits or attitudes that contradict who you want to be. For you to grow as a professional you need to abandon negative thoughts about power and recognize power as an attribute of leadership.

I personally admire Elizabeth Dole, a United States Senator from North Carolina. She personifies elegance and dignity. Her image is of poise and sophistication. She is gracious and calm in her manner and dedicated to her causes. How she conducts herself creates images of excellence and leadership in my mind. She has an aura of personal power. She doesn't have to tell you that she is powerful. Her body language, self-confidence, and appearance, convince you that she is accomplished. Elizabeth Dole said, "We have learned that power is a positive force if it is used for positive purposes." What you do with your power is a choice.

> **Excellence + Leadership = Personal Power**

Personal power arises from excellence and leadership. When you are performing to the best of your abilities and are gaining credibility and recognition as a professional, then you are amassing personal power. Personal power gives you control over your environment and influence over change that might be necessary to further your career.

Remember the AP, decribed earlier, who approached her manager and became a key employee, gained additional responsibility, and earned a trip to Thailand? This AP has personal power. We all possess some degree of personal power, although most of us go about our day and give it little thought.

I never thought I held any personal power at Ryan Companies until a co-worker pointed it out to me. An associate wanted my opinion on a topic specific to women in the workplace. I asked why she sought my opinion. Her response caught me off guard. She said that she felt I possessed power in the organization and could probably influence a change in this area. I remember being surprised by her response because I had never thought of myself in that way. So I asked her to explain. In what way did she feel I had power in the organization? She said that I was respected in the organization for my contributions and that management listened to me. To her, I held personal power. After this eye-opening conversation, I began to think differently about power.

I realized that power is not simply a position or title. Power is much more subtle than that. I knew several managers in the organization respected for their knowledge, their personal integrity, and their ability to establish trust in relationships. I also knew several respected and powerful co-workers who didn't hold a management position or a significant title. Colleagues respected these co-workers for many of the same reasons they respected those admirable managers.

Unquestionably, your job does not define you; you define your job. Leadership and power are available to you, regardless of the position you hold, because your personal practices drive these two influencing factors.

Exercising Leadership

How you exercise leadership will be as unique as your fingerprints. When others are impressed by your abilities, benefit from your skills, and respect you as an individual, you gain professional credibility. When others seek your advice and listen to your input, you gain a voice. With this kind of admiration, you are respected as a leader in your organization. Leadership is not something you either have or you don't. It's a learned ability.

I think APs can demonstrate their leadership in three simple steps:

1. Be a role model. Consistently display the **Five Ps** of administrative excellence. Others will notice.

2. Offer solutions to problems, mentor or teach others, or do what is necessary to get the job done. Others will benefit.

3. Show consideration and treat people with respect. Others will reciprocate.

Leading Change

After one of my first corporate presentations of the excellence and leadership philosophies presented in this book, a middle-aged AP approached me and said "You have taught me a whole new way of thinking. I have never thought about organizations needing leadership at all levels before nor has anyone ever told me I had potential until you did today." I will never forget this women or this feedback. How unfortunate for her that it took more than 20 years for her to hear these messages. I am confident that she became a better employee after that presentation and that her organization gained an AP dedicated to excellence and leadership.

When you are capable of leading, you are capable of influencing others and leading change. You can exemplify leadership and affect change through your relationship with your manager. Consider again the Monster.com survey referenced in the Introduction. Recall that 71% of respondents said that APs were not valued in their organization. Your leadership skills, especially when applied strategically in partnership with your manager, can influence such opinions.

Taking Advantage of Opportunities to Educate

Administrative leaders effect change by educating managers of our professional value. APs know how vastly different the administrative world is from the world of management but managers rarely think about that. Managers busily focus on their business objectives, so the needs of the APs become secondary. Therefore, you must take any opportunity that presents itself to educate them.

How you "educate" them, however, is very important. Don't try to teach them a lesson. An aggressive approach will likely backfire. Instead tactfully and professionally convey your points. Act the way you think a manager should act with you. Since managers do not understand what it is like to be an administrative employee, many managers welcome the insight into employee needs that our "education" offers. Let me give you several examples of educating managers from my own experience.

When I joined Ryan Companies, the APs in my department were called contract assistants. This job title didn't make sense to me because it seemed to limit all of the work the APs did to support their project teams. I proposed that management change the title from contract assistant to project assistant to better reflect the AP's broad value to the team. Excited by the change, the APs took new pride in their role.

Shortly after, I suggested that our APs should have business cards. I believed they deserved a business card to identify and introduce themselves to the many clients, vendors, and subcontractors that they meet. Management thought the cards to be an unnecessary expense. I convinced them and surprised the APs with business cards. The new cards, in addition to the title change, sent messages of importance and validation. The APs felt their efforts were recognized and appreciated. This small financial investment showed the APs that they were respected and valued team members.

In another example, I spent six years as an executive assistant and administrative manager working in the open environment of a cubicle. I handled many confidential, private matters. In addition to my administrative responsibilities, my day included everything from resolving conflicts, reviewing performance, handling personal issues, interviewing, and making employment offers. Every time I needed to speak with someone directly or to place a confidential phone call, I had to find an empty office or conference room. Not having my own office was ineffective, but offices were reserved for department heads and project manager positions. Historical practices at the company determined that I sit in a cubicle. The cubicle wasn't an intentional power play on my manager's part. Rather, it was "just the way it had always been."

However, when the company remodeled office space, I asked to be included in the new "office" layout. After voicing my predicament and its effects on my productivity, the revised layout included a hard-walled office with a door for me. My job and life as an administrative manager became much easier. Had I not spoken up, the new layout would not have happened. And getting an office elevated the perception and credibility of my administrative position.

My last example concerns administrative management meetings. As the company grew regionally, administrative managers were located in several states. Collectively, we managed 25% of the company staff. It became harder and harder for us to communicate effectively via phone or e-mail, so I suggested that we meet regularly in structured meetings similar in content and format to regional department head meetings. Management approved quarterly meetings.

What did a manager say to me when we returned from our first meeting? "Do you actually get anything done on those trips or is it just for fun?" This question created an opportunity. And here's what I mean by taking the opportunity to educate when an opportunity presents itself: My response was, "Well, when you have your quarterly meetings, do you get anything done or is it just for fun?" I didn't say this sarcastically or rudely. The point was well-taken (and well-received) and the manager agreed that I was right. Managers never again questioned the purpose of our meetings.

Ryan Companies had a healthy culture and respected all employees when I joined the organization. However, some residual stereotypes remained concerning the administrative support staff. That is why I took the opportunity to educate when appropriate to effect change.

Is your organization willing to consider such changes? If you see possibilities to enlighten your manager or your organization, then give it a shot and let the education process begin. No one else will do it for you or for the profession. The task requires your leadership.

The Administrative/Management Partnership

Below are some other ways to work as a partner with your manager, display your leadership qualities, and change or enhance your professional value:

Administrative Leadership

1. **Speak up.** Tell your manager what is causing frustration and offer solutions in return. Managers are not mind readers. They cannot know your work problems unless you tell them. Together you can work toward resolution.

2. **Be resourceful.** Research all avenues for getting or finding additional information or completing an assignment. This proves your ability to think progressively and imaginatively. Your manager will respect you as someone who will "get the job done."

3. **Increase your effectiveness.** Find ways to continually add value to your manager or your team's effectiveness. This will build trust and establish loyalty from your manager(s). Your growing effectiveness and increased trust will distinguish your partnership as exceptional.

4. **Ask questions.** Get clarification before moving forward. Make sure you understand the expectations of an assignment and have the information you need to bring it to completion. This will reassure your manager that you think comprehensively and will consider the details.

5. **Share your successes.** Don't be modest! Let your manager know what you do well and what motivates you to succeed. This gives your manager an opportunity to build on your strengths.

6. **Assert yourself.** Ask if you don't know. Make suggestions. Challenge the norms. Your manager will appreciate your willingness to bring things to his or her attention for the betterment of the team.

7. **Educate yourself.** Stay current with technology and the most efficient means of completing responsibilities. Learning is the key to innovation and new and better ways of doing things. This is a mutual benefit to you and your manager.

8. **Challenge yourself.** Push your personal limits and continue to broaden your experiences. As you take on more responsibility, you become more valuable to your manager and to your organization.

9. **Perform.** Produce quality results and proactively anticipate needs. Prove yourself to be committed to excellence and your manager will be committed to you.

10. **Lead.** Show confidence in your abilities and demonstrate self-respect. Become an administrative role model and influence others. Your manager will respect you as a capable, effective business partner.

A Conversation with Your Manager

I list seven questions below. Imagine your manager is asking you these questions in a face-to-face conversation. Answer as if you are responding directly to him or her.

1. What can I do to contribute to a strong and successful working relationship?

2. How can I improve my communication to you?

3. Are there ways in which I could help make your job easier each day?

4. As a manager-admin team, what is the best way for us to overcome obstacles or avoid potential for inter-personal conflict?

5. In what ways do you prefer to be recognized and rewarded for your contributions?

6. If there is one thing you could change about your job what would it be? How would this change benefit our relationship and organizational sucess?

7. What can I do to support your continued growth and on-going personal and professional development?

Do your answers reveal any opportunities to engage your manager? To educate him or her? What issues would be beneficial to discuss with your manager? Would addressing these issues or opportunities improve your relationship? If so, think about the best way to approach your manager with these ideas. To help structure your conversation, refer to the suggestions for "Professional Resolution" in Chapter V.

When you exhibit leadership to your manager, you will earn the trust and respect necessary to elevate your responsibilities and professional visibility. Everybody benefits. The next chapter reviews the merits of empowered APs.

The Seeds of Potential

It has been said, "The best time to plant a tree is 25 years ago. The second best time is today." It is never too late to become the person you want to be. Are you satisfied to think you've reached your full potential? If not, then excellence, leadership, and personal power may help you realize your potential and fulfill your ambitions. You, your organization, and APs in general will benefit.

Chapter VIII - Empowerment

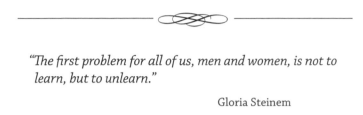

"The first problem for all of us, men and women, is not to learn, but to unlearn."

Gloria Steinem

The definition of empowerment is to *enable, permit,* and *authorize.* As an AP your empowerment largely depends upon how your manager directs and delegates work.

Managers can empower or encumber their administrative staff. Managers trust that AP leaders will exercise greater responsibility, make decisions, use good judgment, and do the right and necessary things to achieve results. Managers grant this trust and empowerment because AP leaders have proven their reliability and earned the trust and confidence of their managers. Empowered APs make decisions in much the same way as effective managers do, by asking themselves, "What's the best thing to do in this situation? What's in the best interest of the organization?" Empowered APs perform their responsibilities by thinking and acting like managers.

In contrast, many APs unknowingly disempower themselves. Here's how:

- **Corresponding ineffectively.** The use of cutesy terms or symbols to convey an idea or make an announcement undermines a serious, professional message. For example, expressing excitement in business correspondence by using words like "yeah," "yippee," or "hooray" or inserting a "smiley face" is often ineffective. Although I respect enthusiasm, such words and symbols appear childlike and make workplace messages appear frivolous.

- **Responding softly.** Women, more than men, tend to soften their response or reaction to situations. Here's what I mean by this. Has anyone ever asked your opinion and you respond by saying, "Yes...well maybe...no...I guess I'm not sure?" Another example is the comment, "I just need a tiny bit more time" when you are behind schedule or running late. Such uncertain or diminutive responses diminish your personal power and erode others' confidence in you. Choose words that are strong, powerful, and convey confidence. Use statements that will work for you, not against you such as, "Yes, I agree and here's why," or "I need more time. How about Friday?"

- **Apologizing.** It is not uncommon for women in general to habitually apologize. This happens whether an apology is warranted or not. "I'm sorry. I don't understand what you're asking." "I'm sorry. I must have misunderstood." You don't need to apologize unless you did something wrong and someone deserves your apology. Yes, you want to be polite to other people, but overused apologies can make you seem "less important" or "inferior" to someone else.

- **Asking for permission.** Many APs ask permission. "Excuse me, can I ask a question?" or "May I say something?" I notice this often in many meetings. Male associates rarely ask permission to ask a question, but female associates commonly do. Another example is seeking approval too frequently from managers on work-related tasks or responsibilities. You can counter this by clarifying the parameters of your job responsibilities in order to "take the ball and run with it." Such clarity *enables* you to work independently and "check-in" when necessary.

- **Rejecting a compliment.** It is very hard for many APs to accept a compliment. How many times have you heard (or said), "Oh, it was nothing." Or, "I had help. It was a team effort." If it was a team effort, great. If not, then graciously accept the compliment with a *"Thank you,"* and take pride in your accomplishment.

■ **Cluttering a workspace.** Your workspace is a reflection of you. Make sure it conveys an image that is consistent with your working environment and doesn't detract from your capabilities. Overly feminine decorations, inappropriate pictures or expressions, or an abundance of trinkets and useless items can interfere with your credibility in the workplace. For example, is the colleague with the stuffed animals glued to her computer top taken seriously by others?

As Gloria Steinem suggests, we need to "unlearn" some of these behaviors. "Unlearning" is not easy, but awareness of the detrimental impact of such behaviors in a corporate environment is the first step in making changes to empower yourself.

I do not mention some of these things to suggest that you become aggressive or arrogant in your approach to work or working with people (or that you hide your personality and enthusiasms). I don't know too many APs that aspire to aggressive, arrogant behavior, but I have known many that would like to become more assertive and self-confident. These are small ways in which you can strengthen your workplace presence and project yourself as someone with self-confidence and personal empowerment.

APs as a Collective, Powerful Workforce

There is power in numbers, and APs are clearly a powerful group making invaluable contributions to the success of the American economy. If you don't think so, or don't feel powerful in your workplace, think about it this way: What if all four million APs were to walk off their jobs tomorrow for an extended time, and what if future openings are not filled or are filled with poor performers? What would happen to Corporate America? What would happen to your organization? The resulting disaster and organizational chaos would cause serious disruptions, reduce productivity, and significantly affect bottom lines. Collectively APs hold a lot of power in the workplace. Individually, however, you may be empowered or disempowered in your working environment.

You've worked for or heard of organizations that disempower and encumber their APs, but I imagine you prefer organizations that encourage and empower their administrative staff. Let's revisit the "Encumbered" and "Empowered" AP models. I offer these models based on my real-life, personal experiences. These experiences give me a perspective and understanding of how culture and environment affect the productivity and attitudes of administrative employees.

Because of my experiences and perspectives, this chapter will now focus heavily on management and will speak to both management and APs in reference to the empowerment or disempowerment of APs in the workplace.

The Encumbered AP Staff, Feelings of Exclusion

Below is the Encumbered AP Model *(Figure Intro-2)*.

Fig. Intro-2
The "Encumbered" AP Staff

This model represents APs as behind-the-scenes, foundational employees viewed by managers as short-term, interchangeable workers. Since APs are paid to perform a specific function, management is unconcerned with APs' professional development. Most APs feel powerless in this type of organization and likely experience feelings of exclusion:

- bogged down by layers of management and bureaucracy

- excluded from departmental or organizational meetings that affect specific job responsibilities

- marginalized and outside the scope of important activity

- overlooked in respect to recognition and contribution

- hindered by limited communication from manager(s) regarding workload, deadlines, and client requests

- saddled with unclear and minimal expectations regarding job performance

- denied feedback on skills, abilities, and growth opportunities

- ignored when they mention problems or suggest solutions

- treated as unimportant or insignificant as an employee

- excluded from important communications

- denied or limited opportunities to improve or change how things are done

- perceived as an inferior class of employees

This environment often leads to a dissatisfied, frustrated, even angry, administrative staff. These emotions are a breeding ground for cliques. Negative leaders frequently emerge and influence the attitudes of others. Jealousy, envy, and resentment become normal behaviors. In addition to the emotional turmoil that ensues, profitability suffers through the abuse of sick time, high turnover rates, and lost productivity. Although symptomatic of their environment, many APs discredit themselves by behaving in these unseemly ways. Often, organizations that view the administrative role from this perspective get what they expect, which by outward appearances is a staff that is largely unprofessional and seemingly uninterested in their jobs.

Barry Oshry, author of *Seeing Systems: Unlocking the Mysteries of Organizational Life,* describes this type of organizational structure or culture as a "tops-middles-bottoms" arrangement. Encumbered APs sit at the "bottoms" of these organizations. Oshry describes life on "the bottom:"

- Bottoms feel *oppressed* in the system.

- Others (higher-ups) make decisions that affect their lives in major and minor ways – reorganizations happen *to* them; initiatives come and go; health and retirement benefits are diminished; plants are closed; workforces are reduced.

- Bottoms feel unseen and uncared for. They see things that are wrong with their situation and with the organization that higher-ups ought to be fixing but aren't.

- Bottoms feel isolated in the system; they don't have the big picture; there is no vision they can commit to; they don't see how their work fits into the whole; they don't get feedback on their work.

- Tops are invisible to Bottoms except for ceremonial acts (like Christmas visits), which seem patronizing.

- Bottoms feel that Middles add little value – they are uninformed; they may be well-meaning, but they are powerless; they are inconsistent and uneven.

- Much of Bottoms' energy is focused on "them" (higher-ups); Bottoms are angry at "them," frustrated by "them," resentful of "them," disappointed with "them."

Mr. Oshry's findings validate my own experiences in corporate cultures that produce an "encumbered" AP staff environment. Among the many disadvantages of operating this way, perhaps the most negative is that discontented employees tend to be high-maintenance employees. Frustrated individuals and poor performers absorb vast amounts of a manager's time and energy.

You can significantly control your own experience by pursing administrative excellence and gaining the trust and confidence of your manager. However, for a lasting change to occur, your manager and your organization must be willing participants in the empowerment of APs.

The Empowered AP Staff, Feelings of Inclusion

Now refer to *Figure Intro-3,* the Empowered AP staff. In this model APs are at the forefront of an organization, producing results and meeting the needs of customers and clients. From this perspective, APs are more valuable to the manager and to the organization because they are recognized as critical to the end result. With this direct connection to the customer, it makes good business sense to empower APs to do their jobs most effectively. As a matter of fact, it is in the best interest of a manager to do this. The more empowered you are, the more efficient your manager is. I refer to this as a delegation philosophy for encouraging the growth of APs. Simply stated, the more responsibility you are given, the more professional growth you will experience.

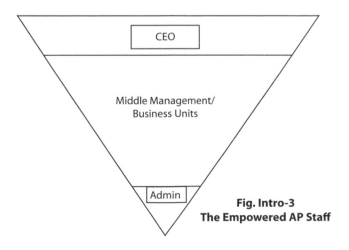

Fig. Intro-3
The Empowered AP Staff

In an empowered environment an AP will likely experience feelings of *inclusion:*

- respected by others for performing her roles and responsibilities

- valued as important and significant to the overall success of the team or organization

- recognized for achieving individual and team goals

- communicated with directly on issues that affect workload and performance

- included in meetings and events that clarify customers' needs and APs' corresponding job responsibilities

- connected in strong partnerships and relationships with internal and external customers

- asked for input and opinions

- encouraged to speak up, voice concerns, and share ideas

- encouraged to make decisions, within realm of responsibility, that support corporate goals and objectives

- encouraged to suggest change, job enhancements, and organizational improvement

Most importantly, managers in this environment value APs as colleagues. The performance of APs increases exponentially when they know they matter and that they have the necessary knowledge to adequately perform their job.

For several managers and APs, the Empowered AP model is an enlightened view of the role of the administrative professional. If your manager is remiss in this regard and you want to move toward this type of working environment, then use the leadership skills identified in Chapter VII to influence his or her actions. Through your own initiative, you can achieve many of the items listed above. Empowerment is often a natural response to one's leadership ability.

Satisfaction Levels of an Empowered AP Staff

APs typically thrive in empowered environments. Because of their inclusion they are focused on outcomes, results, and accomplishments. APs treated as active participants become involved in many aspects of achieving company goals and, as a result, their business knowledge expands. Since they are valued members of the team, APs that work in such environments are more likely to be productive and satisfied.

Below are several charts measuring the bi-annual satisfaction of APs working in an empowered environment. These charts show a progression of cultural changes and management initiatives over a six-year period. This feedback represents about 60 APs working in the Minneapolis office of Ryan Companies.

These APs were asked to rate their level of agreement or satisfaction in each of the following areas. The rating system is designed to represent a scale of 1 to 5 (one being the lowest level of agreement or satisfaction and five being the highest level). The organization strives for ratings between four and five in each area. Areas that score lower than 4 become targets for improvement.

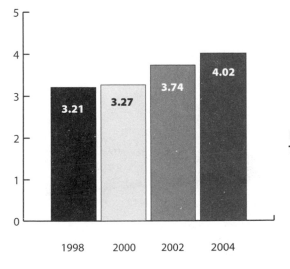

Fig. 8-1 Survey Results, Training To Do Your Job

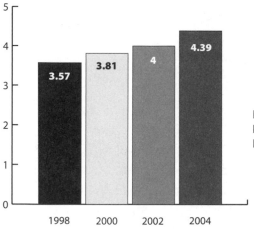

Fig. 8-2 Survey Results, Resources Available To Do Your Job

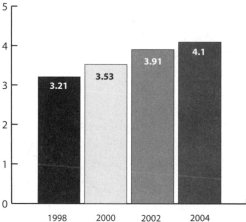

Fig. 8-3 Survey Results, Opportunities To Increase Responsibility

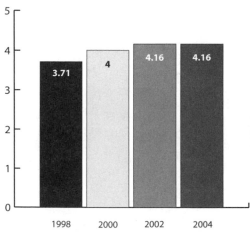

Fig. 8-4 Survey Results, Manager Provides Timely Feedback

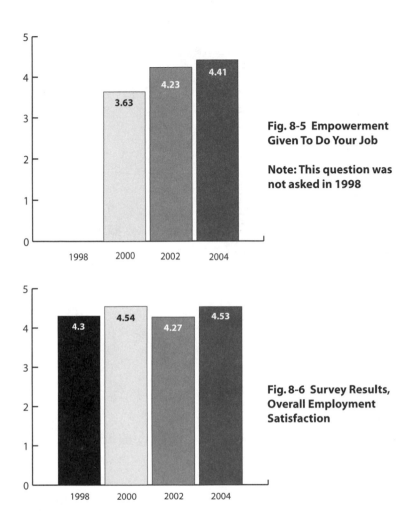

Fig. 8-5 Empowerment
Given To Do Your Job

Note: This question was
not asked in 1998

Fig. 8-6 Survey Results,
Overall Employment
Satisfaction

These results indicate the staff feels relatively empowered. This is good news for APs and for the company since these feelings and conditions are in large part due to a structured professional development plan created specifically for this staff *(see Chapter IX for details)*. This plan created an atmosphere that empowers the AP staff and maintains a high level of AP job satisfaction. (The small dip in the 2002 Overall Employee Satisfaction rating may reflect challenging economic conditions, downsizing, and organizational changes—all residual effects of the 9/11 terrorist attacks. But if so, note how little the satisfaction dropped amid the broader economic turmoil.) Overall, Ryan Companies benefits from an AP staff that enjoys and is satisfied by its work.

Increased morale, professionalism, and productivity are some of the rewards of the partnership between APs and management.

If your company does not administer an annual or bi-annual employee survey, then I strongly suggest that you talk to your manager or Human Resources Department about the advantages of such a tool. Surveys provide the opportunity for employees to respond candidly, honestly, and anonymously to questions important to company success. Results provide the company with much-needed insight about the "temperature" of the organization: Are people generally satisfied? Are they frustrated? How do they feel about their jobs? Analysts can then sort the answers into important and identifiable groups, such as particular work groups, departments, or teams. Such results give companies vital feedback from their most valuable asset, employees. Employee surveys, however, should not be administered unless a serious effort will be made to improve working conditions. To ignore the results would be devastating to organizational credibility.

Creating a Partnership Between Managers and APs

Below are ten simple things that managers can do to empower an AP staff. An AP exhibiting excellence and leadership should expect these responses from an effective manager. These actions correspond to the ten administrative leadership qualities outlined in Chapter VII, the chapter addressing leadership. Together, these actions allow you—whether you are a manager or an AP—to participate in a successful partnership of management and administrative support. Each description demonstrates how the actions empower APs.

Management Empowerment

1. **Listen.** Many APs are intimidated to approach a manager—if they approach at all—with a concern or frustration. An effective manager alleviates your fears, banishes the threatening feeling, and welcomes your insights. If you can go directly to your manager with workplace concerns, then you have the opportunity to handle matters constructively, professionally, and proactively.

2. **Guide.** A manager that guides your efforts also facilitates your success. A successful manager gives you enough information to perform your task ably and precisely without a lot of time-consuming follow-up. This information and guidance enables you to take full responsibility for your assignment, complete it promptly, and, in turn, save time for your manager.

3. **Trust.** Effective managers understand that most people want to do a good job. These managers show their confidence in you, trust you to do the right thing, and have faith you will successfully complete your responsibilities. Effective managers also realize that mistakes are normal, often a valuable learning experience, and that some mistakes help you become a better employee.

4. **Specify.** Effective managers set specific expectations: how, when, where, with whom. This does not mean the micro-management of delegated responsibilities.

5. **Capitalize.** A manager who knows your strengths is a manager who can capitalize on those strengths. Playing to your strengths is enjoyable to you and frees your manager to focus on his or her own talents, abilities, and responsibilities.

6. **Communicate.** An effective manager will communicate and share as much information as possible. This permits you to anticipate the needs of your job and have a larger view of your organizational surroundings.

7. **Invest.** An effective, successful manager recognizes that training is an investment, not an unnecessary expense. Such managers realize that further instruction and continued education will help you to meet the demands of your job. They support you, your job, and the organization by supporting your training efforts.

8. **Encourage.** A manager cannot motivate you, but he or she can provide a motivating, encouraging environment. By encouraging your potential, a manager develops an increasingly valuable employee.

9. **Praise.** "Thank you!" "Good job!" "Well done!" A manager's simple gratitude and appreciation will refuel and energize you.

10. **Manage.** Feedback is part of managing. An AP cannot perform effectively without receiving periodic feedback. Effective performance assessments confirm an AP's strengths, but also provide the opportunity to make adjustments and improvements.

Boss or Manager, What's Your Preference?

Many of you still refer to your manager as your "boss." I want to discourage you from doing that. I believe this is another way in which APs "disempower" themselves professionally. "Boss" is a remnant of the manager-secretary power structure of the 1950s and 1960s. Just as APs went through a name change from secretary to administrative professional, you need to make the same psychological adjustment with those that lead you. Here's why.

"Boss" is a word derived from the Dutch word baas, meaning master. The dictionary defines boss as: 1. To supervise and, 2. To command in a domineering manner. Unless you need constant direction you probably don't need to be supervised, and you never need to be commanded in a domineering way.

"Manager" seems a far more appropriate term. The dictionary defines a manager as: 1. One who manages and, 2. One in charge of the business affairs or training of a person or group.

Which description seems more appropriate to you? I certainly hope that most managers prefer to be leaders and trainers rather than masters and commanders.

Barriers to Job Satisfaction and Empowerment

Some of you, regardless of your performance or initiative, fail to achieve the job satisfaction or the empowerment that excellence and leadership provide others. If so, then let's examine four specific areas. These four areas are adapted from *The Heart of Change* by John P. Kotter and Dan S. Cohen. Any of these four areas may hinder job satisfaction or personal empowerment:

1. **Structure:** This includes the structure of an organization, the culture of a department, the make-up of a team, and the specifics of a job description.

   ■ **Structure of an organization.** Think about encumbering and empowering businesses. Do stereotypes circulate in your organization that make it difficult for APs to perform effectively?

   ■ **Culture of a department.** Are the objectives of the department clear to all employees? Is there a shared understanding of purpose and mission? Is there strong leadership to direct the goals and objectives of all employees?

   ■ **Make-up of team.** Is your team evenly balanced? Does everyone contribute equally? Is everyone respected, appreciated, and included in the bigger picture? Does each team member understand his and her roles? Do the members have the tools and skills to perform their responsibilities?

   ■ **Confines or absence of job description.** Is your job description outdated? Does it restrict your growth and advancement? Do you even have a job description? If not, how can you and others measure your success or know what is expected of you?

2. **Systems:** Do established procedures or systems limit productivity, create more work than necessary, or cause frustration?

3. **Supervisor:** Do you have an issue or concern with your supervisor or manager? Are you given enough information? Are you able to perform your task without constant supervision? Are you empowered to make decisions to complete the task most effectively?

4. **Skills:** Do you have the necessary skills to perform your job adequately? Do you have access to training and education to enhance your performance?

These four areas will help you isolate barriers. If you are challenged in any of these four ways, then think about what you can do to make a difference and improve your circumstances. You may be unable to resolve some of these issues. However, you control many more matters than you realize. Determine what you can control or influence and then create a plan for effecting change. This is how personal leadership can directly lead to professional empowerment.

Organizational Empowerment

I believe APs must work harder than many other professionals in the workplace to be viewed as contemporaries. I believe this for several reasons: One, we have professional stereotypes to overcome. Two, the administrative profession is female-dominated. Three, our salaries are meager in the big picture, so many managers conclude that we are meager or inconsequential too. And four, we do not generate revenue for our organizations. These conditions place us at a disadvantage in a business world that remains largely traditional and male-dominated. As a result, I believe there is a much lower tolerance for mediocre or poor performance amongst the administrative staff, and less understanding about how and why such performance may occur. As such, APs are often seen as "easily replaceable."

We've come far as a profession. But the Monster.com survey tells us we have miles to go to gain the respect that we deserve. The past 50 years have seen an administrative evolution of growth and change. In the 1950s and 1960s the role of the secretary was to react to requests, answer phones, type, file, and make the coffee. In some organizations secretaries were required to wear uniforms, as if they were waitresses, stewardesses, fast food clerks, or members of other service professions. In the 1970s we started to take risks and ask questions, but always with the proper amount of respect for those with "the important" positions. We even earned the right to wear pant suits. Perhaps not a fashion highlight, but a breakthrough nevertheless. The 1990s saw more major changes. We are now called "administrative professionals." We now need highly-honed technical skills and effective interpersonal skills to foster teamwork, work in partnership, and develop and maintain relationships with internal and external customers. These changes didn't come easily and they didn't come overnight; they were gradual, but significant.

Our administrative forebearers pushed boundaries and sparked many of these changes. In turn, we are the trailblazers for APs of the future. Carry on and keep up the momentum! We need to further empower ourselves and our organizations. We must face today's challenges as a unified profession. We determine who we are. We can influence how others perceive us.

To shift an organization from an encumbered framework to an empowered workplace, you need to work with your administrative peers. Each AP needs to take ownership of her or his personal situation and exhibit the behaviors that will earn respect and gain the trust of the manager. This can be accomplished by setting high professional standards so that your organization has no choice but to take you seriously because your collective presence and impressive performance will demand that they do. As this happens, you gain empowerment as a profession in your workplace.

The next chapter will share the successes of two administrative teams that valuably changed their working environment.

Chapter IX – Growth

"We commit to develop as an empowered, professional team through shared knowledge and communication, and to earn respect by helping our organization to achieve its business goals."

AP Mission Statement
United Properties – Minneapolis, MN

The May 2004 edition of *OfficePRO* magazine contains an article entitled *"Support Groups—administrative professionals come together in company-wide networks to build professional development and share expertise."* The article tells us something important:

> Administrative assistants are extending a helping hand to each other. By creating support programs designed for and by administrative professionals, office pros can create better work environments, improve their individual performance, help advance their careers and that of other support personnel, and help their companies function better and with lower overhead.

In-house professional development plans are gaining momentum in organizations committed to helping APs grow and thrive. These plans, sometimes called administrative networks or support groups, formally organize resources for the growth and development of APs. Such plans, and the associated organizational structures, unify administrative support staff in meeting the goals and objectives of an organization. A significant advantage of an administrative network is that APs recognize themselves as a team functioning within their organizational structure.

The Silo Effect

An AP supports a team. In a team setting the AP may support one manager or several people. Naturally, the AP focuses her attention on the team. The downside of such focus is the "silo effect." Human Resource Departments use the term "silo" to describe a streamlined team or a tight focus. A silo effect is created when you become so focused on your work and your objectives that you lose sight of your surroundings. Wearing blinders. Tunnel vision. Working in the dark. Silo = solo. You know the experience.

Here are APs working in four silos embedded in one organization.

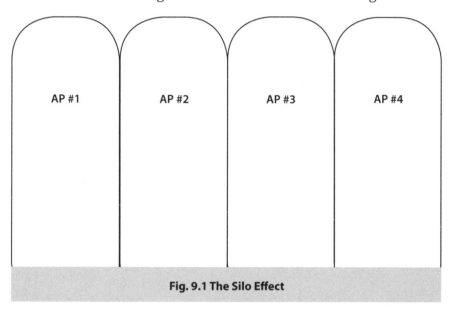

AP #1   AP #2   AP #3   AP #4

Fig. 9.1 The Silo Effect

The APs may work in the same department or not. It doesn't matter. What is important is that they work independently, interact little with each other, and focus solely on their team or manager. The limited communication between the APs restricts the flow of information and ideas, forcing them to rely on their own thinking and ideas to perform their job. This is not necessarily an ineffective way to perform tasks, but it is a constrained way of performing tasks. Don't managers and upper-level executives meet and coordinate efforts and ideas?

Your tight, in-silo focus prevents you from noticing other APs performing many tasks you do, shouldering the same responsibilities, and desiring the same success and achievement. These colleagues and peers are invaluable resources. They have different knowledge, experiences, and expertise that can help you. And you possess knowledge, experiences, and expertise that can help them. Unless you break down barriers and encourage communication between and among APs, you will continue to work autonomously and isolated in your own dark silo.

Let me offer an example of what can happen when you are accustomed to working this way. I once joined a group discussion on leading-edge ideas for administrative growth. I was excited to be a part of this group and was eager to hear what other organizations were doing to advance the role of their APs. This group consisted of twelve APs with varying levels of experience. Within minutes of our introductions the conversation focused on how we could quickly sort through our daily mail to weed out the junk mail. From my perspective this didn't seem leading-edge. This is routine practice. I understand it wastes time to sort through the stacks of junk mail, but discussing it is a waste of time, too. By focusing—and commiserating—on this issue, the group restricted wider discussion and wasted the opportunity to share ideas that could lead to powerful changes for the role of the AP.

This example illustrates APs so engrossed in their "siloed" responsibilities that they fail to recognize—and grasp—their opportunities to expand their thinking and profit from the deeper knowledge of colleagues and peers. This "administrative myopia" is highly contagious and an all-too-common condition among APs. I don't say this to insult the intelligence of APs. Instead, I offer this example because I think siloed thinking and behavior is a side-effect of work driven by narrow, ingrained processes rather than a comprehensive sense of organizational goals.

Motivational speakers and trainers often note that "there is no 'I' in 'team'." Yet you've probably noticed that there is an "I" in "silo"; indeed, a capital "I" looks like a silo. And to make the point in painfully obvious fashion, as APs *sigh* their performance is *low.* How apt. A *team* of APs—both in practice and outlook—will be able to work more effectively, productively, and happily, and will be working shoulder-to-shoulder with managers toward the same corporate goals and objectives.

The Collaborative Effect

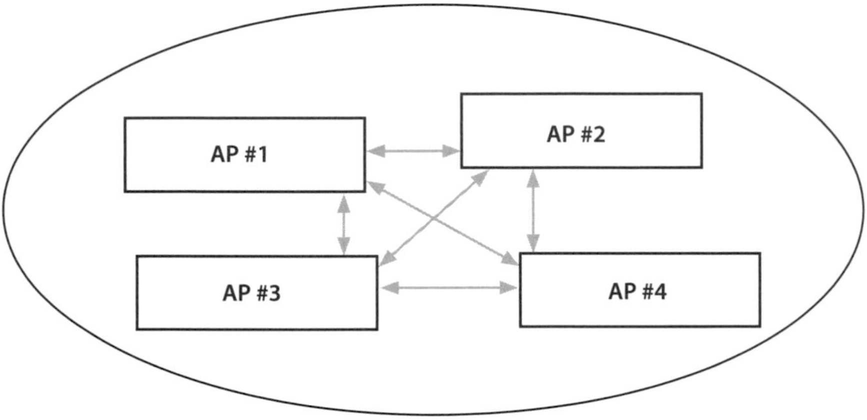

Fig. 9-2 The Collaborative Effect

The APs in this environment have escaped their silos and now perform as a team, support each other, and build on each other's ideas for efficiency and growth. When your own progressive thinking combines with the progressive thinking of others, synergy and ground-breaking change can occur.

The *OfficePRO* article mentioned above notes that the APs at Hewlett-Packard's facility in Vancouver, Washington are recognized for "saving Hewlett-Packard over one million dollars in 2002-2003 alone." In-house administrative network initiatives sparked this stunning accomplishment. This is the million-dollar magnitude of AP collaboration. APs can more readily demonstrate their merit and professionalism and can create big organizational advantages when the work environment significantly improves, when APs are empowered rather than encumbered, when they are free to share ideas, experiences, and perspectives, and when they can envision, contribute to, and shape the big-picture.

Two Business Models

I want to share with you the accomplishments of two organizations that created in-house professional development plans. I was differently involved with both of these plans.

RYAN COMPANIES US, INC.

Ryan Companies employs approximately 500 people in several states. I was involved in formulating Ryan's plan from its inception. As an HR manager responsible to the administrative area of this company, I recognized an opportunity to promote the growth and development of our APs.

Like many companies, Ryan experienced substantial growth during the late-1990s, and the AP staff grew in proportion to the organization. With waves of new employees and increasing workloads, tensions mounted. No one felt this tension more than the AP staff. Their performance suffered, professionalism deteriorated, and they were discontented. They felt overlooked and undervalued.

We considered a professional development plan for the APs. I spearheaded this task as a Human Resources initiative. I did internet research to determine what was being done to promote the growth and development of administrative employees. I found little. I called local organizations in Minneapolis and St. Paul (MN), where I live, to see if they were doing anything unique or specific to the training and development of APs. I remember one call very well. I was speaking to the vice president of a Human Resources department and explaining my vision for administrative growth to her. Her comment was, "You have more energy than I do. No we don't do anything for them." End of discussion. She was right, I did have more energy than she did, and I was committed to a vision.

Gathering Administrative Feedback

It quickly became obvious that a professional development plan specific to APs was a novelty—or a distant fantasy—in many organizations in 2000. It didn't matter. We knew that it was important to meet the needs of our APs. The next bi-annual employee survey confirmed what we already knew based on conversations with our APs and our observations of performance and attitudes. They were discontented and didn't mind telling us about their frustrations and concerns:

- Insufficient training to perform job skills

- Insufficient resources available to perform job responsibilities

- Insufficient opportunities to increase job responsibilities

- Lack of timely and candid feedback from managers

Building a Knowledgeable Team

Armed with the feedback from the survey, we pursued the idea of a professional development plan with upper management. They told us to "Go ahead and do what needs to be done." We were empowered to move forward. We formed a team of key APs to develop this plan. In total, there were five of us involved in this process. We met and brainstormed ideas to benefit the growth and development of approximately 60 APs. As we agreed on initiatives and components of the plan, we determined why each had value and why it would benefit APs and Ryan Companies. We connected all of our ideas to the overall goals and objectives of the organization. Once we had a viable plan, and a corresponding budget, we presented our suggestions to department heads for final approval.

Implementing the Plan

We launched our plan with a "kick-off event" to show APs that we had heard their feedback, and we were willing to meet their needs for professional development. We also let them know that this was an initial framework and that we expected they would ultimately decide the direction of the plan and take ownership of further improvements.

We designed the Ryan plan to be broad and flexible. We offered initiatives that would apply to a diverse staff with varying time constraints and unique skills and interests. All of the initiatives were voluntary and left to the discretion of individual APs.

Ryan's original professional development plan included the following initiatives:

- **Internal AP meetings–twice a year**
  The purpose of these meetings—facilitated by APs, not managers—was to break down the barriers between departments and to provide APs an opportunity to network, share ideas for improving the work and workplace, and to rely on each other as a team. These meetings addressed issues specific to Ryan processes, procedures, and corporate-directed initiatives.

- **External AP meetings–twice a year**
  These meetings specifically addressed the professional development of APs. Outside speakers or consultants spoke on topics such as committing to workplace professionalism, practicing business ethics, maximizing personal potential, and enhancing communication skills.

- **Administrative mentoring program**
  Ryan Companies established a formal mentoring program to recognize and build on the strengths of tenured APs by partnering them with less experienced APs. The program provided senior APs an opportunity to develop leadership skills, and share their knowledge and experience. The program allowed newer APs to learn and grow more quickly. All APs benefited from each other.

- **International Association of Administrative Professionals (IAAP) and the Certified Professional Secretary® (CPS®) certification**
  Ryan Companies encouraged and funded all involvement of APs in IAAP chapters and programs and in the CPS certification process. The initial expense included registration and instructional fees for eighteen APs who registered for the CPS

certification. The high number of participants allowed Ryan to bring instructors from a local college on-site to help the APs prepare for the examination. To date, several APs have gone on to obtain their Certified Administrative Professional® (CAP®) designation as well.

- **Administrative career paths for "families" of related jobs**
  We created progressive, sequential job descriptions that traced a path of promotions that recognized and rewarded APs who attained advanced skills in areas where several APs performed the same job. The new titles matched the skill and expertise of the individual to the job. For example: Project Assistant-I, Project Assistant-II, Senior Project Assistant.

- **Centralized reporting structure for administrative staff**
  Ryan Companies recognized that for any of the above initiatives to work over the long-term, continuous leadership and management were necessary. As part of this plan, we centralized the administrative structure of the Minneapolis office and expanded the responsibilities of an administrative manager to lead all APs. This centralized and focused structure promoted consistency and equity among the AP staff.

- **Mid-level management opportunities**
  This initiative provided additional opportunities for APs to grow professionally and develop leadership incrementally. New positions were developed (administrative trainer and administrative coordinator) to assist the administrative manager with the demands of training and workload issues. These positions were temporary and rotating, thereby creating valuable, routine opportunities for APs to acquire a feel for employee relations and the professional development of others. These opportunities also expanded skills and experience.

As the Ryan Companies' plan evolved, subcommittees formed around many of the initiatives: training, mentoring, internal meetings, and external educational meetings. APs led and directed the subcommittees. Participating in the committees gave the APs the opportunity to improve organizational skills, practice public speaking, assign projects, and give work direction. These skills and abilities transferred to their respective jobs.

This plan continues to evolve and change depending on the current needs of staff and management. A recent addition to the Ryan plan is an administrative leadership group. This group selects a current leadership book and meets twice a month to discuss ideas, concepts, and beneficial ways to apply the knowledge to their jobs.

A Successful Plan

This plan successfully transformed the AP staff. APs embraced the opportunities for personal and professional development and challenged themselves to become better at their jobs. The administrative manager worked with each AP as an individual to promote her or his strengths and abilities. In short, APs' needs were getting met and Ryan was getting a better, stronger, more productive, and more professional administrative support team. Subsequent employee surveys confirmed the success of this plan *(see Chapter VIII on Empowerment)*.

The height of success came when we were approached by the Minneapolis Chapter of IAAP for nomination of the IAAP 2001 Award for Excellence. Although we were initially skeptical of the nomination, because it was too soon to be certain of the success of this program, we decided to submit ourselves for consideration. It did not occur to us we would win. Yet not only did we win, we also won the 2002 Innovation Award presented by the American Management Association (AMA). These unexpected awards caused employees and managers at Ryan Companies to view our administrative team in a new light. We were award-winners, and we had done it in a short time. Our APs quickly gained professional credibility.

Ryan's plan was "piloted" in the Minneapolis office. APs in Ryan's five regional offices are now led by administrative managers that share a vision to "Create a supportive environment that provides opportunities for the growth and recognition of the Ryan Administrative Professionals." Each office has since developed a professional development plan specific to its needs.

UNITED PROPERTIES

United Properties, a full-service commercial real estate company located in Minneapolis, employs approximately 400 people. APs in the Brokerage Department approached the department vice president for ways to increase the value and recognition of their roles. He listened to their ideas and pursued resources. United Properties then contacted me to discuss possibilities with the vice president, a Human Resources representative, and several of the APs.

United Properties created a professional development plan unique to them and their environment. As a first step, working as a consultant to United Properties, I conducted informal interviews with the administrative support team and with managing brokers to determine the needs of the AP staff and management. This needs assessment produced basic benchmark information and identified areas of opportunity.

Based on feedback from the needs assessment, a plan materialized:

- At separate meetings with the APs and the brokerage staff, the department vice president and I reviewed the findings of the needs assessment and outlined a plan of action. These meetings clearly demonstrated the commitment of management to implementing a plan to promote the growth and development of the twelve administrative associates in the department.

- A meeting management and team building training session for APs launched the professional development plan. This session provided the APs with the skills and knowledge to run effective team meetings, to share information, and to work collaboratively on projects and issues important to departmental success.

- The first official AP team meeting produced a mission statement for (and by) the newly formed administrative team. This mission statement is the opening quote to this chapter and lays the foundation for their shared objectives and desired outcomes.

- Bi-weekly meetings were scheduled, coordinated, and led by APs to tackle issues of process and procedure that surfaced in the needs assessment. These meetings address the efficiencies of the department and encourage stronger communication and teamwork among the APs.

- Job descriptions were updated and expanded to recognize skill advancement and job growth for varying levels of administrative expertise.

- The Human Resources Department facilitated a training session on workplace behavioral styles to educate APs on their own style, as well as the style of others. The objective of this training was to improve communication and strengthen the relationships among administrative staff and brokers.

- A training session on workload and time management encouraged APs to become more efficient by reducing wastes of time and lowering barriers to productivity.

- A new position, administrative lead, was created. The newly hired administrative lead mentors, coaches, and guides the AP team to help them develop personally and professionally.

- An in-house administrative leadership certification program, taught by a local college and offered to APs throughout the organization, is the most recent addition to the United Properties plan.

The United Properties plan continues to grow and gain momentum. Signs of success are evident. The APs have solidified and affected many changes. According to the department vice president, "They have never been a stronger team." They are embracing opportunities for leadership, empowerment, and growth. As a result, they are more confident in their communication and proactive in meeting workplace challenges. This is a good example of a company on the right track to developing the full potential of their APs.

The department vice president notes how "revolutionary it is to develop administrative professionals in this way." As a manager he recognizes that many managers do not consider such an undertaking. Now that he sees the rewards of a professional development plan, he promotes the value to other organizations by saying, "It makes sense. APs are front-line employees critical to organizational success and customer satisfaction."

A Wise Investment

Professional development plans are a wise investment in any organization. The costs are minimal in the larger scheme of things and the pay-offs are tremendous. A professional development plan taps into the abilities of each AP and brings her potential, talent, and self-confidence to the surface. The organization develops better employees who recognize their value and appreciate the opportunity to use their minds, skills, and abilities to help the organization achieve results. Everyone wins.

The New Administrative Team

As you form a "new" administrative team via a professional development plan, your team will go through the normal stages of development:

- **Forming.** In this initial stage people are unsure of their roles, goals, and expectations. People may be reluctant to speak up or share ideas and may resist change. They may feel intimidated or lack confidence in outcomes and success. People may not know each other very well at this point, which will be uncomfortable for some APs. Many may feel "We've tried this before and it didn't work," or "This will just mean more work for me."

- **Storming.** Objectives and ideas begin to surface. People become more comfortable with each other as they get to know each other and establish trust. Brainstorming and creativity are necessary at this stage to pave a shared path to achievement. This is where APs will "understand what is expected and what we are striving for."

- **Norming.** The comfort level stage. APs know what is expected of them and where their skills and abilities fit into the big picture. They have normal routines and know how they are a part of this team. Members of successful teams will think, "I really enjoy being a part of this team and value our goals and objectives."

- **Performing.** The premier stage. The team is now fully functional and is seeing results. Goals and objectives are being met and others outside of the team are recognizing these accomplishments. The team is making a difference and affecting organizational effectiveness. APs now take pride in their participation.

Developing Your Own Professional Development Plan

Professional development plans vary from company to company. Different organizations have different needs. The size of your organization is irrelevant. Although I shared examples from two mid-size organizations, large and small organizations can also develop such plans. I have worked with various organizations that have successfully implemented plans unique to their corporate culture and environment.

Development plans invite you to use your imagination. There is no right or wrong. You can be as creative as your environment will support. As long as you have a team of APs that support the organization, you have the necessary foundation for a successful professional development plan.

Can you see the value of in-house networks? If you think you and your AP peers could benefit from this type of plan, then I challenge you to use your administrative leadership to spearhead a plan in your organization. Here are some tips:

1. Understand the needs of your administrative associates. What's important to them? How can their needs to do their jobs effectively be met? Gather this information through dis-

cussions, a formal needs assessment, or an existing employee survey.

2. Approach the Human Resources Department or a manager who will support your ideas and help champion the cause of administrative development. This individual will be your liaison should you need additional support in selling your ideas to the appropriate people.

3. Form an administrative committee that is a cross-section of the department or organization and will represent the concerns and ideas specific to your organization.

4. Tie the goals and objectives of APs to the goals and objectives of your organization. There should be direct correlation between what you want to accomplish and what the organization seeks to achieve.

5. Present your ideas to the appropriate person or department. You want and need others' agreement to any proposed course of action. Prepare a budget and know what expenses may arise. Most importantly, know what "return on investment" the organization can expect. In other words, "What's in it for them?" Perhaps decision makers in the organization want more productivity, more satisfied employees, or lower costs. Know how your ideas will affect the bottom-line.

Don't overwhelm yourself by thinking you have to develop a comprehensive plan immediately. Perhaps you get started by offering one AP initiative per year, or perhaps you focus on one particular department. It doesn't matter what you do, it only matters that organizations do something to promote APs.

Visualizing a Professional Development Plan

If you could create a professional development plan in your organization, what would it look like? What do you want to accomplish, and who must be included in your vision? How would you begin to implement such a plan? Have I shared tips that will help you begin? Here's some space to jot some notes.

My professional development plan would include the following initiatives:

My challenges are:

I can overcome these challenges by:

Facing Opposition

Some of you are thinking, "What about companies that dismiss the needs of the AP staff?" Not all HR Departments, managers, or organizations will reject your ideas. Think about the words of the United Properties vice president, "Many managers do not consider such an undertaking." He meant that many managers just don't think about doing something like this—that is, it never occurs to them. Yet if you mention it respectfully and collaboratively, then perhaps you will have created that small space for a seed, an idea, to grow and take hold. A thoughtful approach to a professional development plan may become a consideration in your organization.

However, some organizations will discard even the most well-thought-out plan. If that is your experience, then you must decide whether this organization deserves you, whether this is the right organization for you and your long-term professional growth. Only you can make that choice.

Many APs tell me they want to do something like this in their organization, but their administrative peers dismiss the idea. They have encountered fear of change. A professional development plan promises change, and many people are uncomfortable with change. Some are terrified by it. These reluctant peers may think, "I don't have time to participate," "Things are fine the way they are," "I just want to do my job and go home." Professional development plans push the comfort zones of some people because the effects are unknown when the plans are first discussed. Reluctant colleagues don't know how the plan will affect them, so they withdraw from the idea.

For these reasons, almost every professional development plan that I've seen is **voluntary.** Make yours **voluntary** too. I can't emphasize this enough. People should participate to the extent they choose to participate. Broad, non-threatening plans are more likely to arouse the curiosity of your administrative peers. Freedom is a great motivator. The freedom for each AP to choose her level of involvement or to participate in those things that interest her is often precisely the hook to attract her participation and enthusiasm. When APs can see the value of proposed changes, and when they understand how it benefits themselves and others, then they may recognize "what's in it for me" and choose to participate. But let's be clear: your most reluctant peers will engage only after good coaching and leadership from management.

An Administrative Management Structure

Since leadership from management is so fundamentally crucial for professional development programs to set root and thrive, I support a centralized management structure for APs. An administrative manager who understands the administrative role and its challenges, frustrations, and rewards is more likely to motivate and inspire an AP than could a technical or process-oriented manager, such as the executives, lawyers, doctors, engineers, and the like that we work with. Such managers have only a limited understanding of the administrative role, limited time to manage administrative concerns, limited interest in devoting time and energy to administrative issues. In general, they may also have traits of personality and behavior that differ from their administrative staff. The objectives of these two types of managers are different.

Administrative Manager	Technical Manager
■ Devotes time to the goals of administrative professionals—views APs as valuable keys to achieving organizational results	■ Devotes time to the goals of the organization—views APs as a vehicle or means for achieving organizational results
■ Manages in a hands-on style	■ Manages in a detached style
■ Stays closer to personal and professional development	■ Stays closer to productivity and work volume
■ Places emphasis on the balance of "soft skill and hard skill" knowledge	■ Places emphasis on "technical and hard skill" knowledge
■ Views self as supportive of APs	■ Views self as superior to APs
■ Coaches, leads, and encourages	■ Supervises, maintains, and directs

Fig. 9-3 Two Styles of Management

Some of you have technical managers with comprehensive management styles. Perhaps you find that your needs for personal and professional growth are met. However, others may find something lacking in feedback and guidance and may flounder as they work for such managers.

You can probably see how a professional development plan becomes more effective when it is led by an administrative manager. This one person has the "bird's-eye" view of the administrative aspect of the department or organization (depending on the size of your company). This person can champion administrative development, hold each AP accountable for performance, and "raise the bar" for the administrative team as a whole.

If you think administrative management may be a good career path for you, then see if these words describe you:

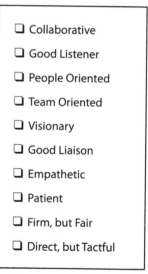

❏ Collaborative

❏ Good Listener

❏ People Oriented

❏ Team Oriented

❏ Visionary

❏ Good Liaison

❏ Empathetic

❏ Patient

❏ Firm, but Fair

❏ Direct, but Tactful

Fig. 9-4 Strengths of an Administrative Manager

These are some of the attributes I have seen in successful administrative managers.

Administrative managers must be equipped to deal with numerous personal and sensitive situations. The above characteristics make this part of the job easier. Another important ingredient of a successful administrative manager is passion. This individual, without question, must value the profession and be a role model of administrative excellence herself or himself.

Individual Growth for APs

We have talked about AP growth through professional development plans. Now let's talk about your growth as an individual AP. Some organizations have well structured performance management plans in place to support the growth and development of employees. Others do not.

A good performance management plan is consistent, fair, and equitable to all employees. It allows everyone to be evaluated and held to the same high standards of performance.

A well structured performance management plan for APs includes several specific characteristics:

- *Current and progressive job descriptions.* Job descriptions are the guidelines for growth, not a checklist for duties. They should set clear expectations for your job, clear criteria for evaluating your performance, and specific steps for ascending to the next level of administrative success.

- *Corresponding annual review.* A good performance management plan includes an annual review that corresponds to existing administrative job descriptions. This review should consider appropriate hard and soft skills necessary to perform your job. A comprehensive review may include:

   ### Personal Attributes or Soft Skills

   ▲ Work Habits
   ▲ Dependability
   ▲ Self-Motivation
   ▲ Communication Skills
   ▲ People Skills
   ▲ Team Player Ability
   ▲ Professional Judgment

Technical Expertise or Hard Skills

▲ Job Knowledge

▲ Computer Skills

▲ Administrative Skills
   Document Preparation
   Time Management
   Planning and Organizing

▲ Project Management

A fair performance review allows opportunities for both the AP and the manager to give input. The performance review is a vehicle for open communication and two-way dialogue about the AP's successes and challenges throughout the year.

- **Individual Strategic Plan.** This plan provides a strategic approach to achieving projects, goals, objectives, and personal improvement for the upcoming year, based on the results of the annual performance review. It then becomes the benchmark for measuring results throughout the year. Successful APs tie their goals and objectives to the goals and objectives of the manager, department, or organization.

- **Quarterly Goals.** Quarterly goals are informal discussions with your manager to talk about your individual strategic plan and how you are doing in meeting your objectives. It provides the opportunity to discuss obstacles or problems and also discuss your accomplishments and successes. These conversations are critical because they offer the feedback you need to achieve and maintain a peak level of performance. Such conversations prevent surprises in an annual review.

If your organization does not yet have a performance management plan in place for APs, then the above outline is a good starting point. Creating a performance management plan that meets the needs of your organization and reflects your corporate culture can be a great growth opportunity and another effective way to demonstrate administrative leadership. By striving for excellence you send a message of seriousness about the growth and development of the administrative profession. Ultimately your efforts will help to raise the level of performance expectations for all administrative associates in your organization.

The Importance of Feedback

Perhaps your organization has a review process already in place. You can refer to some of the above suggestions to supplement your existing plan if necessary. Keep in mind that your growth is only as good as the feedback that you receive from your manager. An AP once explained her review process to me:

> A half hour before review time, my manager is going around to the other managers that I support asking for feedback on my performance for the last year. This is being done in front of me and is clearly an imposition for my manager. My manager and I then meet to discuss his feedback and my input. I am told that I am doing great and that I don't have anything that I need to work on. It's suggested that I just keep doing what I'm doing. This kind of feedback is de-motivating. I want suggestions for improvement and opportunity for increased responsibility and growth. Being told I'm doing great does nothing to inspire me to perform at a higher level. It tells me that there are no expectations of increased contribution.

This kind of feedback is common for many APs. "Hey, you are doing great," "You don't have anything to worry about," "Relax and keep up the good work." In defense of managers, some believe they are putting you at ease, defusing any potential conflict, and quelling your concerns about performance. They misguidedly think they are offering you a professional compliment. They don't realize that when they give this kind of simplified, clichéd, empty feedback that they marginalize your contributions and suppress your potential. I don't believe this happens intentionally. More likely, they don't realize or understand your aspirations, goals, and visions for growth and development. It's doubtful the same manager would tell one of his or her sales or production associates the same thing about performance. After all, where would companies be if the feedback to sales associates or engineering staff was, "Just keep doing what you're doing. You don't need to get better or increase volume."

In most cases the empowerment that you learned about in the last chapter will foster your professional growth. But what should you do when your manager gives little to no feedback? What if your organization minimizes, ignores, or dismisses the needs of its administrative associates?

1. Focus on yourself and your performance.

2. Commit to your personal and professional development.

3. Take a realistic view of your capabilities and your limitations.

4. Set personal goals and expectations that are practical and consistent with your working environment and complement your skills and abilities.

5. Benchmark and measure your own success: compete with yourself.

6. Assert yourself and let your manager know what you need to improve your skills and increase your contributions.

7. Seek input from other administrative associates before championing change that will affect them.

8. Continue to push for improvement and change without being overbearing or aggressive.

9. Voice appreciation of those advances that are made concerning administrative growth and development.

10. Never lose sight of leadership possibilities and the opportunities to make a difference.

Go and Grow

Former First Lady Barbara Bush believes, "If human beings are perceived as potentials rather than problems, as possessing strengths instead of weaknesses, as unlimited rather than dull and unresponsive, then they thrive and grow to their abilities."

Never stop growing. As an AP you can grow and achieve individually and as part of a strong, capable, administrative team contributing to the success of your organization. When you grow, you gain, and you get. You get what you deserve and what you expect. Go and grow!

Chapter X – A LEG to Stand On

"Saying yes and no clearly builds confidence and rids us of the misconception that we are powerless."

Marsha Sinetar

Leadership, empowerment, and growth are the culmination of excellent behaviors and will position you for professional respect. Professional respect gives you standing in the workplace. This is the book in a nutshell, the book reduced to a bumper sticker.

An astute AP once told me after one of my presentations that the **L**eadership, **E**mpowerment, and **G**rowth activated by administrative excellence would give her "a LEG to stand on" in her workplace. Until that time, I hadn't seen it precisely that way myself. I couldn't have said it better.

These three principles will take your career to the next level and give *you* "a LEG to stand on" with your manager and within your organization. In other words, as you model administrative excellence, you develop professional clout. From this standpoint you have the ability to say "yes" or "no" to those things that directly affect you and your performance.

Filmmaker Robert Altman stated, "If you don't have a leg to stand on, you can't put your foot down." Leadership, empowerment, and growth are your leverage for a better working environment. So, we've talked about your head, heart, attitude, and behavior. Now you have the LEGs to move yourself forward!

Part III

Conclusion

Chapter XI   New Beginnings

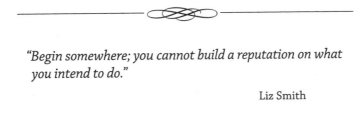

> *"Begin somewhere; you cannot build a reputation on what you intend to do."*
>
> Liz Smith

In *The 7 Habits of Highly Effective People,* Stephen Covey encourages his readers to "begin with the end in mind." Mr. Covey explains: "We may be very busy, we may be very *efficient,* but we will also be truly *effective* only when we begin with the end in mind."

I want you to fast forward to a future event. This event may be a farewell party as you transition from one employer to another. Perhaps it is your retirement party. What are people saying about you at this event? What is your greatest contribution to this employer? To your manager and co-workers? What experiences are your co-workers remembering from having worked with you? What legacy or lasting impression did you leave?

I once attended a retirement party for an office manager who worked for the same organization and the same executive for over 30 years. The office manager's employer, the company president, spoke words of gratitude and respect for their long, successful partnership. His exact words escape me. But I do remember the emotional comment of an AP who was also listening to this glowing tribute. The AP said, "Wow, can you imagine having someone say those things about you? I hope that someone will feel that way about me some day."

They can, and they will, depending on your contributions and the experiences generated from working with you.

John Maxwell, author of several leadership books, reminds us that, "The real test of leadership isn't where you start out. It's where you end up."

You no longer have to leave your successes to wishful thinking. You now have the knowledge and skills to determine your outcome. Practicing and applying the behaviors and tools in this book will make a difference and put you in control of your professional journey.

I realize some of you may think my views are idealistic in the complexity of the real world. I understand that in the reality of your workplace that things are complicated and convoluted by politics, hierarchies, and real people with real attitudes and strong opinions. I intentionally offer much of my insight in simplistic terms. I have done this because basic, easy-to-apply methods are practical and usable. You are more likely to use straightforward approaches rather than complex theories and ideologies.

I also realize, as I conclude this book, that I have taken a risk. I have shared my thoughts, beliefs, and experiences with you. In so doing, I expose myself to criticism, judgments, and opposing opinions. Reactions to this book will be part of my own continued journey to personal and professional growth.

Like each of you, I too, must make an effort to practice the **Five Ps** of administrative excellence in my worklife. Having knowledge of the rewards these behaviors can bring is one thing. Practicing them and bringing them to reality is another. It takes effort and commitment to become your best.

Oprah Winfrey believes, "Not only are you responsible for your life, but doing the best at this moment puts you in the best place for the next moment." As a successful career woman, Oprah recognizes the need to position herself for continued opportunity and success.

My hope is that you are inspired by such messages. I hope this book helps you discover your latent potential. I also hope you develop a vision for further career opportunity and accomplishment that unlocks your potential. Remember, as you take action and gain strength in your AP role, the administrative profession is strengthened. The concerted effort to revolutionize our profession starts with you. One by one we will make a difference. Together we will make an impact.

A social epidemic of administrative excellence will benefit you in several ways. Imagine every AP promoting herself and the profession by exhibiting the **Five Ps** of administrative excellence. Now imagine a world where every manager views his or her AP as a strategic business partner, integral to the bottom line, vital to success. Imagine a world where APs command higher salaries because the profession has gained unquestioned recognition and respect. Imagine a profession that has career paths and a professional development plan available. Imagine seeing the possibilities for AP growth when you interview for a job. Imagine a world where APs are taken seriously and the profession is admired, revered, and shares equal importance in the workplace.

None of this will ever happen without you and your commitment to the profession. It doesn't matter if you are the only AP in a small office or you are one of many APs in a huge corporation. You now have a "leg to stand on." A better future is the responsibility of each of you who considers yourself an administrative professional.

I leave you with an Irish proverb that puts this responsibility in perspective:

"You never plough a field by turning it over in your mind."

Do your part. Make a difference. Reap the rewards of administrative excellence!

In Memory

Christine O'Hara Daly
1925-2002
A Respected
Administrative Professional

Bibliography

Authored References

Becker, Esther R. (1962) *How to be an Effective Executive Secretary.* New York, NY: Harper & Row Publishers.

Covey, Stephen. (1990) *The 7 Habits of Highly Effective People.* New York, NY: Simon & Schuster, Inc., A Fireside Book.

Elmer, M.C. (1925) *A Study of Women in Clerical and Secretarial Work in Minneapolis, Minnesota,* Minneapolis, MN: Women's Occupational Bureau.

Fitter, Fawn. (1995) "Why Not be a Secterary?" *Cosmopolitan,* August: 121-122.

Hutchinson, Lois. (1979) *Standard Secretarial Handbook.* Revised ed. New York, NY: McGraw-Hill, Inc.

Kotter, John P. and Dan S. Cohen. (2002) *The Heart of Change: Real-Life Stories of How People Change Their Organizations.* Boston, MA: Harvard Business School Press.

Maxwell, John C. (1998) *The 21 Irrefutable Laws of Leadership.* Nashville, TN: Thomas Nelson Publishers.

McCune, Jenny C. (2004) "Support Groups." OfficePRO 64(4) May: 8-10.

Oshry, Barry. (1996) *Seeing Systems: Unlocking the Mysteries of Organizational Life.* San Francisco, CA: Berrett-Koehler Publishers.

Peters, Thomas J. (1999) *The Brand You 50: Fifty Ways to Transform Yourself from an 'Employee' into a Brand that Shouts Distinction, Commitment, and Passion!* New York, NY: Knopf.

Pry, Pauline. (1888) "The Earth is Theirs." *Daily Globe* (St. Paul, MN), March 18.

Thomas, Marlo, and Friends. (2002) *The Right Words at the Right Time.* New York, NY: Atria Books.

References from Newspapers and Corporate Sources

Daily Globe, St. Paul, MN. (1888) "At the Hello Center," February 26.

Monster Meter Poll Results. (2004) "Are administrative professionals appreciated at your office?", annual survey, April.

Star Tribune, Minneapolis, MN. (1940) An employment advertisement, September 29.

Background Information

American Management Association, *7 Ways to Empower Your Employees*, www.amanet.org/editorial/7ways_empower.htm

Arkansas Encyclopedia, provided by the *Anything Arkansas Directory*, Helen Gurley Brown Biography, www.anythingarkansas.com

Hecker, Daniel E. (2005) *Occupational employment projections to 2014.* Monthly Labor Review.

Herman, Roger E. (2003) *Labor Shortage Ahead.* Greensboro, NC: The Herman Group. www.retentionconnection.com/article_labor_shortage.htm

Schlereth, Thomas J. (1991) *Victorian America: Transformations in Everyday Life 1876-1915.* New York, NY: HarperPerennial.

Sutherland, Daniel E. (2000) *The Expansion of Everyday Life, 1860-1876.* Fayetteville, AR: The University of Arkansas Press.

Suggested Readings and Good Ideas

Burke, Michelle. (1997) *The Valuable Office Professional.* New York, NY: AMACOM.

DeMars, Nan. (1997) *You Want Me To Do What? When, Where, and How to Draw the Line at Work,* New York, NY: Simon & Schuster, Inc., A Fireside Book.

Frankel, Lois P., Ph.D. (2004) *Nice Girls Don't Get the Corner Office: 101 Unconscious Mistakes Women Make That Sabotage Their Careers.* New York, NY: Warner Business Books.

Maxwell, John C. (2003) *Thinking for a Change.* New York, NY: Warner Books.

Professional Resources

American Management Association – www.amanet.org

International Association of Administrative Professionals – www.iaap-hq.org

National Association of Executive Secretaries and Administrative Assistants – www.naesaa.com

Personal Report for the Administrative Professional, a monthly newsletter www.admin-pro.com/extra

The Effective Admin, a free bimonthly newsletter and informational website for administrative professionals – www.admin-ezine.com

Acknowledgments

I have been blessed with a tremendous support system over the years, and I would like to thank many people and organizations who have been instrumental in my career:

Ryan Companies US, Inc.
A wonderful company to work for
that provided the forward-thinking environment
for many of the concepts
outlined in this book to take root and flourish.

The Minneapolis Chapter of IAAP
for recognizing the value of administrative staff development.

The International Association of Administrative Professionals and
The American Management Association
for providing a platform for administrative achievement and
for recognizing leading-edge companies.

United Properties for believing in
the potential of administrative excellence.

C.T. Main and the New York Power Authority
for an invaluable learning experience
so many years ago.

A special thank you to several people for either their unique contribution to this book or their support in bringing my business to life: Pat Berk, Cathy Bruno, Kim Byham, Sandy Caughey CPS, Bob Cutshall, Nan DeMars CPS, Susan Fenner PhD, Cindy Gross, Terry Hauer, Kim Howard, Wayne Kirchgasler, Amy Beth Miller, Wendy Madsen, Jim Nahrgang PHR, Mike Ohmes, Lisa Oliver, Jill Parrish, Carrie Patton PHR, Martel Robinson, Jody Schliemann CPS, Donna Seamans, Pam Shives, Terri Steinhoff CPS, Melissa Tofte, Nancy Torell, and Gidget Wegener.

And, last but not least, the staff of Beaver's Pond Press and, especially, Kurt Burch, my editor who forced my thinking and challenged my abilities to make this book strong and valuable, and Ronna Hammer, my designer for beautifully depicting my vision.

About the Author

 Erin O'Hara Meyer was raised in Prattsville, New York. She attended Bay State College in Boston, Massachusetts and obtained an A.S. Degree in Secretarial Science and earned her Professional Human Resources (PHR) certification in 1998. She is the president of Administrative Excellence, Inc. an international training and consulting firm dedicated to the personal and professional development of administrative professionals. Erin lives in Rosemount, Minnesota with her husband, Steve.

Administrative Excellence, Inc. provides the following professional development initiatives. Presentations can be custom-designed to meet the specific needs of administrative teams and organizational objectives.

- *Understanding DiSC® Dimensions of Behavior*

- *Building a Reputation of Excellence*

- *Managing Time, Workload, and Multiple Responsibilities*

- *Partnering Effectively with Your Team and Manager*

- *Leading Your Organization to Administrative Excellence*

To learn more about the training and consulting services of Administrative Excellence, Inc. please visit:

www.adminexcellence.com
or contact Erin at:
651-322-3678
erin@adminexcellence.com

tered a few tourists who naively believed in the law that gave them the right-of-way. Feeling a twinge of annoyance, Jerry figured his passenger might not be quite as smart, or as much in love, as he appeared. "Aren't you listening, man? Love gives you wings."

Love could rescue. If you had faith in it you could jump off a building and land safely. Love could redeem.

The passenger smiled. It was not every day that a hardened New Yorker experienced something new. Most had already been there and done that—whatever "it" happened to be. Yet as much as the passenger loved his own girlfriend, it was apparent that this slightly nutty cabby was infatuated in a truly spectacular way. "She must be some girl."

She was. In fact, she was so terrific that Jerry did not know how to articulate how absolutely sensational she actually was. Jerry's words could not come close to conveying the feeling in his heart. "I love her so bad. She just . . . wrecks me. I would die for her."

As Jerry was about to turn south on Seventh Avenue, he stopped reluctantly for a red light. A road crew worked a block away and a white strobe light flashed a warning to motorists: proceed with caution. Jerry could not help but notice the strobe. To most people the light would have been nothing more than what it was intended to be. But to Jerry, the strobe was utterly spellbinding—even though he did not know why. He tried to look away as his passenger asked a question Jerry would have preferred not to hear. "Does she feel the same about you?"

"I don't know."

His eyes blinked rapidly—almost in sync with the strobe. It reminded him of something. What exactly

he could not be sure. Whatever it was, it was not good, but it was inescapable.

For a moment sitting in a yellow cab on Seventh Avenue and Twenty-third Street, Jerry Fletcher was in hell. Not literally in hell, of course, for there were no pointy-tailed demons to be seen, no lakes of fire, and no naked sinners running around looking for an emergency exit. Nor could it be said that Jerry was experiencing something esoteric like a spiritual crisis or an old-fashioned nervous breakdown.

Not at all. This was worse than the real thing. A few fallen angels and a goateed kingpin with a pitchfork would have been welcome. Instead, in the flash of a strobe, Jerry was transported to a uniquely terrible place where he found himself forced into a cruelly uninviting chair. Worse than the dentist. Worse than economy class on a long flight. Shadowy, faceless figures strapped his arms down and then his head. Incapacitated and frightened, Jerry shut his eyes to the blinking strobe which seemed to have made the trip with him. Maybe he could make it all go away. Please God. If only the light would stop.

It worked. Darkness. Peace. Safety.

None of which lasted very long as several meaty fingers wrenched at his eyelids and taped them open.

Now the single strobe light was joined by others until Jerry faced a bewildering and terrifying kaleidoscope of penetrating beams. Never before had something so harmless as light seemed so menacing.

It was all over in an instant.

Jerry blinked and looked around. He was back in his cab and happier than he had ever been before to be stuck in traffic.

The roadside strobe was still blinking, however, and before he knew it Jerry was transfixed all over again. He struggled desperately to resist being dragged back into the world of the chair and the faceless people but found himself stuck somewhere in between the reality of Seventh Avenue and his hallucination. He could hear his fare asking a question and Jerry tried to answer it, hoping that a conversation could serve as a lifeline to reality. He tried to focus on the question. Did his girlfriend feel the same way about him? Jerry couldn't say—for he had never told the woman that he loved her.

"Why the hell not?"

"I, uh, I have some problems."

A point which Jerry was about to prove to his passenger.

When the traffic light turned green Jerry did not respond. Normally he would have hit his accelerator as soon as the light for the cross traffic turned yellow. Not this time. Instead, Jerry cocked his head to listen as the sound of conspiratorial whispers filled the taxi. Voices. Men and women. Speaking urgently but just softly enough that he could not actually make out the words. What were they saying? Could the passenger hear them? He didn't seem to. Were the voices warning him about impending danger?

Whatever the voices were trying to help Jerry avoid, they were a little too late with their advice. A flash of the strobe and Twenty-third Street disappeared all over again. Much to his chagrin, Jerry found himself back in the miserable chair and surrounded by blank-faced thugs. He watched helplessly as the hallucinogenic figures pumped the contents of a syringe into his immobilized arm.

Maybe Jerry was wrong about those voices from the cab. Maybe they were not on his side after all. Maybe they were part of the problem in the first place. As if to confirm his suspicion, once the syringe was empty and Jerry's perspective had gotten woozier, the whispering voices continued. Except now they were louder and increasingly disjointed. Jerry tried to figure out what the hell was going on, but all he could establish was that the sounds were increasingly threatening. Cabalistic. The voices were working in league with the fingers and soon they were joined by impossibly stretched-out human forms that melted through walls.

Jerry watched the drug-induced spectacle and tried desperately to make sense of what he saw. Suddenly, the voices fell silent and Jerry felt momentarily relieved. Then he realized that the devil you know is usually better than the one you have yet to meet. The quiet was ominous and then interrupted by approaching footsteps. The devil himself was on the way. Jerry's eyes darted back and forth trying to spot whoever or whatever was nearing.

Then he stopped and stared directly at the advancing danger. It was close by. Without warning, Jerry Fletcher's eyes widened with unanticipated agony. The room and the figures within it may have been an illusion but Jerry's scream was the real thing.

And Jerry was not the only one screaming.

A Volvo blared its horn and its passengers shrieked in terror as Jerry Fletcher's yellow cab hurtled toward them at sixty miles per hour on a narrow crosstown street. Fortunately, it was a street-cleaning day and Twenty-third Street's northern curb was free of parked cars. Jerry snapped out of his tormented reverie in just enough time to veer his car out of the Volvo's path and narrowly averted a deadly head-on collision.

The screaming was in the past but now the yelling began. The passenger in the backseat was no longer feeling cynical, but panic-stricken. Minutes earlier he had hailed a cab driven by an incurable romantic, wise enough to ignore his crusty exterior and understand the true feelings of a stranger. Cyrano had turned kamikaze, however, and now seemed determined to splatter both of them against the grillwork of oncoming cars and trucks. The warm afterglow of the passenger's amorous interlude collapsed into cold, sweaty fear. He did not understand what was going on and shouted stupidly to Jerry, as if hoping for a rational explanation, "Are you crazy?!"

Jerry did not think so. "The guy came right at us!"

The passenger didn't bother with any more questions, for the answer was obvious. The cabby had lost his mind. "You turned up a one-way street!"

Jerry peered out his window as they reached Ninth Avenue and spotted a One Way sign pointing in the opposite direction. There was no disputing the evidence but he was not one to give up easily. Jerry muttered to himself as he turned left and headed south toward the Village. "I was only going one way."

With the imminent danger past, the passenger's panic subsided and he had a good idea. "Drop me off here!" Jerry tried to apologize but his fare had made up his mind. "Just drop me off." Jerry pulled to the curb as carefully as he could and flipped off the meter. The fare was three dollars and sixty cents. Before Jerry could tell the passenger what he owed, the man handed him a twenty and was out the door.

On another day Jerry might have been impressed

by his tip. Normally a friendly guy, he would have wanted to thank the cynical lover appropriately. But considering the places his mind had traveled during the last few minutes, Jerry Fletcher just wanted to clear his head and get on with the shift. Rubbing his eyes, he did his best to regroup and reassert control over reality.

As far as he knew, Jerry had never hallucinated before in his life. He had no idea what it was all about and no inkling where the images had come from. The only thing that Jerry knew for absolutely sure was that he never again wanted to go back to the miserable chair and the whispering voices.

Later that night he regained a grip on reality. The evening was fairly busy and he'd already forgotten the momentary business with the evil chair, the disjointed human figures and whispering voices.

During the last few hours his fares had been exceptionally normal. A young actress rode with him from Chelsea to Times Square in time for her curtain. Jerry drove a businessman to Kennedy Airport and hauled a family of tourists to their midtown hotel. Now he was cruising north on Fifth Avenue, nearing Central Park, hoping for a decent fare.

A well-dressed man in a Burberry trench coat stepped off the curb and hailed the cab. As usual, Jerry checked the rearview mirror for a tail and seeing none, pulled over and stopped a few yards away from the new customer. Jerry watched the man approach through the passenger-side mirror. The closer he got to the curb, however, the less certain Jerry was of the man's intentions.

What created the bulk under his trench coat? Was the man armed? What was wrong with the briefcase the man carried? It bulged in a way that suggested he wasn't carrying documents but something entirely different. Why did he keep looking to his left, across the avenue, toward the park? Was there someone there? An accomplice? Jerry quickly looked into the street to make sure no one was approaching him from his blind side. What about the man himself? White. Early fifties. Sharp features. Did Jerry recognize him from somewhere? He was not sure. It was possible.

Suddenly, Jerry was worried. His pulse began to race and his mouth went dry. He did not like the situation. He was not sure why, but something in his gut told him that there was something very wrong going on here. When the man was closer, Jerry took a good look at him. He was entirely nondescript. Just the sort of forgettable face that worked for the CIA or other less high-profile agencies. There was no doubt about it—the guy who hailed him looked increasingly sinister. Jerry had to do something. Fast.

The passenger reached for the door and was disconcerted when all the locks in the cab clicked into their down position.

The engine roared as Jerry gunned it and the cab sped away from the curb and into the traffic along Fifth Avenue.

Stumbling backward, the would-be passenger shouted after the fleeing car. He was angry. He was trying to catch the next train from Grand Central so he could be home in Scarsdale in time for *Nightline*. Now he didn't stand a chance. The furious commuter began to swear as he hoofed his way to the taxi stand at the Park Plaza.

Where Jerry Fletcher saw a highly trained intelligence operative intent upon murder, there was only a tired, irritable businessman. Sometimes Jerry saw things that other people didn't, and sometimes he saw things that just never were.

Jerry's adrenaline rush carried him uptown and over to the West Side. Like many things in his life, however, it was not a direct journey. After escaping from the sinister man in the trench coat, Jerry raced north, cut through Central Park, across to the West Side Highway, and headed south before exiting again on Thirty-fourth Street. After weaving through the empty streets of the Garment District, Jerry was sure he had eluded whoever might be after him and headed back uptown toward the Upper West Side.

Jerry had a date with the woman he loved and it included dinner. He did not want to be late.

If the major avenues on the Upper West Side teemed with people going about their business, the crosstown streets were altogether quieter and more of a refuge. It was not especially late as Jerry flipped off his headlights and pulled to the curb, but Eighty-first Street was already asleep for the night. It was a neighborhood of young professionals, some with families some without, successful members of the performing arts community, and a sampling of elderly residents.

Jerry reached into a brown paper bag and pulled out a sandwich. Just as he was about to take the first bite, Jerry paused and removed a single slice of bologna from between two slices of Wonderbread. Jerry put the rest of the sandwich down and stared at the single slice, regarding it as though it somehow stood apart from the rest of his dinner. After a moment's consideration, Jerry peeled off the edge of the bologna slice until he held a clear piece of lunch meat casing in his hands. Jerry raised the casing to the dull glow of a streetlight and tried to find something printed that he could read, as though the casing possessed a hidden code.

Normally, Jerry was not the kind of guy to look for hidden messages in sandwiches. Hidden messages had their place in Jerry's world, but usually they were located in more traditional locations like magazine articles or billboards. But his experience earlier with the sinister man on Fifth set him on edge and Jerry began to think that if "they" were brazen enough to chase him down on a well-trafficked street in Manhattan, they might just be clever enough to communicate with him via his dinner.

Jerry's logic was a bit confused and even delusional, but it made perfect sense to him.

There was not a lot of time to think it through, however, as Jerry's attention was quickly diverted from his bologna to something outside of the cab. Jerry put down his sandwich, picked up a pair of binoculars, and focused on something located across the street.

A beautiful young woman stood in the window of a second-floor apartment and then abruptly disappeared from view. For someone afflicted with more than a touch of paranoia, Jerry took the young woman's vanishing with surprising equanimity. A moment later she reappeared and started another stretching exercise in which she stretched her calves but stayed very much in Jerry's line of sight.

Some people might have called Jerry a Peeping Tom. He would have been offended by the suggestion. As far as he was concerned, Jerry's intentions were entirely honorable. After all, the woman who appeared in his binoculars was the woman he loved.

Alice Sutton was twenty-eight years old, although she had already crammed in more life experience than a person ten years her senior. Her Yale Law School sweatshirt testified to her intelligence, and the intensity with which she pursued her exercise emphasized her driven nature. Jerry could read it on her face as she worked out; Alice had to be the best at whatever she did—no matter what it was.

Jerry thought they were a match made in heaven.

Right now Alice was taking her exercise very seriously and focused her entire being on stretching the tightness out of her leg. The world she inhabited was reduced to Alice against her aching body. Her apartment did not exist. Manhattan did not sit outside her window. The future of Western Civilization was less of a concern than working out the tension in her ornery limb. If at that moment Jerry Fletcher had jumped out of his cab and mooned her from under the streetlights, she never would have noticed. Alice was lost in herself. Her world revolved solely around setting goals, working toward them, and personal achievement.

It did not look like Alice Sutton was having any fun.

Conversely, Jerry Fletcher was blissing out. If he could have swooned while sitting in a cab, he would have. Jerry sighed deeply with Alice's every movement. He was hopelessly, head-over-heels in love with Alice Sutton. Jerry even cherished the way she sweated.

If Jerry's obsession with secret messages hidden in his bologna sandwich was suspect, his taste in women was not. For even while she worked out with the humor of a crusader converting the infidel at swordpoint, Alice Sutton was a remarkably attractive young woman. Her chestnut-colored hair was pulled back in a functional ponytail, but it still managed to make Jerry's heart pump a little faster. The elegant, fine lines of Alice's face were classically beautiful and could have been intimidating. But to Jerry her exquisite looks were only a cause for amazement. To his mind she could have been a miraculously animated piece of sculpture that had stepped off a pedestal in the Metropolitan Museum of Art and yanked on a sports bra and leggings. The only thing that troubled Jerry about the woman he was spying on was her mouth. Not that there was anything at all physically wrong. On the contrary, Jerry imagined that under the right circumstances it would be a wonder to behold. The only problem with Alice's mouth was something that Jerry had never before observed.

In all the months Jerry had known Alice Sutton, he had never seen her smile.

Jerry sighed again as Alice began her final stretching exercises, fiddled with her Walkman, and began to sing along with her radio. Jerry wanted to share the moment. He wanted to perform a duet. Peering through the binoculars, however, was not good enough. He could not read her lips. He had no idea what song she was singing.

Jerry had an idea. Flipping on the radio mounted in his dashboard, Jerry hit the scan switch and then stared at Alice, hoping to figure out what station she was tuned to. Alice's lips were out of sync with everything on the radio. Jerry, however, was not the sort of person to give up easily. He had to sing with Alice. They had to share an experience, even if she had no idea she was one half of a couple. Suddenly it was a matter of some urgency. He wasn't going to give up until he found her song. Jerry tended to get carried away by his enthusiasm and suddenly his mission to sing with Alice grew into a matter of life and death.

The radio flirted briefly with a traffic report before moving on to a local rapper. Olivia Newton-John. No. Natalie Merchant. No. Frankie Valli. No. Wait. Frankie Valli—maybe. Jerry watched Alice sing and was thrilled when her lips synched up with his favorite love song of all time.

Pumped up by his success, Jerry slapped his steering wheel a couple of times before launching into his own sincere if entirely off-key version of Frankie Valli's greatest hit.

> You're just too good to be true.
> Can't take my eyes off of you.

Jerry was euphoric. He was serenading the woman he loved. He couldn't ask for much more than that. Sure, it was true she had no idea at all that he was anywhere in the vicinity. And he had to admit that if she knew he was watching her, Alice would probably call the cops.

Some things were worth waiting for.

For the moment, Jerry Fletcher was a happy man. In his mind "You're Just Too Good to Be True" would forever be "their song."

> I love you, baby
> And if it's quite all right
> I need you, baby
> All through the lonely night.

Then, without warning, well before the end of the song, Alice stopped singing. Jerry trailed off too. If they weren't singing together, Jerry didn't see the point in carrying on alone. Instead, he watched as Alice walked aboard her treadmill and cranked it up.

Alice was not one for wasting time and her walk quickly evolved into a jog. Soon the jog was a run. And not just the lazy run of someone going through the motions on a piece of expensive exercise equipment. Clearly, Alice did not expect the machinery to do the work for her. She was running hard. Running like she was trying to get somewhere fast. Alice turned up the speed of the treadmill to a truly challenging pace. Now she was running like she was trying to get away from something. Her lovely face was caught in a somber expression. Alice was not experiencing "release" in her workout and she certainly was not having a joyful time.

It was clear, even to a guy as blinded by love as Jerry Fletcher, that Alice Sutton was punishing herself.

Jerry had no idea why she was so tough on herself. He only knew that if there was some way he could rid her of the demons that were chasing her, he would do whatever it took. Whatever the cost. Even if the price tag was his own life. His euphoria quickly dissipated into melancholy. It was painful to watch someone he loved being so sad and angry.

> You're just too good to be true.
> Can't take my eyes off of you.

Frankie Valli was still crooning at the top of his lungs. Jerry didn't want to hear it and he flipped off the radio. He didn't feel like great love songs all of a sudden. Jerry lowered his binoculars and tossed them onto the seat next to him. He could not bear to watch Alice hurt herself this way. It was better just to go.

Jerry put the cab into gear, took a last painful look as Alice ran her night away, and drove off into the busy city.

Chapter 2

The stars of *Mad About You* stared down from their perch on a billboard high above Times Square as Jerry drove his cab down Broadway and pulled over by a classic New York newsstand. It was after midnight but it could have been early evening for all the crowds and traffic. The only oasis from the milling tourists was the eastern sidewalk where a large newsstand was located.

Normally this stretch of pavement would have been as packed with strolling people as any other. Often it would be busier, for the newsstand and its proprietor, Flip Tanner, were veritable landmarks in a neighborhood dominated by massive neon signs pitching soda and underwear.

But tonight was different. A visitor from far away would have been forgiven for mistaking this particular stretch of Broadway for either the Hudson or East rivers. Churning down the avenue and sweeping up over its curb onto the sidewalk was an angry torrent of water.

Life was difficult enough for Flip Tanner without the added problem of saving his newspapers and magazines from the Broadway Flood. Long hours in an unheated newsstand and the challenge of living in Manhattan while consigned to a battered wheelchair could have broken the spirit of many lesser men. But Flip learned years before to take things in stride. When the little tsunami came hurtling down the boulevard hours before, he rigged the newsstand for extremely foul weather. Papers that normally sat on the sidewalk were now stacked on milk crates and glossy magazines were protected with plastic coverings.

Flip watched Jerry pull over as his cab plowed twin fountains of water toward the newsstand. Flip pointed to his vulnerable papers and Jerry slowed enough to keep the splashing to a minimum. At fifty, and crippled by a land mine during a tour of duty in Southeast Asia, Flip's upper body was all muscle, sinew, and tendon. Even without his bulky old overcoat it was clear from the massiveness of his chest and arms that Flip was not someone to mess with. Even in a wheelchair Flip Tanner was a formidable figure.

But few people would have been conscious of this, for Flip's demeanor was generally cheerful. Tough as he might be when angered, the impression people had of him was that of a likable, hardworking guy with the life experience and wisdom of a gritty sage. The Yoda of Times Square.

As Jerry pulled up, Flip heaved a stack of newspapers and magazines onto his lap. After rolling over to meet the cab at the curb, Flip handed Jerry the collection of reading material through the passenger side window. Jerry commented on the water raging through the spokes of the wheelchair and Flip explained, "Water main. Broke all the way over on Fortieth street and Seventh. Subway's a damn river."

Jerry processed this information and then looked back at Broadway, where water gushed out of a manhole in the street. A certain look came to his face and

Flip watched the change in Jerry's appearance. After a moment Flip could not help but smile. "What're you thinking, Jerry?"

Jerry paused a moment as his mind worked through the facts. "Water mains usually go in the winter. It's October first." Flip knew exactly how Jerry's mind worked and tried to nudge him in a less suspicious direction. "Reminds me of life in the Delta."

"Mississippi?"

Life in the Mississippi Delta had been difficult, but there was a tougher Delta in Flip's life. "Mekong, my friend, Mekong."

Jerry knew that Flip had been paralyzed during the Vietnam War but they had never really talked the issue through. Jerry had an unusual opinion about the origins of the war, as he did about many subjects. "You know, Flip, the Vietnam War was fought because of a bet Howard Hughes lost to Aristotle Onassis."

It was the classic construction of a slightly paranoid mind. The world was controlled by a handful of wealthy men who treated everyone else on the planet like pawns.

Flip heard a lot of explanations for the tragedy of the Vietnam War over the years but he had never heard this one before. He wanted to laugh, but he figured Jerry might be insulted if he did. Instead he played along with his friend's theory. "Sure. And Hughes and Onassis used my legs for a wishbone. Nearly snapped me in half."

Oblivious to Flip's lighthearted skepticism, Jerry accepted the comment at face value, thanked him for the papers, and drove off. He was already behind his normal schedule and there was still a lot of work left to be done tonight.

Flip watched Jerry's cab dart into traffic and head south. He smiled and shook his head. Jerry was sort of a lunatic. A nice lunatic to be sure. But not your average, everyday guy on the street. He had his own way of looking at the world. It certainly was an unusual perspective.

Jerry's political view of the world was not the only unusual thing in his life. Jerry also had a distinctive way of going home at the end of the day and entering his apartment. After dropping off his cab on Eleventh Avenue, he walked back to his Greenwich Village brownstone in a slightly roundabout course.

Still carrying his stack of magazines and newspapers, Jerry climbed a fire escape and made his way to the roof of an apartment house. Before he went any further, Jerry scanned the area for trouble. Finding the coast to be clear, he started across the building, hesitating only to open the door to a pigeon coop and offering the birds inside their freedom.

But this was not Jerry's home. It was the building next to his home. Jerry leaped the expanse between the two buildings, soaring above a garbage strewn alley as he went. Even with his arms full, his balance was good, and Jerry landed on the roof of his own apartment on his two feet. Then, checking the neighboring buildings for unwanted guests, he climbed down the fire escape to a window on the fifth floor.

The window opened easily and Jerry dropped into the hallway of his dingy apartment building. It was hardly a slum but it wasn't especially well maintained either. The white ceramic tiles lining the floor were embedded with decades of urban grit and the walls were a faded brown color, sorely in need a new coat of paint. The decor didn't matter to Jerry. He just wanted to get into his apartment without bumping into anyone who might be after him.

Footsteps climbed the well-worn stairwell.

Jerry froze and waited to see who was approaching. He relaxed only when he saw the elderly woman who lived above him make her way to the sixth floor with her hands full of laundry.

The old lady knew Jerry climbed in from the fire escape but she paid no attention. She was used to the antics of the good-looking but meshugganah young man in apartment 502. As long as he did not play his TV too loudly or cook strange foods that stunk up the building, he could use the fire escape as his front door as much as he liked. Young people nowadays were a quirky group—this one in particular. Still, the young man in 502 was always polite and seemed a genuinely nice person.

Agreeable but weird. A few months back when her cable TV had gone on the blink, Jerry explained to her that the government used cable TV to monitor the activities of its citizens. He was happy to fix her connection as long as she did not mind different government officials watching what she was doing all the time. The old lady was a lifelong Democrat but she would be damned if Bill Clinton was going to watch her eat dinner and fall asleep in front of the tube.

At Jerry's urging they kept the cable disconnected and began a letter-writing campaign to the *New York Times*.

Jerry waited for the old lady to continue up to the sixth floor and then checked the seam between the door and the frame casing to his apartment. The tip of a toothpick was just visible—stuck into place. Assured that no one had opened his door while he was working, Jerry unlocked it, watched as the toothpick fell, and entered his apartment.

Jerry locked the door behind him, picked up an empty beer bottle from the floor and balanced it upside down on the door handle. If someone were to open the door this low-tech alarm system would alert him when the bottle crashed to the floor.

Tossing his jacket onto a hook, Jerry leaned against a wall and made his way along a dark, crowded corridor. What normally would have been walk-through space was instead the storage center of a mad professor's filing system. Jerry was a trim man but he had to squeeze his way along a narrow path that was left by a crazy labyrinth of overly stuffed file cabinets.

The cabinets were all old and battered, no doubt the cast-offs of an office redecoration project or a thrift shop. Each file cabinet was meticulously labeled. Some even had cartoons of their subjects next to their names. Jerry passed files with likenesses of George Bush, Patti Hearst, and then some more obscure subjects such as "Delta 30," "Blue Flood," and "Sirhan2." Rounding a corner in the maze, Jerry passed a few more cutting-edge topics like "Nazis and Nutrasweet," and something called "M.K. ULTRA," which featured a silhouette of a man holding a handgun. Presumably the person who had done the drawings was Jerry, and despite the odd subject matter it was clear that he had real talent.

Jerry stepped out of the congested hallway and into an almost equally crowded living room—the nerve center of his obsession. The Spartan, rundown room was devoid of creature comforts—no couch, no lamps, no easy chair, no carpeting. Nothing. Instead, Jerry's life was concentrated on work. An old Xerox machine sat next to an old electric typewriter, a shelf was crammed with magazines and a number of files lay strewn around the room.

It couldn't be said, however, that Jerry didn't pay attention to decoration. Hanging from the walls was a pastiche of framed newspaper headlines and magazine photographs. More than anything, Jerry's apartment was a gallery of disasters, tragedies, and assassinations. Beginning with a *Times* front page showing the burning Hindenburg, Jerry's "wallpaper" covered the decades: The attempted assassination of Roosevelt in Chicago. The declaration of war on December 8, 1941. The atom bomb drop on Hiroshima. The attempted assassination of Harry Truman by Puerto Rican separatists. Ike's warning about the military industrial complex. The Cuban Missile Crisis. The assassination of President Kennedy. Johnson's exponential buildup of the Viet Nam conflict. Nixon's secret bombing in Cambodia. Watergate. The assassination attempts on President Ford by Squeaky Fromme and Sara Jane Moore. The assassination of Lord Mountbatten and his family. The Los Angeles quake of '71. The murder of John Lennon by Mark David Chapman. The assassination of Anwar Sadat in Egypt. The mysterious circumstances surrounding the death of Pope John Paul I. The Son of Sam serial killer. The assassination attempts on the lives of President Reagan and Pope John Paul II. The Mexico City quake of '85. The Persian Gulf War.

It was a hall of fame of catastrophe and a shrine which called attention to the dark history of the modern human spirit.

But the myriad newspaper headlines were not the only eccentricity of Jerry's decorative scheme. Another strange aspect to the apartment's decor was an

unusual material that appeared to be a peculiar form
of paneling. The walls, floors, and ceilings were completely covered by sheets of a silvery toned material
that resembled particle board. It certainly did nothing
to improve the appearance of the space and if Jerry
ever entertained guests, an unlikely possibility, they
would have had no clue as to its actual purpose.

If the files cluttering the hallway and the bizarre interior design of the living room provided a suggestion of Jerry's irrepressible derangement, then the
kitchen offered proof positive. Jerry ambled in hungry and considered his snacking options.

There was plenty to choose from as he gazed over
well-stocked cabinets that sat behind reinforced steel
bars. The imprisoned food might not have been safe
from New York's omnipresent cockroach community,
but it was certain that no human being was going to
help themselves without permission.

It may have been that Jerry once had a roommate
who stole his food. Or, it may have been that Jerry
was truly worried about somebody tampering with
his corn flakes. Whatever the explanation, his mania
for security also encompassed his ancient refrigerator.
The old Frigidaire was wrapped in padlocked chains
that ran through steel rings bolted to the sides. It was
an easy bet that nuclear material in the former Soviet
Union was kept under less stringent safeguards than
the interior of Jerry's fridge. Nevertheless, Jerry spun
the combination lock with a casualness that accepted
this arrangement as an everyday affair. Before he
opened the door to the treasures within he paused to
consider a set of magnetic words stuck on the refrigerator door.

Jerry had what he considered to be a profound

thought and rearranged the magnets into a form of
instant poetry.

> The essential goddess death could
> chain bitter men.

He rearranged a few more words and completed
his creative effort.

> And crush the ugly moment . . . like
> life pounding eggs.

If it was clear that Jerry wasn't meant to be a cab
driver it was also equally apparent that he wasn't
born to be a poet either. There was something else,
some other task waiting for him, that he was destined
to perform.

But at the moment all he was interested in was a
bite to eat. Jerry opened the fridge, revealing ten individually padlocked stainless steel containers. He removed one labeled "Tapioca" and carried his
late-night snack into the bedroom.

The only thing that distinguished the bedroom
from the hallway was a narrow cot that passed for a
bed tucked up against the window. Other than that,
the room seemed merely an extension of the jumbled
hallway and living room. The dirty walls were covered with more disaster headlines and any free space
was crammed with more files. The only seemingly
normal feature of the room was a small wooden night
table sitting next to the cot. While hardly a piece of
any distinction, it stood out in its sheer ordinariness.
Despite all of Jerry's quirkiness, he was like anybody
else in some ways. He kept a water glass next to his
bed and had an alarm clock to get him up in the
morning.

Just another guy trying to get by in the big city.

Jerry took his bowl of tapioca to bed and began to work his way through the pile of magazines and newspapers given to him by Flip Tanner. Using a red magic marker to highlight articles of interest, Jerry digested the information in various publications. *The New York Times. The San Francisco Chronicle. Le Monde. Time. The Economist* and *Popular Mechanics.*

After his initial examination of the headlines, Jerry began a more careful review of the news and made notes on three-by-five-inch index cards. Today he focused on a wide swath of stories—the launch of the space shuttle, military base closings, and an escapee from a state mental hospital. What seemed to interest him most, however, was an obituary for a world-famous industrialist. Jerry seemed fascinated by the story of Ernest Harriman's drowning at his home in Greenwich, Connecticut.

Later on during the night, Jerry flipped through hundreds of index cards which were filed in massive Rolodexes. He was cross-referencing information, pulling cards off their hoops and lining them up against the cards he had drawn up from the day's papers. Amidst the clutter of the cards and highlighted articles a trend became apparent. Jerry was now focusing his attention upon the amazing coincidence that linked that launch of six different space shuttles over the years with the occurrence of six major earthquakes around the world.

Jerry whistled softly to himself. Despite his obvious obsession with plots and intrigue, Jerry was not so jaded that he couldn't still be shocked occasionally.

Later, after another bowl of tapioca, Jerry settled at his desk in the living room and began pounding away on his old typewriter. The subject of his article was his newly discovered connection between space shuttles and earthquakes. After proofreading and editing it, Jerry typeset the article into a small newsletter. The title of his publication was *Conspiracy Theory* and it boasted one of his hand-drawn illustrations featuring a pair of lips whispering into an ear. Once *Conspiracy Theory* was ready for duplication, Jerry coaxed his tired Xerox machine into producing half a dozen copies.

Just before the sun rose, Jerry wrote out five mailing labels and stuck them onto copies of his newsletter. It was hardly a massive subscription list but Jerry had high hopes for the future.

As dawn settled over Manhattan, Jerry left the apartment and rushed around the city, dropping each newsletter into different mailboxes in varied locations across Manhattan. After sending off the last newsletter, Jerry started for home. Before he was a block away, however, he stopped in his tracks. Jerry looked at the last mailbox with a sense of dread and then returned to it, checking to make sure the copy of *Conspiracy Theory* had made its trip successfully down the slot.

Relieved, he started to walk away. Even before he got to the other side of the street he stopped once more. Turning back, Jerry was uncertain whether or not the newsletter really *had* made it to where it was supposed to go. He returned once more to the mailbox, pulled open the little door, and peered into the darkness, reassured that *Conspiracy Theory* had in fact dropped into the safety of the box's storage area.

In addition to his loopy paranoia, Jerry Fletcher also had other issues that might be described as obsessive-compulsive. Still, it was a fine line between earnestness and madness, and as outrageously as

Jerry might behave at times it was impossible not to find his idiosyncrasies just a little bit endearing. For all of his neuroses, Jerry Fletcher went about his derangement with such conviction that he was almost credible.

It was midmorning by the time Jerry went downtown and climbed the steps to the imposing, if slightly decrepit, offices of the United States Department of Justice. Despite the somewhat sooty appearance of the massive building, it contained what was in many ways the flagship division of the powerful government agency. This was where the best and the brightest worked.

Once inside, Jerry made his way through metal detectors and stopped to stare at a statue of a blindfolded woman representing Justice. The message was easy to interpret—Justice knew no favorites. Justice was fair. Jerry turned to a federal cop who stood guard several feet away. Jerry could not contain his awe. "Smart girl."

"How's that, sir?"

Jerry kept his eyes on Lady Justice. "She's got a blindfold on." The guard sensed something suspect about the man who was entranced by the statue. Most people entering the halls of the Department of Justice were rarely lighthearted and irreverent. Those with legitimate appointments in this building were usually consumed by their business and not given to admiring the artwork.

"Do you have an appointment, sir?"

Jerry's focus never broke. He continued to stare at the blindfolded piece of marble, "Depends on your definition . . ."

* * *

Several floors above where Jerry stood ogling the symbol of American justice, a morning meeting for the investigative section of the Department of Justice was about to begin. Conservatively dressed lawyers milled around a conference room that boasted a view of New Jersey. There was no mistaking what these people did for a living. Despite a wide range of ages and appearances, the attorneys in this room were all singularly notable for their seriousness of purpose.

The men and women standing around the dingy conference room made the employees of the Internal Revenue Service look like the fun-loving staff on Carnival Cruises. Woe be to the lawbreaker who crossed paths with these grumpy servants of justice.

Standing out in the crowd was one of the few people who was sitting down. Alice Sutton ignored her coworkers who chatted over weak coffee and artery-clogging donuts. Instead, Alice sat at the conference room table by herself and organized her notes. When the meeting began she would be ready for whatever came her way.

It could not be said that Alice distinguished herself from the crowd by being any less solemn than the others. As Jerry witnessed, when he watched her working out with single-minded determination, Alice Sutton was not a lighthearted woman. What set Alice apart from her compatriots, however, was the motivation behind her resolve. The other men and women in the room focused on their work because they sought to punish people who broke the law.

Alice's drive came from a need to punish herself.

While Alice reviewed her briefs, thirty-five-year-old Jim Young introduced a new member of the staff named Roger Davies to the routine. "This is the conference room. We start 9 a.m. sharp, except Tuesday . . ."

Young never got to finish his introductory lecture. Department chief Phil Wilson strode into the room and commandeered it without bothering with social pleasantries. After twenty-five years with the Justice Department, Wilson had risen to the top of his field. A medium-sized man with a barrel chest, Wilson's no-nonsense appearance echoed his approach to life and work. As far as he was concerned, they worked at the Justice Department to catch bad guys. That was all there was to it. There was nothing personal in it for him at all. He expected people to obey the law. If they did not, his troops would build a good case, track the offenders down, arrest, prosecute, and convict.

Wilson expected the men and women who worked for him to pursue their cases with zeal and to win. Above all, Wilson demanded that his staff live up to the highest standards of the law. He insisted that they take advantage of every opportunity the law offered, but at the same time they could never deviate from its well-designated limitations.

"People. Give me this room!"

It was apparent to everyone in the room that Wilson's arrival, not unlike an angry bull entering the ring, meant bad news for somebody. No one wanted any part of their boss's anger and the attorneys headed for the door with an uncharacteristic meekness.

Alice noticed a long computer printout in Wilson's hand and knew she was doomed. Not one to surrender easily, she took her papers and tried to slip out of the room without being noticed by the human volcano who was glaring at her. Just as she was about to cross the threshold into the sanctuary of the hallway,

Wilson reeled her back inside. "I want to talk to you, Miss Sutton."

The other lawyers all breathed a sigh of relief. Rookie Roger Davies watched as Alice walked back into the conference room to deal with whatever was causing Wilson to erupt. Whoever she was, and however much trouble she may have been in, Roger could not help but notice her great beauty. If the blindfolded symbol of Justice looked more like Alice, the criminal world might be inspired to abandon their wicked ways.

Roger turned to his mentor. "Who is she?"

"You heard of Tom Sutton? The federal judge. Alice is his daughter."

Roger did know of the late Judge Sutton. Almost everyone did. A respected legal authority, he had been the face of justice to many Americans who only knew the law from television and radio. After numerous appearances on *Nightline*, *All Things Considered*, *Charlie Rose*, and various network news programs, Tom Sutton had earned a place in the American cultural pantheon. He was one of the people who explained complex ideas in easily accessible terms and was as respected a figure in law as former surgeon general C. Everett Koop was in medicine and Norman Schwarzkopf was in military affairs. His untimely death had saddened millions.

Davies wanted to offer an encouraging word to Alice as she entered the conference room but she brushed past him and he missed his opportunity. Wilson shut the door in his face.

Alice was calm, for she knew exactly what was coming her way. Her mind raced as she plotted a strategy for dealing with her boss. It was not that she was afraid. Not at all. It was just that Alice did not want Wilson to prevent her from pursuing a case in which she had a particular interest. After thinking it through, she concluded that as the ultimate straight arrow, Wilson would be a sucker for a no-nonsense response. To a leader of the most prestigious division of the Department of Justice, honesty was the best policy. Alice steeled herself to withstand the opening onslaught.

Wilson waved the lengthy computer printout in Alice's face. "This is a request, from you, for eighteen wiretaps. On the Ezekial Walters case. A case we are no longer investigating."

The Department of Justice sent Ezekial Walters to a federal penitentiary sometime before. Walters was a notorious white supremacist allegedly involved in the militia movement. After bombing several federal buildings and robbing a number of banks, Walters was going to be a guest of Uncle Sam's hospitality for the rest of his natural life.

Alice was not intimidated by Wilson's tirade. She had a perfectly logical explanation for her behavior. "I've been doing it in my spare time." That was not good enough for her department chief, however. He worked himself up into quite a state when he learned of Alice's wiretapping requests and now he was going to vent. "This is the Justice Department, not Alice Sutton, PI! Walters is serving a life sentence on the bank bombing. That'll have to satisfy you because we don't have the evidence to charge him with anything else."

Now Alice was having difficulty restraining her temper. It was one thing to be reprimanded for doing something that pushed the envelope of legitimacy. It was another for her boss to personalize the issue and take a low blow at her. He knew her history. The "Alice Sutton, PI" remark was out of line. Still, Alice was a self-controlled person and managed to keep her cool. "Do you know what it's like, Mr. Wilson? To think you know what happened, but to never be sure?"

"I've been here twenty years. I know what it's like."

So much for Alice's cool. It vaporized in an instant and Alice took on her boss regardless of the consequences. Where did Wilson get off telling her he "understood" her problems? "No. Unless you've investigated your own father's murder, you have no idea."

From their safe positions in the hallway, the lawyers who scurried out of the conference room watched the confrontation with awe. None of them would have ever considered doing such a thing and all of them enjoyed a vicarious thrill. Sutton versus Wilson packed a better punch than any fight card scheduled at the Garden.

As the lawyers rooted silently for Alice, Jim offered an unnecessary explanation to Davies about the background of the argument. "Judge Sutton denied a writ of habeas corpus to the cult leader Ezekial Walters. A week later the judge was dead."

Davies knew the history and was interested in more vital information, "Does she have a boyfriend?"

Jim and the other attorneys considered the rookie with sardonic weariness. The kid was warming up for the big mating dance. They wouldn't have been surprised if he started squawking, hopping up and down, and flapping his arms like an ungainly tropical bird on the make as he stared at Alice through the window. They took Davies' behavior in stride, however, for they had seen the effect Alice had upon men many times previously. Who among the male attorneys present could have denied their own urge to squawk at Alice?

But the new kid was barking up the wrong tree and they were all too happy to share the bad news with him.

"She doesn't date." "She doesn't socialize." "She just works. Relentlessly." The lawyers sounded like they were commiserating. The truth was, however, that having all barked up that same tree at one time, the lawyers enjoyed the hangdog look on Roger Davies' face.

And while their explanation of Alice's social life might have sounded like an exaggeration to the up-start lawyer, it was in fact absolutely true.

Alice had not always been such a workaholic. Nor had she always been so obsessively private and chilly. If nowadays she was known for her uncanny imitation of a humorless parochial school marm, a few of the older staff members remembered a different Alice. They recalled a warm, outgoing, vivacious woman fresh out of Yale Law. While Alice had been one of the youngest appointees in division history, and some initially blamed her assignment on nepotism, the senior staff were quickly charmed by her. What Alice had not understood because of inexperience, they were happy to teach her, because she was a pleasure to have around.

But Alice had changed. Ever since her father's murder she struggled with inner demons and frightened off anyone who was once close to her.

A commotion at the end of the hallway diverted everybody's attention.

Two cops struggled with a man they all recognized. The man was heading their way and managed to drag two of the law officers with him. While the man was not violent or especially threatening, he was loud. The cops seemed embarrassed that they could not keep him under control.

Jerry struggled to elude the grasp of the gorillas who were trying to eject him from the building. Who the hell did they think they were? He was a taxpayer. Or at least he had been once. Nowadays he was too busy organizing his files and watching out for the welfare of his nation to actually fill out the paperwork. Nevertheless, he had as much of a right to be there as any citizen, "I'm an American and I demand to see Alice Sutton!"

The attorneys rolled their eyes and laughed. Alice Sutton had this effect on men. Whenever this head case showed up they liked to joke that he was simply another victim of the Sutton frostiness. It was rumored that anyone who refused to accept her absolute lack of interest in their romantic attention was driven stark-raving mad.

At least that was the quip everyone in the department shared. The truth was that whenever Jerry bothered Alice, they all breathed a sigh of relief, for he could have just as easily been obsessed with one of them.

Like any law enforcement agency, the Department of Justice attracted a certain following from the lunatic fringes of American society. People called with "new" information about presidential assassinations. Members of the staff were not surprised when witnesses came forward with startling revelations about JFK's murder. That kind of thing was routine. Conspiracy groupies loved to call their office and usually were handed off to whichever administrative assistant was least popular at the moment. The veteran attorneys were sometimes surprised, however, by some of the more creative tips they got. Just the previous week someone called who claimed to have been an eyewitness to the 1881 murder of President James Garfield during a previous life. The staff usually laughed off the ravings of their disciples and even set up a bulletin board illustrating the best conspiracies never told.

But everyone in the office knew that as funny as some of these people were, many of them also possessed a terribly dark side. They were all aware that their groupies were often consumed by fantasies of persecution and could easily turn violent. While someone like Jerry Fletcher seemed harmless enough, the Justice Department staff knew that his goofy charm could well be masking a threatening persona.

They bandied around their joke about Alice driving Jerry mad because it imbued their coworker with a sense of control over an unpredictable situation. The fact was they were all afraid of people who were a little too much in love with international plots, conspiracies, and intrigues.

Inside the conference room, Alice and Wilson both noticed the heads of their colleagues turn simultaneously toward an unseen object further down the hallway. Alice was reminded of the deftly executed movements of synchronized swimming teams she watched while on assignment to the Olympic bombing case in Atlanta. Any pleasure that memory might have offered faded quickly as Alice saw who was coming to see her.

Jerry Fletcher was just about the last person on earth Alice wanted to see at that moment.

Today was going badly enough without adding him to the mix. Alice began to shake her head, caught somewhere between anger and despair. Wilson's mood also changed as soon as he saw Jerry talking and pushing his way past the two befuddled guards. Suddenly the stern disciplinarian softened. The angry boss transformed into a protective figure, a man who was not happy to see the arrival of someone who was harassing an employee he cared about. "Ah, your psychotic is here."

Alice was willing to go to undignified lengths to avoid talking to Jerry. As she crouched down onto the floor and hid behind a chair, she practically begged Wilson for help. "Not today. Please. Tell him I'm on vacation. That I won't be back for two weeks."

Wilson was amazed to see one of his toughest attorneys hiding behind the furniture like a blushing teenager. While it was true that Wilson was feeling an uncharacteristic flash of sympathy for his employee, he was not the type who could put it into words. He headed for the door and left Alice with a gruff reprimand. "I don't know if you're the best lawyer I've got or a high school sophomore."

Shaking his head as he left the room, Wilson was prepared to translate his unspoken sentiment into deed. Talk was never his strong suit. Action was what he did best. Wilson and his staff watched as the two hapless security guards battled with the still-struggling Jerry. Fists were flying as well as outrageous explanations of everything that had gone wrong in the world since the discovery of America. It was as though Jerry figured the future of the world depended upon his convincing the Department of Justice to listen to him. His earnest ravings covered everything from terrible storms during the winter of '97 to the former Duchess of York's endorsement of a cranberry juice as evidence of a resurgent Communist movement in Great Britain.

Despite everyone denying that Alice was cowering in the conference room, Jerry seemed to know she was there. But the closer he got to his objective, the more physical the beefy guards got. Wilson did not waste any words. He was not the sort of man to empathize with Jerry's concerns. "Get him out of here."

Alice watched from behind her chair and for a brief moment she felt a sense of relief. Wilson was going to get rid of this annoying pest and she could continue on with her day. But as the guards grew tougher on Jerry it became clear that they were hurting him. As they dragged him down the hallway back to the elevators, Alice felt an unusual feeling of sympathy for the man who was single-handedly driving her crazy with his constant phone calls and unsolicited visits. She could not have explained what she did, but on impulse Alice ran out of the conference room and put a halt to the proceedings. "It's okay! Let him go!"

The guards were having a good time strong-arming Jerry and were reluctant to stop. He had embarrassed them and they wanted to make sure he did not bother to come back ever again. They were, however, well trained. They looked to Wilson for confirmation of the new order and he nodded. Disappointed, the guards let Jerry go and headed back to their posts.

Jerry beamed at Alice, who gestured wearily for him to follow her. The other attorneys watched in shock as she led Jerry toward her office. They were even more amazed to hear the suggestion of warmth, or at least an absence of outright enmity, in her voice. "Jerry, you are a restraining order waiting to happen."

She said the nicest things. Jerry was elated and would have kissed Alice there and then. But he knew there were limits. He had to behave himself if he wanted to win her over. Still, it was a great way to start the day. Jerry had beaten the system designed to keep him out, and the woman he loved showed him mercy. Maybe she was finally beginning to like him. Despite the various threats to the future of democracy and the survival of the human species, there was hope for the world after all—Alice Sutton was giving him a chance.

Maybe she was ready to listen.

An hour later, Alice was still listening, but was no closer to understanding the logic of Jerry's theories. They sat together in her tiny cluttered office with the door wide open so Alice's secretary Jill could maintain a protective vigil. Jill kept an eagle eye on Jerry. If he hiccuped the wrong way she was ready to call security and tell them to shoot first and ask questions later.

Jerry certainly did not notice it, but Alice's office bore an uneasy resemblance to his own littered apartment. While there were no file cabinet mazes to walk through, and no newspapers hung on the walls, the office was strewn with papers and files. There was nothing methodical about the mess and no hint of organization underneath the different piles. Instead the chaos bore witness to Alice's complete addiction to her work. Certainly she wasn't as far gone in her obsession as Jerry was. But there was more than a hint of an unhealthy compulsion evident to anyone who stepped inside.

As unlikely as it might seem, Jerry and Alice were not entirely different. Not at all. They were simply at different ends of the spectrum of fixation. Alice could still function effectively in the real world even if the people around her thought she was an ice princess. Jerry, on the other hand, was only a few flamboyant incidents away from checking into a rubber room for a long stay.

At some gut level, Jerry understood their bond, and that might have been why he was madly in love with her. Conversely, Alice had absolutely no awareness that she resembled this congenial crackpot in any way, shape, or form. She was not sure why she was humoring him, but that is exactly what she was doing.

Jerry had just filled her in about last night's discovery. Alice was not quite able to follow his logic. "I don't see the connection."

Jerry's heart beat even faster. Her innocence in the face of incontrovertible evidence proved her unadulterated decency. He loved her all the more for it. Still, he had a point to make and she needed to open her eyes to the dangers of the real world. "Come on! Six major earthquakes in the last three years? The space shuttle in orbit for every one of them?"

Now, Alice understood what Jerry was getting at. She tried to take him seriously but could not hide the incredulity from her voice. "The shuttle is testing some top secret seismic weapon?"

Close but not quite. Jerry spelled it out for her, "Not testing. *Using.* Nukes are passé. This is the weapon of the future." Mid explanation, Jerry paused as he noticed a framed photograph sitting on the credenza behind her desk. He admired the picture of a twenty-year-old Alice in full riding gear as she gracefully jumped a horse over a set of competitive rails.

The sudden change in Jerry's focus was disconcerting. But it gave Alice a chance to exchange a look with Jill, who was listening to the whole business from her post. They had heard some whopping stories in their time but Jerry's transcended the usual run-of-the-mill paranoia and took it to a whole new level. Jerry was not just another nut. He was an artist, a visionary. Someone who saw extraordinary things where others saw nothing.

Jerry might have been a prophet of sorts, but Alice was uncomfortable with him staring at her picture. She tried to steer him back to a territory that was relatively appropriate. It was one thing to discuss nefarious plots, however it was unacceptable for him to be interested in her personal life. "Jerry, I still don't see what it has to do with the President."

But Jerry's mind had switched tracks and the unstoppable locomotive in his head was now hurtling toward an area that was taboo. "Do you still ride?"

"Not for years."

"So why do you keep the picture up? You wish you hadn't quit?"

"Well, I . . ." Alice caught herself before she told Jerry more than she wanted him to know. What *was* it about him? Why did she keep cutting him slack? Alice was not known for her tolerance. Normally questions like those posed by Jerry would have been met with a stony silence and an instant termination of the conversation. Alice needed to take control of the discussion immediately. "Jerry, the point of all this. Get there. What does it have to do with the President?"

Jerry seemed momentarily dazed as he tried to focus on what mattered. Alice watched as he forced the hyperactive gears in his mind to return to the reason he had come to see her in the first place. It seemed to be a real effort.

Suddenly, Jerry reached into his pocket, pulled out

a large seismic survey map, spread it out over Alice's desk, and began a hurried lecture about his latest theory. "The President's in Europe. Tomorrow he'll be in Turkey." Jerry pointed to a stretch of territory outside of Istanbul. "Right along this fault line. They launched the space shuttle yesterday."

Alice did not get it. "Motive?"

"He's cutting funding for NASA. The milk cow of the aerospace industry. We're talking billions. Motive enough?"

So maybe there was motive. But the method was still the stuff of madness. "*NASA* is going to kill the President of the United States with an earthquake?" Jerry nodded solemnly. The expression on his face in no way reflected the preposterous nature of his hypothesis. Alice looked to see if he was kidding. Nope. No joke. He was entirely serious. Jerry looked as though he had just explained something entirely mundane to Alice. Something on a par with predicting that the sun would rise in the east tomorrow morning. Jerry continued. "An earthquake. Not exactly the kind of thing a Secret Service agent can throw himself on top of."

Alice did not know how to respond. Jill saved her the trouble by calling from her desk, "Mr. Wilson wants you back up in conference, Alice!"

Alice's frustration built to the point of detonation. "You hear that? He probably wants me up there so he can fire me." Oblivious to the fact that he was a major part of her problem, Jerry confidently offered to help her out. The damsel he loved was distressed. He was delighted to ride to her rescue. "You want me to talk to him, smooth things over?"

Alice exploded. She had tried to be patient but Jerry had pushed her too far. "No! I want you to go home or to wherever it is you go! I want you to make an appointment next time! You can't keep bursting in here."

He did not understand. Jerry actually looked hurt. "Why not?"

"Why not?! Because I have a job! I have a boss! Jerry, you're going to get me into a lot of trouble one day!"

For the first time since Alice had met Jerry, he was chastened. Instantly, Jerry fell quiet and acknowledged he might have done something wrong. "I'm sorry." He was a different person when he was not spouting insane conspiracy theories.

Alice stared at him and began to feel bad about yelling. "It's okay. Just use your common sense . . . even though I guess you wouldn't be sitting here if I was using mine."

And then for the first time, she smiled. Jerry had never seen anything like it before in his life. Alice's smile was not merely dazzling, it was something more. It was inspiring. Jerry no longer felt like he had done something wrong. He was revitalized. "Okay. Deal. So, you gonna warn him?"

"Who?"

"The President."

The smile was gone. It was like talking to a brick wall. Jerry was a lost cause. Alice tried to humor him—anything to get him out of the office. "I can't promise you anything."

Jerry might have been over the edge, but he was still sane enough to know when he was being indulged. "You think I'm crazy."

"I think you're different."

And then, as mad people often can, Jerry displayed a perception of reality that was discomfiting. "You know, to be 'normal' and live in the 'real world,' to swallow Coca-Cola and eat Kentucky Fried Chicken, you have to be in a conspiracy *against yourself*." Alice sat up straighter and listened. Jerry actually was making some sort of sense. "I can't lie to me, Alice. And the more I learn about the truth, the crazier I look to people like you. Can't you see that's what they're counting on?"

Paranoia again. He blew his chance to get Alice on his side and never knew it. While Jerry spent most of his time worrying about what other people would do to him, he had just stabbed himself in the back. As far as Alice was concerned, he was his own worst enemy.

He was clueless to her dismay, however, and took a shot at winning Alice's heart. "You want to go out sometime?"

"No." Alice didn't waste much time thinking over her answer.

And then he turned the tables on her all over again. He nodded as though accepting her rejection, looking away with embarrassment. In that instant the distrustful, unbalanced Jerry Fletcher transformed into an appealingly boyish suitor. Alice knew that if he had not been a candidate for a straitjacket, her answer would have been different.

Jerry did not mope over his defeat. Instead, he gathered up his seismic map of Europe and headed out the door before turning back to ask a last question. "What was your horse's name?"

"Johnny Dancer." Alice thought his question was odd. There was something more she wanted to know. "You've been in my office ten times. How come you never asked me about that picture before."

The answer was simple. "I was waiting till I knew

you better. Johnny Dancer, huh? Sounds like a race-horse."

And then he was gone. She watched him leave and felt something that she was entirely unaccustomed to.

Alice Sutton was confused.

Chapter 3

Something had been nagging at Jerry since the previous night. After leaving the Department of Justice, he pointed his cab north and rushed up Broadway. Traffic was normally bad during the day and it did not help any when he found water still flowing past Flip Tanner's newsstand like the wild Mississippi.

If anything, the situation was worse than it had been the previous night. Jerry parked the cab behind a massive food truck that was unloading goods to a restaurant. The cab was hidden from view of the police and Jerry raced out to see exactly what was going on.

The intersection of Fortieth Street and Seventh Avenue was completely cordoned off and the sidewalks were now sandbagged. Traffic cops redirected cars. Meanwhile real cops encouraged drivers not to kill the men and women who were forcing them to take a detour. The fact that the avenue was submerged under a massive puddle that could have been classified as New York State's newest Great Lake seemed not to discourage anyone. Horns blared. Expletives were exchanged. Fists were shaken and an occasional driver was hauled off to jail after badmouthing the overly harassed cops. The commotion allowed Jerry the opportunity to move around the scene without being chased off. Some guy looking at the inland ocean of Manhattan was the least of the cop's worries.

Jerry waded into the puddle and spotted massive diesel-powered contraptions pumping water up out of the subway that ran beneath the street. The water itself was not what interested Jerry. He wanted to know what had caused the calamity in the first place. There was something wrong and he was determined to find out what it was. Jerry flagged down a Department of Water and Power employee and asked a question as politely as he could. "Excuse me, don't water mains usually go in the winter?"

"Hey, pal, all I know is it's beaucoup overtime."

Apparently the DWP wasn't especially interested in public relations. Although his sneakers were already soaked and he was catching a chill, Jerry snooped around the location some more until something caught his eye.

A harmless-looking American sedan sat inside the cordoned-off area.

Most people would never have even noticed it. But as Jerry knew all too well, that was exactly the point. Sloshing through the water, Jerry took a closer look at the vehicle. Just as he suspected, it had official U.S. Government plates. Jerry was beginning to think that maybe the flooded street was a lot more serious than just an inconvenience. As he frowned and tried to fathom what was going on, two guys in suits marched up the steps from the subway and got into the sedan. Feds. Without a doubt. As clearly as if they had been wearing big signs on their backs.

Things were heating up and Jerry ran to his cab so he could follow the sedan wherever it was headed.

Whoever they were and whatever they were up to, Jerry Fletcher was on the case.

Forty-five minutes and a lot of traffic later, Jerry was back downtown again. He watched as the sedan double-parked in front of the Federal Building and the two suits ran inside. Jerry improvised a parking space by leaving his cab in an active alley and followed.

Inside the lobby, he looked around and spotted the two suits entering an elevator headed somewhere between the fourteenth and twenty-fifth floors. As the doors to the elevator closed, Jerry checked a directory of the building's tenants. The Central Intelligence Agency occupied the eighteenth to twenty-second floors. Jerry couldn't prove anything but it certainly looked like his suspicions were confirmed. "*Spooks.* I knew it."

Somehow, and for a convoluted reason that even Jerry could not possibly fathom, the CIA was involved with the broken water main in Times Square. Jerry tried to work it through. It didn't make sense. Legally the CIA was limited to overseas operations. Maybe it had something to do with the end of the Cold War and the absence of traditional enemies like the Soviet Union. But even to someone like Jerry, the possibility of the CIA being involved in road maintenance seemed a real stretch. Then again, you never knew.

Aware that he couldn't just barge into Central Intelligence headquarters as he had into Alice's office, Jerry left the building and returned to his cab. The whole business required some reflection.

What Jerry did not know, however, was that his

visit, no matter how brief, had already been noted by surveillance cameras hidden in the lobby ceiling.

The watcher had been seen.

Later that day, Jerry ate lunch at one of the few diners he trusted the cooks not to poison him. The joint was near the Brooklyn Bridge and was a favorite destination of cabbies throughout the city. There, seemingly far removed from the dog-eat-dog world of Manhattan, he relaxed, allowing himself to participate in what were for him fairly normal conversations. Surrounded by other drivers, Jerry felt as though he truly blended in. In the diner, he was one of a crowd. It was his refuge. One of the few places in the world he could truly feel at ease.

After a lunch of chili and a slice of pie, Jerry left a few bills on the Formica counter and walked out to the street.

Standing before him were the two suits from the CIA.

Jerry had trained himself for just this situation for a long time. In some ways it seemed that his whole life had been building up to this moment. He had finally stumbled across a criminal government operation and now they were after him.

Unfortunately, all his preparation came to nothing as Jerry froze. For an instant the man who was convinced that the world was aswirl in bizarre conspiracies could simply not believe what he saw.

The CIA man on Jerry's left was named Piper. The guy on the right was Clark. As Jerry stood dumbfounded they yanked him out of the doorway and began to drag him toward his cab.

As soon as they lunged for him, the gridlock in Jerry's brain loosened. He struggled to break their grip and did a fair job of fighting for someone who was outnumbered two to one. But before he could get away, Clark pulled an air syringe from his jacket pocket and injected it directly into Jerry's neck.

Jerry felt a surge of intense heat bolt from his neck right up into his brain. A dark curtain seemed to be crushing him down into the pavement. Two seconds later he was unconscious. His body went slack, the two spooks dragged him silently to the cab and shoved him inside.

The street was empty and Jerry's kidnapping was only witnessed by one lonely person. An elderly man sitting in the diner window watched the battle briefly before returning to his meatloaf with mushroom gravy. People got mugged every day but the old man had not eaten a hot meal in almost a week.

As far as the world was concerned, nothing had just happened to Jerry Fletcher. No one had seen a thing and therefore nothing had taken place.

Just because Jerry was paranoid, it didn't mean that everyone wasn't out to get him.

Chapter 4

Sometime later Jerry awoke to find himself strapped into a moving wheelchair. He had no idea where he was but the hallway he was rolling through looked as though it were some kind of decrepit institution. Maybe a school. Maybe a prison. The wheelchair was pushed around a corner and a groggy Jerry entered a dingy old hospital room.

The space was cavernous and filthy in a way that would have offended even Jerry's lax housekeeping sensibility. Windows were shattered and glass lay over floors that were encrusted with layers of dirt. Once grandiose lighting fixtures hung sadly from the ceiling and now served as homes for pigeons, bats, and enterprising rats. But the most distinguishing characteristic of the room was an enormous hydrotherapy tank set in the middle.

The beneficial effects of warm bubbling water have long been known to the medical community. Used today mainly for orthopedic injuries, it was not that long ago that a good soak was seen as therapy for the mentally ill. Stick one agitated person in the tank, let soak for half an hour, remove, and find a significantly calmer person. The medical principle involved wasn't that different from taking a hot tub at the end of an aggravating week. Basically the hydrotherapy tank was simply a rectangular Jacuzzi built into the floor, without the wine and naked party girls.

None of which was readily apparent to Jerry. While his consciousness was slowly returning, he was still unable to see further than a few inches in front of his nose. Although he could not focus his eyes he was aware that there were at least two other people in the room. Probably the spooks from the CIA. What worried him most, however, was the sound of rapidly running water. Like someone was filling a tub. He didn't know what they had planned for him, but Jerry was pretty sure they weren't going to give him a bubble bath.

Hazy figures moved around him before the water was abruptly turned off. All Jerry could hear now was the thugs' breathing and the quiet, steady drip from the unseen faucet. Drip. Drip. Drip. Somehow the absence of the roaring water was more ominous than the noise. The soft trickle of water was suddenly terrifying. Growing up, Jerry had heard stories of something called Chinese water torture. He didn't know exactly what it was, and the goons who dragged him here didn't look Asian, but he was profoundly scared nevertheless. He would have loved to hear the sound of someone yelling at him, threatening him. The quiet room was getting on his nerves and Jerry realized that he was righteously screwed.

And then, cutting through his palpable fear, Jerry enjoyed a moment of triumph. Never one to do things the way everybody else did, Jerry reached a new level of perversity by claiming victory just as truly terrible things were about to be done. To Jerry's way of thinking, his success might not rank up with Ed McMahon arriving to announce he had just won the Publishers'

Annual Clearinghouse Sweepstakes, but he was pretty thrilled even so.

Half blinded, bound to a wheelchair, and pretty much immobilized, Jerry crowed over his success. "I was right. Wasn't I? *I was right.*" All those long nights checking through newspapers and magazines, trying to find out the real news behind the headlines. All the carefully maintained files on government officials, agencies, and programs had finally led to something tangible. The plots and intrigues he had investigated were not merely the product of his imagination. They were real. Nobody could deny it after today. If they had been only fantasy, he wouldn't be where he was now. To someone else it would have been a dubious triumph, but Jerry was ecstatic.

Now that he had ascertained the authenticity of this particular conspiracy he wanted to know more. If they were going to torture him, Jerry should at least know which group of schemers could claim credit for doing him in. "I was right—so what was I right about?"

The shadowy figures ignored the question. Dogged as ever, Jerry was not about to give up easily. "Are you guys from NASA?"

He didn't get the answer he wanted to hear. Instead, one of the figures grabbed Jerry's head from behind. Jerry tried to struggle but there wasn't much he could do when the ape behind the wheelchair incapacitated him. The second figure stepped forward into Jerry's line of vision and taped his eyelids open.

Suddenly there was something all-too familiar about what was happening. Jerry didn't care for their sense of hospitality one bit. "I was wrong! I was wrong!"

Amazingly that seemed to work. For just after admitting his error, the two figures walked out of the room. Jerry was left alone to struggle futilely. Unable to loosen his bonds, he did the only sensible thing—he gave up and waited to see what was in store.

Footsteps approached the doorway to the room and then entered. With his eyelids taped open, Jerry didn't have a lot of choice but to watch the man who joined him in the gloomy room. Jerry frowned. The man looked familiar but he couldn't recall who he was. As usual Jerry was not one to be intimidated into silence. "Do I know you?"

"Yes you do, Jerry. Quite well."

The silken voice belonged to Dr. William Jonas, a genteel-looking, professorial man in his early fifties. Jonas was not large but beneath his tweedy exterior there was an imposing presence. Whether it was a lurking physical threat, something more cerebral, or just an apparent ruthlessness, Jerry couldn't be sure. At the moment, Jonas's calm demeanor was oddly soothing. Still, under the best of circumstances Jerry didn't trust many people. So after being jabbed in the neck with a tranquilizer, kidnapped, and tied into a wheelchair with his eyes jammed open, Jerry wasn't about to be lulled into trusting this new arrival. Even if the rational-looking son of a bitch suddenly pulled off a rubber mask to reveal the kindly, wrinkled face of Mother Teresa and spoke Hindi with an Albanian accent, Jerry wasn't likely to relax.

The two men stared at each other without blinking. Jerry had no choice, but Jonas was proving himself to be a cool customer. It was clear that Jonas thought a lot of himself and Jerry had to admit that the other guy had the upper hand. He would have preferred Jonas to be stark-raving mad, foaming at the mouth, screaming all kinds of frightening threats. At least

Jerry would know what he was dealing with. But that wasn't Jonas's style and instead Jerry was subjected to a velvety but puzzling warning. "Have you ever been in a place from which hope has gone? All that's left is patience. Everywhere. Like a fog."

It might have been that Jerry was having a lousy day, but he just wasn't in the mood for abstract threats. Worse, he had no idea what this quietly dangerous clown was talking about. Jonas gauged Jerry's silent reaction and continued. "I'm a very patient man."

"That's great. Good for you." Jerry did not want to go out of his way to piss off the smug bastard but he had to say something. Clearly some response was needed. But what could be said if he didn't have a clue as to what was going on?

"Who have you been talking to, Jerry? Who else knows what you know?"

He was doing it again. Jerry's mind raced as he tried to find the right answer. Jerry wasn't exactly a coward but he would have said almost anything to be released from the damn chair and blink his burning eyes. "Could you be a little more specific?"

Apparently those weren't the magic words and it didn't look like Jonas was about to be helpful. Jerry watched with grave apprehension as Jonas methodically loaded a syringe with clear fluid. Never one to be fond of needles, Jerry groaned. Two in one day. Nor did he expect Jonas to inject him with anything approaching the tender-loving care of his childhood pediatrician. At least he wanted to know what to expect. Was he going to be knocked unconscious again or something worse. "What's that?"

"Gravy for the brain. With a little kicker of my own

devising. Surely it must be coming back to you by now?"

Nothing was coming back to Jerry, other than the screaming warning in his brain to get the hell out of the chair before that stuff got injected into his body. Jerry struggled as best he could, considering that his arms were lashed so tightly to the chair that they were turning blue. It wasn't much of a show. There was nothing for him to do other than watch the needle pierce his skin. Jonas smiled as he pushed the plunger down with his thumb.

Jerry was now approaching a panic. "What do I know?" Just give him a clue, he'd confess. Nudge him in the right direction and Jerry would tell his captor anything. From the beginning. Leaving nothing out. With great detail and maybe even a few jokes included in the package if the nasty bald guy with the needle wanted some entertainment. But he couldn't say a word unless he was given a hint.

Jonas wasn't a sharing kind of a guy. At least regarding information. Stepping away from the chair, he switched on a row of blinding strobe lights. For some reason this whole exercise seemed strangely familiar to Jerry. He just couldn't figure out why.

The strobes began to flash more quickly and with each painful burst of concentrated light he felt himself pushed closer to the edges of sanity. Jerry would have liked to close his eyes, but the tape was heavy-duty stuff and he found himself obligated to watch the show whether he liked it or not. Jonas grinned at him like a maniacal theater usher and Jerry began to worry that his captor was going to ask to see his ticket.

It was a crazy thing to worry about but the mind-altering drugs were kicking in and Jerry's grasp on reality was tenuous at best. Suddenly it appeared to him that Jonas had taken up dancing. It was an unlikely thing for his tormentor to be doing but as far as Jerry could tell Jones was jumping around the room with each flash of the strobe.

Of course Jonas was not the kind of man to dance. Not at work. Not even during the polyester decade when he still had a full head of hair. Jonas was a serious man and his emotional expression leaned more toward the sadistic. Jerry was dead wrong about his torturer cutting up the floor. The truth was that Jonas was nose-to-nose with Jerry and he had no intention of asking his hostage to dance. "Who else knows what we know?"

There was nothing Jerry could say. He sat in his chair with his jaw hanging slack. He stopped trying to fight the effects of the drug cocktail and went along for the ride.

Then the world behind him collapsed, and Jerry toppled backward into the void.

Jonas released a lever on the wheelchair and Jerry dropped backward into the freezing waters of the hydrotherapy tank. A bad situation had turned exponentially worse.

Jonas stood in a shallow section of the tank and held Jerry's head just above the surface of the water. He put his face distressingly close to Jerry's and dunked him quickly. As he resurfaced all that could be seen was Jonas's distorted face looming in front of him. The sight was terrifying but Jonas's voice was strangely comforting. "Who else knows what we know?"

Jerry could not reply. He did not have the answer nor did he have the ability anymore to speak. Jonas was silent in his disappointment. He looked as though Jerry were letting him down. Then a large hand entered Jerry's field of vision and pushed his head underwater.

He couldn't breathe. He couldn't fight back. He was royally screwed. All he could do was try to ignore the horrible burning sensation in his lungs and the terrible panic in his mind. It was a tall order. Drowning and imminent death have a way of holding a person's attention. What the hell was this all about? Jerry Fletcher was a New York cabby. Nothing more. What did they expect him to confess? Did they really want to know that he sometimes didn't flip the meter on when he picked up an especially beautiful fare? Were they willing to torture him to find out the best shortcuts through Manhattan?

It was true he had a quirky hobby and possessed the definitive collection of conspiracy files outside of the CIA and the *National Enquirer*. But why did the spooks feel compelled to kill him? Jerry was more than willing to talk with anyone about anything he knew. All Jonas had to do was ask about a specific theory and Jerry would be delighted to sit down over a beer and fill him in.

As the hand was removed from his face, Jerry surged up to suck in as much oxygen as he possibly could. Well, at least they weren't intent on drowning him. Not yet anyway. Torture wasn't great, but at least it was less conclusive than death. Jonas watched Jerry gasp for breath. When he had quieted down, the interrogation continued. "Who else knows what we know?"

Jerry tried to answer. He would have said anything as long as he didn't have to go back underwater. But his mouth wasn't listening to the orders from his brain. His jaws flapped up and down but no words came out.

Without any visible sign of emotion, Jonas shoved Jerry's head back under the ice-cold water.

The third dunking was far worse than the first two. Jerry's lungs felt as though they were exploding. This time he had no breath left to hold. Instead, he immediately inhaled a gallon or so of water and began to drown. Jonas looked at him curiously as Jerry screamed underwater. It wasn't a sound a person heard every day and Jonas seemed to enjoy it. Jerry was now in serious trouble and his body began to flail uncontrollably. His will to live was so intense and his body was so strong that his left wrist burst through the heavy duty tape that bound him to the wheelchair.

Jonas was having such a good time he never noticed that one of Jerry's hands was free. Jonas didn't want his fun to end prematurely so he let Jerry up for air before he died. With his head only inches above the water, Jerry gasped and coughed until he could finally speak again. "I'll . . . tell you."

That was what Jonas wanted to hear. He pulled Jerry up out of the tank into a sitting position in the wheelchair. Jonas whispered into Jerry's ear. "From your lips, to God's ear."

Jonas may have had a few kinks in his psyche but a diminished sense of personal empowerment wasn't one of them.

It was an odd thing. Maybe it was the drugs or the near-death experience but Jerry was fascinated that his entire view was dominated by Jonas's nose. As one might imagine, Jerry was not well disposed toward his tormentor and the idea of having this enormous blow hole stuck in his face angered him greatly.

There were some things a man could accept and then there were some things which demanded action.

Using his freed left hand, Jerry grabbed Jonas's shirt and yanked him close. Jerry didn't have a lot of choice in how he was going to fight this battle. In fact there was only one obvious target he could attack.

Jerry bit Jonas's nose as hard as he could.

He had seen this sort of desperate measure in *The Three Stooges*, but the real thing was infinitely more effective and gruesome. Blood began to flow but Jerry would not loosen his hold. He gnawed with all the ferocity that his jaws and teeth could muster up. When Jerry found an artery, blood exploded everywhere.

A howling Jonas tried to scramble out of the hungry reach of Jerry's gnashing teeth.

Jerry held on. It was a matter of life and death. When Jonas tried to retreat. Jerry and his wheelchair were dragged along for the ride. Jonas tripped over his own feet and fell backward. The hard landing knocked the wind out of him, and he lay on the floor struggling to catch his breath.

Jerry spat out a chunk of Jonas's nose and took a look at his former tormentor. The tables were turned. There was a certain justice in the world after all. Now Jonas knew how Jerry felt only minutes before. But Jerry did not savor his victory for long. He knew he had to get the hell out of wherever he was.

Leaving Jonas writhing on the floor, Jerry wheeled himself out the door and into a hallway. Under the best of circumstances his escape would have been a serious challenge. Still strapped into the wheelchair, and with only the partial use of one arm, Jerry tried to maneuver his way toward a stairwell. Jonas's drug concoction coursed through his brain and it appeared to him that the walls were jerking back and forth like giant Slinkys. Jerry pushed himself forward and tried to negotiate the undulating architecture.

He didn't get far. A wall seemed to jump right in his path and Jerry lurched forward as he made contact. Trying to clear his head, Jerry moved as quickly and carefully as he could toward an exit. Ricocheting off several more walls, Jerry finally made it to the stairwell that he hoped would lead him outside. As he arrived, he heard the sound of rapidly ascending footsteps. That route wasn't going to work. Sound the bugle, full retreat.

Jerry spun around to retrace his path through the gauntlet of lunging walls. Walls with an attitude were bad. Men with guns were worse. Jerry knew that whoever was rushing up the stairs to greet him wasn't sent from the front desk to help him with his bags. But Jerry stopped in his tracks before he had rolled ten feet down the corridor.

Jonas hobbled out of the hydrotherapy room. Holding a blood-soaked handkerchief to his nose, murder was clearly on his mind.

Jerry had to make a quick choice. He could take on an unknown assailant in the stairwell or deal with a man whose nose he just had for lunch. At least the guy climbing the stairs had nothing personal against Jerry. That seemed like the safer bet.

Spinning back toward the stairwell, Jerry was confronted by one of the thugs who had kidnapped him from the diner. The man reached the landing half a flight down from where Jerry was glaring at him. Now Jerry was the one who carried a personal grudge. He launched himself down the stairwell and found his wheelchair to be miraculously stable as it bounced along the steps.

The man watched Jerry with widening eyes as the

wheelchair careened down the stairs and slammed into him. He was driven backward through a window, out into the wild blue yonder, where he did a half gainer before continuing his journey to the pavement several stories below.

Meanwhile, Jerry was building up quite a head of steam as gravity exerted its influence upon the rapidly descending wheelchair. As he bounced down the third floor stairway he worried how he was going to slow his chariot down. If there were brakes on the contraption he couldn't have applied them since one of his arms was still strapped down and the other was still weak from the struggle.

Ever since Jerry bit Jonas's nose, luck seemed to be on his side. His braking concerns were put to rest when the second thug from the diner appeared directly in his path on the landing at the second floor. The impact was fierce and a cracking noise resounded through the stairwell. Broken bones? The wheelchair? Someone's skull? Neither man had the time to waste identifying the nature of the sound.

Instead the two men and the wheelchair tumbled down a long flight of stairs. With each step someone or something took the full impact of their combined weights against their body. It was a gruesome journey. At the end of it the thug lay on a landing with a broken neck, and the wheelchair lay in pieces.

All things considered Jerry was in fairly decent shape. Despite a painful spoke that pierced his side, he was alive. After pulling the offending object out of his body, Jerry shook off the remnant of the wheelchair that had held him hostage. Not wasting any time, Jerry charged out of the stairwell and found himself outdoors in the breezeway connecting two buildings of an abandoned hospital.

As he ran toward another doorway, Jerry noticed that there seemed to be people inside. Maybe the hospital wasn't completely vacant after all.

As he bolted into the next structure he found himself in the active kitchen of a busy hospital. It didn't make sense. But Jerry didn't have the inclination to stick around and figure out what was going on. He wanted out. He moved so fast that the kitchen staff was barely aware of his presence. Racing out of the kitchen and into a loading dock, Jerry spotted a delivery truck that was just about to pull away.

Launching himself into the back of the truck with the last energy in his body, Jerry landed with a muffled crash among bags of potatoes and napkins and pulled the door shut behind him.

It wasn't the most comfortable ride, but he was happy just to be out of the grasp of the mysterious Jonas. The truck moved along at a moderate pace and then geared down as it seemed to drive the span of a bridge. As he lay there trying to catch his breath, they picked up speed and took a corner a little too quickly. He was tossed into several sides of beef. A latch became undone and the rear door was flung wide open. A few blocks later the driver rounded another corner at high speed and the centrifugal force flung Jerry out of the back of the vehicle and into the path of oncoming cabs.

The sound of brakes squealing was music to Jerry's ears. He landed on the street and a number of taxis had to swerve to avoid hitting him. Jerry was a bruised but happy man. Surrounded by a sea of yellow cabs, he felt as though the cavalry had arrived to rescue him.

Bloody and battered, Jerry Fletcher waved to his

brother cabbies and began to shout happily, "I'm one of you. I'm one of you!"

The cabbies weren't impressed. All they saw was another nut blocking their path. Jerry was greeted with a chorus of expletives in an astonishing variety of languages.

Undaunted, Jerry began the long walk home.

Chapter 5

It was the end of a long day as Alice Sutton left her office and strode toward the elevators. Falling into step next to her was a young attorney from her division named John Kirkpatrick. John wasn't a bad guy at all and Alice had nothing in particular against him. John considered it something of a triumph when she nodded brusquely to him when he said hello. At least she hadn't ignored him.

John's level of confidence rose and he took his best shot. "So, you doing anything tonight?" Alice hefted her briefcase in front of his face. "Working."

She was hardly coquettish but John felt a surge of warmth course through his body. Alice only offered him one word but at least it hadn't been entirely dismissive. "Hmmm, how about tomorrow night?"

"Working."

Same word. Maybe she wasn't much of a conversationalist. "Night after that?"

Alice smiled and John would have gone out to fight wars on her behalf. But the news wasn't what he wanted to hear. "Look, you're a nice guy, but I'm not really dating right now."

A smile from that lovely mouth and a half a dozen, no maybe even a dozen words. John was feeling his Cheerios. "I'm not that good at 'no,' Alice."

Alice didn't pause but stepped into the elevator and pressed the lobby button. "Too bad. Because I'm terrible at 'yes.'"

The doors closed, Alice disappeared, and so did the romantic ambitions of the Ice Princess's latest victim.

As the doors to the elevator opened, Alice stepped out into her own worst nightmare. She couldn't see him, but she could hear his voice as it echoed wildly through the marble hall. "Alice Sutton! I need to see Alice!!"

She tried to slink away in the opposite direction but Jerry spotted her through the arms of the three brawny cops who were trying to restrain him. One cop tried to calm him down. "You don't leave now, you're under arrest."

Jerry wasn't listening. "Alice! This is it. They just tried to kill me! I don't know what I know, but it's big!"

Despite herself, Alice turned back to look and instantly saw that something *had* happened to her lunatic. Clearly, he had been through the wringer. She was tempted to speak to him, and even considered asking the security service to give Jerry a ride to the hospital. Alice never got the chance.

As the cops tried to restrain him, Jerry lost his cool. Having just survived torture and an attempt on his life, he wasn't intimidated by uniformed law officers. Jerry broke their grip and grabbed one of the cops' revolvers. He waved it in front of their faces and shouted, "Get back!"

Everyone, including Alice, froze. The cops who still had their service revolvers in their holsters, pulled them out and aimed at Jerry. Standoff city. Butch and Sundance just before they took on the Bolivian army.

"Easy, Jerry. Easy." Alice was the only person who could defuse the crisis. She looked at him more closely and was concerned. "There's blood on your shirt."

"I bit the bastard's nose off."

"You bit someone's nose off?" This was extreme stuff even for someone as lost in space as Jerry. Yet, there *was* blood splattered all over his chest. Something *had* happened. It just remained to be resolved exactly what.

"Yes! I bit his nose off. Don't let's get into this thing where I have to repeat myself!"

A guard moved into position to flank the gunman. Jerry followed him with his stolen weapon. He tried to make them understand. "It's a man without a nose you want, you dumb complicit sons of bitches!" Jerry paused, realizing his statement was extraordinary. Outrageous. Out to lunch. He turned to Alice. She was his only chance. "You've got to listen to me."

Alice's voice modulated between calm authority and the fear that Jerry had finally gone entirely over the edge. "Put down the gun and I'll take your statement. Okay?"

"You're the boss. Just don't make me repeat myself. I hate that." Blood dripped from Jerry's side. Now Alice was less troubled about what Jerry had done than what someone else might have done to him. "Jerry, you're bleeding."

Jerry removed his hand from where it was stanching the blood from his puncture wound. "I got a piece of a wheelchair jammed through me."

While Jerry was distracted by his conversation with Alice, the guards moved in for the kill. One forced Jerry's gun hand up into the air, while the other two tried to take him down. Jerry managed to fight back until one of the guards jammed a thumb into a pressure point in his neck. Jerry winced and fell to the ground.

Weakened by everything that had happened to him during this long day, Jerry tried to fill Alice in. "I can't remember them, Alice. I can't remember me. But I know it's on the tip of my tongue." He began to sob as his hands were cuffed. Alice instructed the lobby concierge to call an ambulance and told the cops to back away from their prisoner. Jerry lay on his back. Alone. Bleeding and weeping. Alice never heard such a desolate sound before in her life.

Against her more conservative instincts, Alice knelt beside Jerry Fletcher, put an arm around his battered shoulders, and tried to comfort him.

Her life was never going to be the same.

Hours later, she was sitting in the waiting room of Roosevelt Hospital's emergency room. The facility was definitely an inner city, gritty clinic. Cheap plastic chairs. Depressing commercial prints on the wall. Dreary fluorescent lighting. And worst of all— crowds. Old people. Young people. People who bled. People who smelled. People who cried.

Dressed in her stylish business suit, Alice did not look like she belonged there. Even if she had only been wearing jeans, she would have stood apart. This world was alien to her and she was doing her best to get through the experience.

Alice always used her work to help her get past moments of crisis, and today was no exception. She practically yelled into her cellular phone, "I need the files tonight. Have them sent to my apartment. I don't give a rat's ass what you're doing! Hello? Damn it!" Whoever she had been talking to was not impressed by her phone manner. She was left with an earful of dial tone.

"Sucks huh?" A twenty-year-old prostitute weathering the opening salvos of chemical withdrawal commented upon Alice's abbreviated conversation. Alice didn't bother to even look at her. She wanted nothing to do with the young junkie. But Crystal Wilkes was persistent in her own way and held up a beeper. "You should get one of these. Then use a pay phone. Cell phones can be traced."

Alice had no desire to engage in conversation. But she felt compelled to set the record straight. "I'm not doing anything illegal." Crystal gave her a quick once-over and snorted contemptuously. "Yeah. Right."

A bedraggled doctor who was finishing too many hours on duty walked out of the ER and scanned the waiting faces. "Who's here for Jerry Fletcher?" Alice stood up. "I am." The doctor figured that Alice was his reward after a depressing day on the job. "Jerry has a puncture wound clean through his abdomen, but it didn't touch anything vital. He should be fine. Physically."

He laughed and Alice knew what was coming next. The harassed but amorous doctor continued. "He's insisting he was stabbed with a wheelchair. He says his life is in danger and that . . ." Alice cut him off. She didn't need Jerry psychoanalyzed, she just wanted him patched up. "I know. He's crazy. When can I talk to him."

"They're moving him to the police ward. Maybe in twenty minutes." The doctor slunk back to the ER, reproved by Alice's chilly attitude.

Alice sat back down on her uncomfortable plastic chair and tried to imagine herself anywhere but where she was. But Crystal the junkie was feeling talkative again. Why was it that people like to chat in emergency rooms? Couldn't everyone just shut up and give her some personal space. Crystal's increasingly hyper voice began to give Alice a headache. "You're lucky. I had a boyfriend get shot in the stomach. Now he takes a dump through a plastic tube. I guess that's life, huh?"

Alice reached into her day planner, pulled out a crisp, brand new hundred-dollar bill and offered it to Crystal. "It's yours. Just go sit someplace else." Crystal hesitated, uncertain whether or not Alice was kidding. She wasn't. Plucking the bill from Alice's fingers, Crystal moved to another side of the waiting room.

Alice breathed a sigh of relief. One of the few problems she didn't have to worry about was money. Her father's estate had left her wealthy. It was comforting to know that when people got in your way or were creating trouble they could be made to disappear with such ease.

It was one of the ways Alice managed to keep her life unencumbered by troubling human relationships. Almost anybody would do as she asked for a hundred-dollar bill.

She walked along the police ward where wounded criminals were kept during their hospitalization. The cop guarding the floor barely looked up as Alice proceeded in a businesslike manner.

Alice found room 322, entered, and spotted Jerry lying in bed. Another sleeping inmate shared the room. She watched as a nurse injected something into Jerry's IV. She should have expected it, but Alice gasped when she saw Jerry strapped to his bed. Jerry

watched the nurse suspiciously and despite his infir-
mity seemed as worked up as usual. "What's that?!"
The nurse was no pushover. She knew how to deal
with troublesome patients. "Something to help you
sleep." Jerry protested. "I don't want to sleep! I want
to be checked out." Having answered his question,
the nurse now firmly refused to humor him any
longer. She left the room, passing Alice on her way.

Alice wasn't sure what to say so she simply stated
the obvious. "You're under arrest."

Jerry was indignant. The very image of innocence.
"What's the charge?" Impatient with his self-indul-
gent behavior, Alice snapped back, "You were there,
Jerry. Figure it out."

She had a point. Jerry nodded and actually fell
silent.

Alice began to ask questions. She knew Jerry was a
head case, but it seemed unlikely his wounds could
have been self-inflicted. If only he had offered a more
credible explanation. "If you could remember who
stabbed you with the wheelchair and where it happened, it might help." Jerry was thrilled to be taken
seriously. But suddenly he was fighting to keep his
eyes open. "What a day. Wish I could tell you so it
made sense." Jerry fought the medication and tried to
pull himself up into a sitting position. Alice gently
eased him back down. "Just relax."

"Switch the charts."

Alice wasn't sure she heard right. "What?"

Jerry wasn't kidding. He was as serious as a guy
who was about to pass out could be. "Switch 'em. Or
I'll be dead by morning. Don't want to be dead."

That was it. Alice reached her breaking point. Was
he serious? People getting stabbed by wheelchairs,
people biting other people's noses, and now a homi-

cidal nurse? Jerry Fletcher belonged in a psych ward, not with ordinary criminals. Alice turned to go. "I'll see you tomorrow."

"Wouldn't bet on it."

She didn't respond. Jerry was getting desperate, "Hey . . . I can't control it. It's just something that happened."

Alice was confused. "What is?"

"Love."

They looked at each other a moment. Now Alice was really confused. More than she had been about anything in a long time. He was a nut. What could she be thinking? It was too ridiculous to even contemplate.

Jerry's eyes fluttered as sleep overwhelmed him but there was one last thing he had to say. "Switch 'em. Save my life." He sighed deeply and passed out.

Alice started out the door and then stopped. For someone who was always in control, Alice realized that she was not at all sure what she was doing. Why did she walk over to Jerry and consider the chart hanging from the foot of his bed? Why did she look at his roommate's chart? Was she actually considering his request? Would she really indulge the fantasy of a good-looking guy who just happened to be profoundly paranoid?

Alice stood by the bed, unable to move, incapable of making this decision. She took a long look at Jerry. He was a lot more appealing when he was asleep. Alice sighed and made up her mind.

Chapter 6

The next morning Alice arrived on the police ward to see an orderly wheeling a sheet-covered corpse from Jerry's room. Her heart began to pound as she asked the cop on duty what had happened.

"Guy came in with a gunshot wound, but he died of a heart attack. Go figure."

Alice began to sweat. She pulled back the sheet and stared at the dead body of Jerry's roommate. Before she could think through the implications of what this meant, the cop asked her a question. "Are you Miss Sutton?" She nodded. "They said to send you downstairs."

"Who?"

"The FBI and the CIA. You name the initials and they're down there."

"Any special reason?"

The cop shrugged. "All I know is, they said to send you and the body to the basement."

Now Alice understood. Everyone in the hospital thought the corpse was Jerry Fletcher. Alice told the cop she would go downstairs in a moment. That was fine with him and the cop went back to his magazine.

Alice stepped inside room 322 and found Jerry still very much alive. He was sitting up in bed with his left hand cuffed to the rail. He was a happy man when he saw Alice. "Thank you."

"For what?"

Jerry laughed like there was joke he was supposed to understand. "For switching the charts."

"I didn't switch the charts."

Jerry heard but didn't listen. He was jubilant. There was no question anymore that he had stumbled upon something big. Not only had Jonas tried to drown him but whatever conspiracy he had uncovered had tentacles powerful enough to go after him a second time. Alice looked substantially less thrilled, and Jerry realized that she must be feeling bad about his dead roommate. "It's okay. The guy traded bullets with some man in a liquor store. He had it coming."

Alice was getting frustrated but she wasn't going to let Jerry see that. "You expect me to believe what? That someone came in here last night. Gave that guy . . . something that stopped his heart?"

"Yes. Absolutely. That's exactly what he was saying." Jerry beamed. "You switched the charts; you tell me."

She did not say a word but simply stared at him. Alice was hoping for a clue about whether or not she could take him seriously. Unable to understand, she felt she had to leave. "I got to get downstairs. The CIA, they want to see your body." Jerry was thrilled. The CIA!! It was all true. He hadn't been imagining conspiracies after all. To his way of thinking, he couldn't even be considered paranoid anymore—for this stuff was really happening to him.

Alice, however, still didn't look like she was reading from the same page. Despite the overwhelming evidence, she clearly had doubts.

Jerry was energized by the recent development and

was grateful to Alice for her assistance. "I won't be here when you get back, but I'll be in touch. And thanks."

"For what"

She was still resisting it. Even though the facts were clear for anyone to see. "You saved my life." Alice got mad. "*Heart attacks happen*. And I didn't switch those charts."

And then she was out the door before Jerry could argue any further. He thought about her for a moment, smiled, and then dipped his free hand into a cold bowl of oatmeal and began to smear the sticky cereal onto his chin and chest.

The elevator to the morgue was appropriately depressing. Alice thought the lurching ride would never end and was pleased when it finally reached the basement with a thud. The door opened and she was surprised to be met by a new face. "Ms. Sutton? Agent Russ Lowry, FBI."

The two shook hands. Both felt the morgue was a little less oppressive a place with the other standing there. Lowry was in his late thirties, tall, and darkly handsome. Alice was a quick study of men and while she recognized that he was almost all business, there was clearly a twinkle in his eye. Alice had not thought about romance for a long time, with, of course, the exception of the brief insanity she felt sometimes when she caught Jerry at just the right moment. If she had been at all interested in pursuing a man, Lowry would have made an appealing candidate. She wondered if Jerry's madness was contagious, for when she looked at Lowry she couldn't understand how she had seen something, even momentarily, in the lunatic handcuffed to the bed upstairs.

Lowry got right down to the facts at hand. Alice liked that. "We're waiting for jurisdictional problems to be cleared up. This guy Fletcher's something else."

Alice wanted to laugh. "Tell me about it."

"While we walk." Lowry led Alice toward the operating theater. "The DC police want him for assault. Secret Service for counterfeiting, and we're tracking him on a string of bank robberies. No one knows what the CIA wants him for."

"Wait." Alice wanted to tell Lowry what she knew about Jerry's "demise" but he kept right on going and stepped into a room before she could stop him.

Alice and Lowry faced the backs of a small group of law enforcement officials as they stared at a sheet-covered corpse. Alice was surprised to see her boss, Phil Wilson, standing there. He nodded grimly to her. What was he doing here? Lowry pointed to several other men. "CIA." Another figure stood apart from the rest, but stood in such a way that Alice could not see his face. Lowry whispered into Alice's ear, "Guy's a CIA shrink. Here to ID Fletcher. They knew each other somehow."

"You don't understand . . ." Alice tried again. Lowry shushed her as a pathologist pulled back the sheet to reveal Jerry's former roommate.

No one could see the anger in the CIA psychiatrist's countenance, but his tone of voice was unmistakable. "This isn't him." Wilson turned to Alice for help as the CIA psychiatrist checked the chart at the foot of the gurney.

Alice stumbled over her response. "I was trying to tell, um, Jerry, I mean Fletcher, he's . . ."

Alice's words got stuck in her throat as the CIA psychiatrist turned around to listen. Alice could not believe what she saw.

The man had an enormous bandage on his nose.

It was Jonas. The CIA psychiatrist was Jerry's man without a nose. Alice was shocked as few people ever are. Jerry had been telling the truth. He had bitten this man's nose.

Alice was stricken dumb while Jonas built toward an eruption. Why had the young woman fallen silent? Why wasn't Jerry Fletcher dead? Who was lying on the gurney in his place? Jonas wanted to know exactly where Jerry was. Immediately if not sooner.

As Jonas yelled in the morgue, Jerry was covered in a gelatinous skin of oatmeal. He looked pale as death. The way he groaned and clutched his chest completed the picture. To anyone passing by it appeared that he was on his way to the basement to join his recently departed roommate.

"He's having a heart attack!" Jerry was surrounded by three nurses, two orderlies, and an intern. Frustrated, the intern tugged at the handcuff that chained Jerry to his bed. "Where's that goddamn cop!?" The patient had to be uncuffed. If they needed to jumpstart the man's heart, he couldn't be attached to a metal rail. "Get a crash cart in here!"

The groaning stopped and Jerry recovered enough from his heart attack to offer some clever advice. "No! Get me to the crash cart!"

Alice, Jonas, Lowry, Wilson, and the CIA agents marched toward the elevator, determined to figure out where exactly Jerry Fletcher was. As they walked, Alice couldn't help but stare at Jonas's nose. It was too weird to just be a coincidence.

Jonas noticed Alice staring at his wound. Their gazes met and Alice was deeply unnerved. It wasn't just the missing nose, there was something behind his eyes which was unsettling. Caught in the act, Alice had to acknowledge her error. "Can I ask you something?"

"A dog bit it."

"Excuse me?"

Jonas was fuming inside, but tried to seem as pleasant as he could. Alice wasn't sure what his deal was, but there was clearly something complex going on.

"You were going to ask me about my nose. The poor animal is slated to be destroyed today."

Jonas almost seemed amused. It didn't make sense. Alice probed further. "And you feel bad for the dog?"

"It was my dog." Aside from the polite conversation regarding his wound, Jonas had another agenda. It had not escaped his attention that Department of Justice honcho Phil Wilson had turned to Alice when he needed someone to identify Jerry Fletcher. "Let me ask you a question. How long have you been acquainted with Jerry?"

The elevator announced its arrival with a ping and the doors opened.

Something wild was going on in Jerry's hospital room.

There was a tremendous crash and the intern who was treating Jerry's "cardiac problems" staggered backward out the door, across the hallway, and collapsed against a wall.

Following him out the door was a magically revived Jerry, wearing nothing more than a flapping johnny and a bed rail, which was still attached to his wrist by a handcuff. He dashed down the corridor looking for an exit out of the police ward.

The stunned orderlies and nurses who had unscrewed the rail from the bed in a desperate effort to rush Jerry to the crash cart reeled and wobbled as they made their way to the doorway. They watched their dying patient bolt off like a bat out of hell.

Jerry barreled around a corner and slammed on his brakes as he practically ran down Alice, Jonas, and the rest of the entourage. Jerry swung his arm around, wielding his bed rail like a medieval weapon and drove it into the nearest CIA agent's gut, knocking the shocked man onto his back.

Jerry flashed a panicked grin to Alice. Even with the CIA, FBI, police, doctors, nurses, orderlies, and candy stripers on his tail, Jerry felt compelled to smile whenever he saw Alice. Considering the situation, it didn't make sense, but there it was. Love was a curious and powerful thing.

Then he made a rapid about-face and ran as fast as he could, dressed in only a flimsy hospital gown, dragging a cumbersome bed rail behind him.

After a moment of stunned bewilderment, the various law officers and government agents followed in hot pursuit.

Racing down the linoleum with adrenaline gushing through his veins like water through a broken dam, Jerry noticed a barred security door with a lock facing him. It was the entrance to the high security section of the ward designed for sick prisoners who were active enough to pose a threat.

Jerry had an idea.

Running through the barred door, Jerry ducked into a room on the other side. Spotting another door immediately on his right, he rushed inside a bathroom and through a second door leading to yet another room.

Doors were opening and shutting with a manic rapidity. Cops, secret agents, doctors, and nurses charged through a small maze of rooms in their search for Jerry.

With a little work Jerry eventually ended up back at the original barred door, just as he hoped. With his pursuers only yards behind him, he dove through the security door, pulled it shut behind him, and locked it. Jerry offered a crazy smile to Agent Lowry, who led the pack.

The law enforcement experts and government suits were locked up by their own prisoner.

Lowry tried to pull the barred door out of the door frame but didn't have much success. It was built to survive exactly that kind of stress. As Jerry took off, Lowry bellowed to his fellow captives, "Who's got the goddamn key?"

Meanwhile, Jerry was executing a diversion, hoping to throw his pursuers offtrack. Jumping up onto a hallway chair, Jerry punched a ceiling panel loose, to create the impression he was crawling around among the ventilation ducts and electrical wiring. Instead, he sprinted off down the corridor.

Moments later, Jonas, Lowry, Alice, and the others found someone with a key and released themselves and charged after Jerry. As he planned, they stopped at the chair underneath the broken ceiling panel.

Jonas barked out commands. He ordered two CIA agents to climb up into the false ceiling and investigate whether or not Jerry was really up there. "The rest of you go room to room! I want dogs! I want motion detectors! I want heat sensors!"

Lowry and Alice stared at the CIA psychiatrist suspiciously. Lowry muttered to Alice the question that was foremost in her mind, "Is this guy a psychiatrist or a field agent?"

* * *

Sticking his head inside a small room at the end of a hallway, Jerry saw an orderly dump a load of dirty linens into a laundry chute and amble his way out another door. Jerry launched himself into the room. Considering the chute an excellent if smelly escape route, Jerry gripped its lip and swung one leg into the shaft. Before he could cram his other leg into the soiled abyss, however, a cop entered the room with his service revolver drawn. The cop growled a warning. "Put your foot down."

Jerry tried logic. "If you knew what really happened to Serpico, you'd be doing everything you could to help me out." Frank Serpico had been a New York cop who had uncovered massive corruption in his department. The cop aiming his gun at Jerry knew Serpico had been played by Al Pacino in the movies, but otherwise he didn't make the connection between the film and the escaping perp.

Instead, the cop told Jerry in no uncertain terms to climb out of the chute. *Now.* It was just Jerry's luck to be confronted by the one cop in New York who hadn't seen the movie.

Jerry obliged. But as he pulled his leg out of the chute he placed his hand against a laundry cart and shoved it as hard as he could into the cop. As the cop recovered from the glancing blow, Jerry swung the bed rail cuffed to his arm. The cop went down. Jerry began to squeeze himself back into the chute for a second time, but before he could slide away to safety the cop was back on his feet and grabbing at his arms.

Jerry wrestled with the policeman and began to doubt that this guy could actually be a bona fide New York City patrolman. He was too strong and fought too well to be a regular cop. This guy had to be some sort of secret government warrior. Convinced he was tangling with a foot soldier of a nameless government organization, Jerry tapped into a reserve of strength he had forgotten he possessed. Jerry head-butted the cop.

The cop went down for a second time, releasing his grasp on Jerry's arms. Jerry plummeted down the laundry chute, only to be yanked to a socket-wrenching stop when his bed rail formed a crossbar over the mouth of the shaft. Jerry dangled by his wrist, caught in between dirty bedsheets and a nefarious plot to do him in. He had to do something fast or he was a dead man. Jamming his back against a wall of the chute and shoving his feet against another, Jerry painfully inched his way back up toward the top.

Just as he reached his goal and was about to disengage the bed rail from the position where it was stuck, a face suddenly appeared. It was Alice. Thunderstruck, Jerry lost his grip and plunged back down toward the laundry pile. Again, the bed rail jerked him to a violent halt.

Alice stood next to the semiconscious cop and peered down at Jerry, who was suspended in midair. It was all too strange.

Jerry looked up at Alice with love in his heart and increasing anxiety. He was completely at her mercy. If she wanted, Jerry would be in the hands of the schemers and plotters in less than a minute.

There wasn't a lot of time to waste making up her mind. Despite the madness of the last twenty-four hours, Alice was once again baffled by her inability to pull the plug on this charming lunatic. Puzzling her even further, Alice had to admit that some of what Jerry claimed seemed to be true, as farfetched as it sounded. Not sure what to do, she fell back on her training as a lawyer. Despite the dire situation, she began to ask questions. "He says a dog bit his nose."

"Arf. You gotta help me."

"I can't promise you anything."

People were coming. Footsteps were rushing toward them. The moment of truth had arrived. Alice couldn't believe she was about to help a fugitive but that's exactly what was happening. Reaching into the cop's pocket, Alice removed a key ring. After sorting through half a dozen keys, she chose one and slid it into Jerry's handcuff.

They shared a long look. Alice was about to leave behind the orderly life she had created for herself.

As far as Jerry was concerned, Alice was nothing less than an angel. She was about to save his life for the second time in twenty-four hours. He knew she was going to release him, even if Alice herself hadn't yet made the decision.

She turned the key. The handcuff sprang open and Jerry plunged down two stories to a hard landing made marginally softer by a pile of sheets, towels, and hospital gowns.

Alice went to work. Having aided and abetted an escaping prisoner, she had to cover up her complicity. Pocketing the cop's keys, Alice dragged the bed rail across the room and leaned it against a wall, where it sat inconspicuously next to a pharmaceutical supply cabinet.

Moments later, Jonas and Lowry rushed into the room to find Alice tending to the bleary cop. Lowry was all business. "Which way did he go?"

"I don't know. Didn't see him." Lowry punched a wall with frustration, "No way we can shut a place this size down quick enough." Jonas didn't agree. He sneered at his younger counterpart with ill-disguised contempt. "You have a half naked man chained to a bed rail. Just cover the exits."

Reprimanded, Lowry nodded and headed back to the main hallway. Alice decided to join him. "I'll come with you."

Jonas looked around the room, hoping to find some indication that Jerry Fletcher had been through here. Everything appeared to be normal. Then he saw it. The lone bed rail against the wall. A memory of Agent Wilson asking Alice to identify Jerry's "corpse" flashed through Jonas's mind. Suddenly, it all made sense to him and he shouted to Alice as she walked out the door with Lowry. "*You.*"

Alice stopped cold. Lowry too. Jonas crooked a finger in her direction. "Keep me company. Please."

Jonas was the senior official at the scene of the crime. Alice had no choice but to do as she was told.

Sometime later, Jerry was getting dressed in a doctor's locker room. Fortunately, no one noticed his arrival clad only in his battered johnny. Now he was wearing stolen surgical scrubs and a paper hair net. To anybody who saw him, Jerry was just another surgeon about to take a break from his arduous duties.

Jerry stopped out of the locker room and fell into step with a trio of tired interns who were dressed exactly as he was.

The group headed for an exit that was guarded by two cops on the lookout for a nut with his ass sticking out of his hospital gown. Jerry struck up a conversation with the doctors as they approached the doorway. "Did you see that spleen? I never saw a spleen like that ever."

The cops didn't give Jerry a second look as the four doctors left the building. To them, Jerry was just one of the guys. The interns, however, gave Jerry some odd looks. He didn't care what they thought of him. He wasn't there to make friends. All that mattered was that he get out of the hospital and escape from Jonas. Jerry separated from the doctors and said good-bye with a cheerfully loopy description of a particularly nasty surgery. "It was unbespleenable!"

Then he hit the pavement and was home free.

Alice, on the other hand, was still stuck in the lion's den. Although there was nothing overtly hostile about her conversation with Jonas, the implication was unmistakable. Jonas believed she knew more about Jerry Fletcher than she was letting on. Therefore, Alice was stuck in a verbal sparring session with a tea-drinking lion in the middle of an institutional cafeteria.

"So Jerry thinks NASA is plotting to kill the President?"

"You already asked me that. Why do you insist on making me repeat myself?" Now Alice was quoting Jerry. It was amazing how annoying an interrogation process could be. She would have to remember that in the future.

Jonas wasn't listening and steamrolled along. "And you have no idea where Jerry lives?"

"You've asked me that one three times."

Jonas paused and appraised the young attorney sitting across the table from him. Her ethereal beauty masked a tough-as-nails personality. Wilson had warned him of this but Jonas hadn't quite believed it. She didn't like the way he repeated his questions. "Okay. Here's a fresh one. Why you? Your colleague Mr. Wilson says Jerry won't speak to anyone else. That seems oddly possessive behavior to me."

"I'm sorry. What was the question again."

Tough and clever as well. Jonas realized that Alice was making him repeat himself. He acknowledged her little victory with a chilling smile. Even when this guy tried to appear friendly, he was menacing. *"Why you?"*

Alice figured that honesty was the best policy. "I think he's got a crush on me."

If Jonas had been human he might have been amused. "A charming term. And why him? Why do you tolerate Jerry's visits to your office?"

A good question. One that a number of people at the Department of Justice had asked themselves. There was, however, a perfectly reasonable answer. "Six months ago I was leaving work. Two guys tried to mug me. Jerry came out of nowhere. Rescued me. That's how we met. I know he's probably crazy, but there's something about Jerry that . . ." Alice hesitated and pretended to cough. Jonas was too interested in her explanation. There was more going on here than was apparent. She decided to be more circumspect. "I don't know. It's just hard for me to tell him to get lost."

Then she changed the subject. She had questions of her own. "I didn't know the CIA had psychiatrists." Once again Jonas was impressed. Alice was a bright young woman and a worthy opponent. "We're very specialized."

"Moles digging holes. All that espionage. I guess the boys are under a lot of stress."

Jonas was entirely matter of fact with his explanation. "I retrain the wayward in the ways of polite society. Pull back men who've gone over the edge. It is delicate work."

Alice wasn't sure what she just heard. Was Jonas

talking about Jerry? Paranoid, lunatic, cab-driving, blue-eyed Jerry Fletcher? Was Jonas's pursuit of Jerry an unselfish act? Was he trying to help? Jerry? Involved with the CIA?

It didn't seem likely. Jerry Fletcher saw conspiracies in every passerby, every obscure coincidence. If the sun came up in the east every morning it was indicative of an intergalactic machination. Jerry could never have passed the agency's stringent psychological testing.

As Jonas tended to his tea, Alice noticed he wore a Harvard alumnus ring. Alice hadn't worn her own Stanford ring in years but asked to take a closer look at Jonas's. He offered his hand and Alice took a closer look. Engraved in gold were three open books and the Latin inscription VE-RI-TAS. Alice wasn't a langauge expert but she knew the translation. "*Veritas*. Truth. What is it they say about truth?"

Jonas pulled back his hand and stared at Alice over the rim of his teacup. "The truth will set you free."

After her conversation with Jonas, Alice went to the third floor of the hospital to examine the condition of Jerry's room. A cop stood guard at the door. Alice flashed her Department of Justice identification and was allowed inside.

Other than the fact that one of the beds was missing its left-hand railing, the room looked entirely unremarkable. Perhaps it could have been cleaner but that was the responsibility of the custodial staff. It had nothing to do with Jerry or his escape. Alice opened the nightstand drawer next to Jerry's bed. She found a number of personal items: a key ring, a pack of gum, and a worn copy of J.D. Salinger's most famous book,

The Catcher in the Rye. She flipped through it, hoping to find a clue to whatever mystery it was she was investigating.

The truth was she wasn't even sure what official business she was pursuing. Was she hunting down Jerry or clues to the conspiracy he believed in so fervently? She had no idea.

Nor would Jerry's book offer any insight. Certain passages were highlighted with yellow marker. Others were blacked out. It would have taken someone with more expertise in code breaking than Alice to figure out what it all meant.

"*Catcher in the Rye*?" Russ Lowry joined her in the room. Alice was pleased to see him. She handed the beaten-up paperback to Lowry and he offered the only connection he knew between Holden Caulfield's angst and the criminal world. "That's the book Chapman had on him when he shot John Lennon." Alice knew that. But what did it mean? If it meant anything.

The cop guarding the door overheard their conversation and offered his two cents' worth. "Remember the guy who shot Reagan? John Hinckley? I remember reading how they found a copy of that book in his apartment. Weird coincidence, huh?"

Alice and Lowry processed this information and exchanged a look. They agreed. It *was* an unusual coincidence. Alice considered it further and tried to approach the problem from Jerry's point of view. She knew he didn't believe in happenstance. Jerry would find significance in this. But in this particular instance he seemed to be a participant instead of a whistle blower, for the book was obviously meaningful to him as it had been to two infamous assassins. What did that suggest about Jerry Fletcher?

Lowry checked through Jerry's personal items and broke Alice's concentration. "Gum, keys, and a book." He examined the keys closely, "Car . . . maybe apartment . . . This is an odd one." Alice took a look. The third key was long and narrow. She recognized it instantly. "Safety deposit box."

Just then three CIA suits slunk into the room. One grim-faced man confiscated Jerry's chewing gum and book. Another held out his hand for the key ring. Lowry handed them over without argument. The suits left the room as silently as they had entered. Alice blinked a few times. Had they really been there at all? Lowry shouted after them, "You're welcome!" Then he shrugged to Alice. "Spooks. So, you want to compare notes on this guy?"

Alice wasn't ready. "No. Not yet." There are too many questions floating around in her head. She was no longer sure who her friends were or which people were the bad guys. Alice was pretty certain, however, that Lowry was going to fit into the first category.

She was about to make an encouraging joke, but something caught her eye. A word was scratched into the nightstand next to Jerry's bed. "Geronimo." Lowry found a fork lying on the floor that must have been used to scrape in the message. He was as puzzled as Alice was. "Geronimo? What's that?"

It was the end of a long day and Alice Sutton was finally able to leave the hospital. As she walked out of the busy lobby, she fished a small tape recorder from her briefcase and began to make oral notes. "Jerry Fletcher. Apparently, a major desperado. Subject of a multijurisdictional task force manhunt . . . I don't buy it. He might be nuts, but there's something . . . good about him."

Alice was now more or less willing to give Jerry the benefit of the doubt. For a little while anyway. She might not actually believe his conspiracy theories, but Alice had to admit that she was just a bit curious. As for her personal feelings about Jerry Fletcher—there was something about his eccentric enthusiasm she found appealing. Yet her grudging acceptance of Jerry had more to do with sympathy than affection.

She saw something and began to shout, "No! Please!!" as she ran down the sidewalk. A traffic officer finished ticketing her four-wheel drive Blazer just as Alice reached the car. It was too late. The traffic cop waved and drove off down the avenue. It was the last straw and Alice lost her cool. Furious and frustrated she flung open the door and threw herself behind the wheel.

Still grumbling, Alice started the engine, and prepared to pull out of the space. Fifty-dollar tickets. Talk about conspiracies. She would have loved to be able to direct the attention of the Department of Justice toward the parking bureau. A quick investigation and Alice figured she could dig up enough dirt to make the meter monster who had just ticketed her car rue the day she was born.

Alice glanced up at the rearview mirror, screamed at the top of her lungs, and jumped up with a rocket propulsion provided by jangled nerves. The only thing that kept her from going through the roof was her viselike grip on the steering wheel.

Rising up from the backseat of the Blazer was a hand holding six fanned-out parking tickets.

"They've been coming all day. Nothing I could do about it." Jerry's apologetic face appeared for an instant and then dove back down into his hiding place behind the front seat.

Alice's fear melted into anger and resolved itself into curiosity. "How'd you know this was my car?" Jerry paused, not wanting to tell her that he'd been watching her for some time. "Lucky guess . . . um, I'd feel a lot less naked if we could get outta here."

"Don't tell me you're naked back there."

"Figure of speech. Could we go?" Jerry handed Alice half a dozen parking tickets as she gritted her teeth. Alice hit the gas and pulled out into traffic. Jerry was full of questions. "What took so long? You were in there all day." He escaped this morning and had expected Alice back sooner.

"That's how long it takes to turn a hospital inside out. A lot of people are after you, Jerry."

Instead of acknowledging the fact, Jerry jagged off onto a tangent. "Dead or alive, they'll stick me in there with Oswald. Another lunatic acting alone." What the hell was he talking about?

"Oswald was an assassin. You're not an assassin, are you, Jerry?" He was annoyed. Jerry was trying to warn people about assassins, not get away with murder, "If you're worried about the President, call and warn him about the space shuttle."

"Yeah. Right." Alice wasn't buying and recalled the old saying about "distance lending enchantment." Now Alice understood exactly what it meant. Jerry had vanished from the hospital some eight hours before. In that time Alice had convinced herself that he wasn't such a bad guy at all. Now, less than a minute after their reunion, she was aggravated all over again. More space shuttle bullshit. Besides. It was a pain in the ass to talk to someone you couldn't see. "Sit up, Jerry, so I can see you."

"Uh uh. Don't want *them* to see me."

Here we go again. "Them who, Jerry?"

"Change lanes. Then watch your rearview." A skeptical Alice complied with his request. She changed lanes and looked carefully behind her. Three cars back a pair of headlights followed her into the new lane. She didn't quite believe it. Spy versus spy on the streets of Manhattan? Alice didn't think so. To prove her point, she took a quick left turn as a traffic light turned yellow.

She kept her eyes on the rearview mirror and frowned when she saw the same car make the same turn.

Jerry did not have to ask. He knew he was right. "Flat, wraparound headlights?" Bingo. "Crown Victoria. FBI car. A legitimate tail."

Alice didn't understand. "Legitimate? As opposed to?"

He explained. "People more serious about their work."

Jerry let that notion sink in and then he made a roundabout suggestion. "You know how to drive this thing or do you just like looking good in it?"

Alice played dumb. "You mean I should speed up and try to lose them?" That was exactly what Jerry meant. Alice wasn't surprised. Nor was she impressed. "That's how a man would do it. I'm not a man." Jerry agreed. He had noticed some time before that she wasn't a man.

Alice hit her brakes and stopped the Blazer in the middle of the street. Jerry slid off the rear seat and hugged the floor in a state of serious consternation. *"What are you doing?"*

Behind them the Crown Victoria was forced to slow down considerably. The driver sheepishly crept along, trying his best not to stand out from the rest of the traffic.

Alice stuck her arm out the window and waved to the tail, gesturing for it to approach.

Russ Lowry was behind the wheel of the Crown Victoria and felt like a jerk, realizing Alice had spotted him. There wasn't much he could do but pull up alongside and say hello. Lowry smiled bashfully as Alice greeted him. While he felt foolish for being caught, he was pleased to have another chance to chat with Alice.

"Sorry. Wasn't my idea."

"Jonas?"

Yup. It was the psychiatrist. "It's his show for now. Look, you want to get some dinner? Interagency cooperation and all that?"

From his position hidden on floor of the backseat Jerry grew uneasy. Smooth talk from Joe Ivy League Federal Agent Stud bothered him more than the idea that Jonas and several armies of secret agents were sparing no expense in an effort to kill him.

Alice flashed a rare and transcendent smile but wasn't biting. "When I'm ready to compare notes, I'll let you know."

Lowry accepted his lonely fate with equanimity. "Your call. Have a good night." He would remember that smile on many cold nights in the future.

He drove off without ever realizing that Jerry Fletcher was in the backseat of Alice's car.

After waiting an appropriate amount of time for Lowry to drive off, Jerry popped up from his hiding place, leaned forward, and watched the taillights fade away. Alice wanted him to recognize the effectiveness of her method. "See? Wasn't that a lot easier than squealing tires and knocking over trash cans?"

Jerry wasn't going to give her the satisfaction. "Nothing is easy."

"How long have we known each other, Jerry?"

He didn't have to count. He knew. Precisely. "Six months. Eleven days." Jerry didn't bother with the hours. He didn't want to appear too eager.

Alice was about to make his day. "Till today, I haven't believed a word. Now, I'm curious. Six months, eleven days. I'm going to give you one more hour to impress me. Where to?"

Chapter 7

Times Square. The Great Flood of '97 had receded and the hustle and bustle of the theater district returned to normal.

Flip Tanner sat in his wheelchair in front of the newsstand. Flip made a point of watching the uptown traffic in the evening. He could recognize a regular customer from two blocks away and would have their paper or magazine ready as they pulled up to the curb.

When Alice's Blazer stopped about a foot away from where he was sitting, Flip wasn't sure what was going on. The guy in the car, sitting next to the great-looking young woman looked familiar. But he was out of context. Flip squinted and realized the lucky bastard in the backseat of the sedan was Jerry. *"Jerry?* You didn't show last night. First time ever. Had me worried, boy."

"Sorry, Flip." Jerry cast a knowing look toward Alice. "Got sidetracked."

Flip ogled Alice and thought he understood. America was a great country. The land of opportunity. Two days earlier, Jerry was just another hack in a cab. Now he was being driven around town by a lady who could have graced the cover of any of Flip's magazines. Flip offered Jerry a bawdy wink and Alice looked heavenward, begging relief from the madness that surrounded Jerry Fletcher.

Flip reached down and offered Jerry two stacks of newspapers and magazines. "Saved you last night's too."

Jerry introduced him to Alice. "Flip was a hero in Vietnam."

"Sure was. Pounded the VC for this Greek cat name Ari Onassis." Alice's jaw almost dropped and she took a closer look at Flip. Please God. Not another one. Then she recognized the twinkle in Flip's eye and realized he was joking. They shared a look that acknowledged Jerry's unconventional perspective on the world. And Flip's smile said to Alice that for all of it, Jerry was a good guy.

A day earlier Alice would never have gone through such nonsense. She and Jerry climbed up one fire escape, jumped over an alley eight stories above the pavement, down another fire escape, and into the hallway outside his apartment. As he climbed in through the window, Jerry grimaced and held his side.

"You Okay?"

"Flesh wound. No big deal." Jerry unlocked the door and Alice offered her only comment on his unusual method for going home. "I still don't think we had to park a mile away."

Alice hadn't expected the apartment. When Jerry turned on the light she was astonished to discover the file maze. Not only was Jerry paranoid, but even worse—he was a paranoid pack rat. Jerry's home was as cluttered with suspicion as was his mind. Then she noticed the silvery particle board covering the walls. Some decor. "Is this supposed to protect you from aliens?" If he said yes—a possibility which Alice did not entirely dismiss—then she would walk out the door and write Jerry Fletcher off.

But Jerry didn't answer. Instead, he locked the door and picked up an empty beer bottle from the floor. He had a question of his own to ask, "You know why the Grateful Dead are always on tour?"

"Surprise me."

He did. "The whole kit and caboodle of 'em are British Intelligence agents. *Spies.* Jerry Garcia had a double-0 rating. Just like James Bond." Jerry Fletcher placed the empty beer bottle on the doorknob and disappeared into the file labyrinth. Alice recognized the bottle as a primitive alarm system, laughed to herself, and pretended to be the late leader of the dead, as if he were indeed a compatriot of 007. "Garcia, Jerry Garcia."

If nothing else, Alice was going to gather some good stories to tell to her friends and colleagues. Well, colleagues anyway. Alice didn't have friends anymore. She followed Jerry into the file maze.

Alice had to hurry to catch up to Jerry, who moved through the towering files with expertise. Jerry was pleased to have company and realized he was not living up to his obligations as a good host. "You want something to drink?"

"Um, coffee. If that's okay?" That was fine. Jerry smiled. "Coffee is our friend." He led her into the kitchen and began to unchain the refrigerator. Noticing and misinterpreting the look of dismay on Alice's face, Jerry tried to explain. "I keep the beans in the fridge. They stay fresher that way."

Jerry pulled out a stainless steel container marked "coffee" and began to spin the dial of its combination lock. While he was occupied with this task, Alice took a look at his magnetic poetry sticking to the refrigerator door.

> Must language produce a thousand knives and not recall a whisper?

Alice read another one.

> I love the delicate shadow of she wanting to be me.

There was something significant trying to emerge from Jerry's poetry. Like Jerry himself, there was something Alice wanted to like, but she just couldn't quite penetrate the mystery. Jerry didn't seem to notice as she read the fridge door. After a brief struggle, he gave up trying to open the can of coffee beans and confessed somewhat self-consciously, "Forgot the combination . . . you want some grapefruit juice?"

Alice declined and they made their way into the living room, where Jerry flipped on the Xerox machine. Alice noticed a poster of John Lennon. She remembered the connection between *Catcher in the Rye* and Lennon's assassin. Alice didn't like what she was seeing.

Jerry gestured toward his files and a drafting table that he used as a desk. "If my universe had a hub."

"This would be it." Alice smiled politely. It was disconcerting that Jerry should be proud of the jumbled room. Alice walked over to the drafting table and noticed several competent sketches Jerry had drawn of horses in motion. Next to them lay a book with a photograph of a horse jumping a rail that Jerry had used as a model for his work. Alice seemed to her lose herself in a distant place as she sighed. "Equitation."

The skill of horseback riding.

Jerry tried to explain. "I've been reading up on it." Alice pointed to the sketches and asked a question she already knew the answer to. "Are these yours?" Embarrassed, Jerry nodded yes and turned his attention to the *New York Times*. While he read, Alice noticed two small renderings of herself. Jerry had drawn her sleeping face into the margins of the horse drawings.

Alice's skin crawled. The whole business was getting creepy. Then she relaxed a bit when she thought it through. Hadn't she told Jonas that Jerry had a crush on her? What was the big deal? Two casual pictures. How could she be surprised? Jerry *was* that weird. That was a given. It wasn't news to anyone.

After a quick scan of the headlines, Jerry handed Alice the front page of his paper. "Just look at it. Ten seconds and you'll be scared out of your mind." Alice did as she was told while Jerry picked up several pages that had just been spit out of the ancient copying machine and stapled them together.

Alice gave the *Times* back to him. "Nothing scary there. Sorry." Jerry shook his head and examined the front page carefully, "Oh, well, maybe to the untrained eye." As he read, Jerry made approving noises that could have been mistaken for sounds of passion. He oohed and ahhed and hummmed. Alice wanted to laugh.

Jerry found something important. He pointed to an article about NASA. "More stories about life on Mars. From a rock they found at the South Pole. Explain that one to me. But maybe we should go to Mars and find out? How much do you think that's going to cost?"

Before Alice could reply, Jerry rattled on about another article. "Look at this. The Council of Foreign Affairs is meeting in Zurich. Spokesman says it right out loud: The CFA is a group of concerned citizens with an eye to fostering cooperation among international allies."' Jerry emphasized a point. "They said it, 'with an eye.' *An eye.*"

Alice didn't get it. Jerry pulled a dollar bill from his wallet and pointed to the "eye" on the back side. "Well that's the eye right there. *Money.* And all the power and misery it brings with it. It's a plot to take over the world. The Master Conspiracy."

Alice was beginning to regret the hour she was giving him. It appeared that Jerry was hopelessly lost in the enigmatic world of shadowy international organizations conspiring against the common man. Only a few hours earlier he had started to make some sense. But now he was once again sounding like just another distrustful crank. She scoffed at the whole idea. "Do they have a secret handshake?"

Without missing a beat, Jerry grabbed her hand and put it through a lengthy series of intricate machinations. Once he was done, Jerry waited for her reaction. Alice was shaken. If there was a bona fide handshake and Jerry knew it, did that mean he was more involved in the whole business than she thought? "That's it? That's the secret handshake?" Jerry watched her squirm uneasily before confessing, "I have no idea."

Alice laughed out loud. It was a captivating sight.

Jerry was joking. And she had believed him. In that instant, Alice realized that Jerry wasn't completely out to lunch after all. He could distinguish between fantasy and reality—at least to a certain extent. That was good.

It was also bad. For now Alice could not exclude the possibility that Jerry wasn't making everything up. It seemed outlandish, but there it was. Her laughter faded when Alice realized the seriousness of the implications. "So why are they after you?"

Jerry wasn't sure. "I think I figured something out." He lowered his voice so he could not be overheard. "It must've been my newsletter." This was something new to Alice. "What newsletter?" He reached for the xeroxed pages he had just assembled.

"Here it is. *Conspiracy Theory*. Third issue this year. I bet one of the articles struck a nerve. Pissed someone off." Alice took a look. THE SPACE SHUTTLE'S SEISMIC SECRET. THE OLIVER STONE–GEORGE BUSH CONNECTION. That was going too far. "Oliver Stone?"

It was very simple really. "Stone is their spokesman. You think if someone really had all that information and a national podium to shout it out from they'd let him do it? Stone's a disinformation flunky. The fact that he's alive says it all."

Space shuttle assassins were one thing. Film director Oliver Stone working in league with the Republican establishment, however, was too much to ask anyone to believe. Alice didn't buy it. "Can you prove any of this?"

"Absolutely not. A good conspiracy is an unprovable conspiracy. If you can figure it out, they screwed up."

Alice browsed through the publication and began to read aloud a featured article. "On July 8, 1979, security forces under control of the Trilateral Commission abducted the fathers of all American Nobel Prize winners. The men, many of them octogenarians, were forced at gunpoint to ejaculate into small plastic bottles. The sperm collected is now under study in a secret laboratory located beneath the skating ring at Rockefeller Center." Alice put the magazine down and understood that this was how it was going to be with Jerry. He had moments of clarity but most of the time he was a lost cause. Masturbating octogenarians? Laboratories hidden beneath one of Manhattan's most popular tourist sites? Yeah. Right.

Jerry tried to gauge her reaction. "Pretty scary, huh?"

He had no idea.

Alice hurried the conversation along to less controversial subjects, "How many subscribers do you have?"

Jerry was embarrassed by his lack of success. "Just five. It's the economy . . . You think maybe one of them is not who they seem?" How else would Conspiracy Central have learned that Jerry had uncovered one of their more dastardly plots?

Alice tried to be helpful. "You got a list?"

Jerry nodded and began shuffling through piles of seemingly chaotic papers. It took a minute but he finally remembered where he kept the list. Jerry led Alice into his bedroom and began shuffling through the contents of his night table drawer.

While she waited, Alice checked out a towering bookshelf and noticed ten different copies of *The Catcher in the Rye*. "You're a Holden Caulfield fan."

Jerry didn't seem comfortable with the suggestion. "Umm, not really."

"You obviously like the book."

Jerry clearly would have preferred to change the subject. "Not especially."

"You have ten copies of it, Jerry."

Normally, Jerry could start talking about almost anything without the risk of ever losing steam. But the issue of the book troubled him. It was a moment before he could respond. And when he did, his typi-

cally rapid-fire conversation was now halting. "I just
. . . every time I see one . . . I buy it. I don't know why,
but I need to have them with me." He began to laugh
nervously. "You must think I'm crazy."

No. Never. Such a thought had never occurred to
Alice.

Jerry began to laugh harder. It was not a happy
sound. Instead it edged into the realm of the hysteri-
cal. Alice could hear years of heart-rending pain trying to escape. Alice realized that Jerry had deeper
problems than his manic paranoia. His obsession
with the machinations of international alliances and
government agencies was only a symptom of some
far greater agony. Alice had no idea what that long
buried pain might be, however. But Jerry was no
longer just a nut, he was a man who was suffering terribly.

It was a confusing moment. Ever since her father's
murder at the hand of an unknown assassin, Alice
had steeled herself against emotion. Nevertheless,
she couldn't help but be affected by Jerry's torment.
The rawness and honesty of his feeling embarrassed
her. For the first time in a long while, Alice felt empa-
thy for another person. The whole experience was
making her nervous. To care for someone could only
lead to more pain. She had experienced enough already. Alice didn't want any more sorrow in her life.

Jerry's laughter trailed off when he noticed Alice's
unease. He did not like seeing her unhappy. There
had to be something he could do to make her feel
better.

Had they been living different lives, he might have
had the chance to say the words that would have begun a healing process they both so desperately
needed.

Instead, just as he started to speak, the empty bottle perched on the doorknob of Jerry's front door crashed to the ground.

Without hesitation, Jerry hit a switch and they were plunged into darkness. Jerry pulled Alice down to the floor and kept his eye on the bedroom door.

Alice was angry. He was up to his crazy games again. "It probably fell by itself."

Jerry shushed her and tried to figure out exactly what was going on. It didn't take long.

The bedroom window exploded as tear gas canisters were fired into the room by marksmen positioned across the street.

The front door to the apartment was bludgeoned open with a battering ram. It burst off its hinges and shattered. Chunks of wood and splinters tore through the room. Intensely powerful lights streamed into the apartment.

In the hallway, ten plain-clothed shock troops braced themselves as their mission leader tossed a concussion grenade into the front hallway. The file cabinet maze was ripped to pieces by the explosion. Deadly shards of metal whizzed through the air and embedded themselves deep into the walls.

Jerry protected Alice with his body. As blinding light shone through the broken windows, they were hidden from view by the bed.

The fog of war filled the room and Jerry expected a pause in the assault as their attackers waited to get a clearer picture of the battlefield. Jerry took advantage of the break and shouldered his nightstand several feet across the floor. A barely visible wire loop was revealed. Jerry yanked it and opened a trap door built into the floor. "Go!" Jerry pushed Alice down through the escape hatch.

Meanwhile, ten assault troops burst into the living room with military precision. Several fell to the carpet and covered their colleagues as they whirled into the room, spinning around, aiming their automatic weapons at whatever enemy might appear.

Two commandos rappelled down the side of the apartment house and smashed through the kitchen windows.

Jerry grabbed his list of subscribers to *Conspiracy Theory*, dropped down through the escape hatch, and pulled the trapdoor closed behind him.

Jerry plunged eight feet before landing on a strategically placed mattress. A stunned Alice was flat on her back trying to figure out what had just happened. Hadn't they been about to kiss?

Jerry filled her in. "Always rent a spare apartment!" He stood up and hauled down on a handle attached to a wire that dangled from above. Meeting resistance, Jerry put all his weight into the effort. Whatever he was doing it wasn't easy.

But it did work. The nightstand in Jerry's bedroom slid back into its original position—concealing the trapdoor to the lower apartment. Just in time. For as soon as the nightstand stopped moving, half a dozen assault troops crashed their way into the room, ready to kill an enemy that had mysteriously vanished.

Still, Jerry wasn't about to open a beer and relax. Dashing to a closet, he struck a waiting match. A fuse began to burn its way up toward a hole leading into the upstairs apartment.

"What are you doing?"

"Getting rid of my hub!"

Alice didn't like the sound of Jerry's idea, and then she saw something she liked even less.

The vivid white light thrown by the fuse illuminated a wall covered by an enormous mural. From floor to ceiling the wall was covered in a vividly colored collage of pictures cut from newspapers and magazines: LBJ being sworn in to office aboard Air Force One. A Buddhist monk in Viet Nam committing suicide by self-immolation. Nixon's resignation speech. A victorious Robert Kennedy on the podium of the Ambassador Hotel moments before being murdered. Stunned Civil Rights leaders pointing toward James Earl Ray immediately after the assassination of Reverend King. The ruins of Mexico City after the 1985 quake. Thousands of bodies lying on the streets of Bhopal after the deadly chemical leak.

But for all of the disaster portrayed on the wall, one image dominated the others. Alice focused on it like a laser-guided missile. If she had had any breath left after the attack upstairs and the plunge into the lower apartment she would have lost it.

It was an almost life-sized image of her. In full equestrian gear, she was riding a horse, hands outstretched in euphoria, head thrown back in rapture.

Jerry called the mural his Wonderwall.

But he had no idea that Alice was staring at it. Instead, his attention was completely devoted to the burning fuse. As it disappeared into the upstairs apartment, the light went with it and a few seconds later Jerry and Alice were immersed in darkness.

At first, the assault troops didn't notice the burning fuse entering the apartment. Once inside, it ran into a network of other fuses laced through the maze of file cabinets. Suddenly the apartment was filled by the sizzling sound and buzzing sparklers of a measureless web of incendiary wicks.

The assault team stopped dead in its tracks. They

had no idea what was going on. The lights were dazzling and baffling. It didn't take long to find out.

The fuses reached their targets and suddenly the apartment burst into flames. The troops performed an instant retreat and those pulling up the rear found their backsides scorched. Within seconds the file maze was an impenetrable wall of fire. Everything within the confines of Jerry's apartment was reduced in a flash to melted steel and embers.

The enormous *whoosh* of a blaze coming to life sucked most of the oxygen out of the lower apartment. Alice couldn't see the conflagration but it only took seconds for her to feel the rise in temperature. They had to get out. It would only be a few minutes before the rest of the building became a giant, rent-controlled barbecue.

This was a disaster. A lot of residents might be killed. What in God's name had Jerry done?

In the pitch black it was impossible to see what Jerry was working on now, but he appeared to be strapping something to his chest. Then he seemed to pull on some sort of jacket.

Despite her growing panic, or maybe because of it, Alice felt compelled to grab a match from the box stuck to the wall and light it. She wanted to see what was going on. And then her eyes went back to the mural of her euphoric moment on the horse.

It might not have been the best time to ask questions but Alice was as horrified by the Wonderwall as she was of the fire upstairs. "*What is this?*"

The match threw enough light so Alice could see what Jerry was up to. Now he was wearing a fireman's greatcoat and helmet. Busy as he was, he nevertheless humiliated that Alice had discovered his artwork. He mumbled a lame response. "Don't know what that is. It was here when I moved in."

Alice's fingertips were scorched by the match as it burned down and blinked out. Pitch black again.

Upstairs there was no shortage of light. The apartment had become an incinerator. White hot flame erupted out of vaporized windows and charred door frames. Nothing inside could survive a fire this intense. The housing to Jerry's typewriter melted. The Xerox machine smoldered. And a securely locked can sitting on a kitchen counter exploded, showering popcorn everywhere.

But the most powerful fires burned through the fire cabinets. The steel sagged into Dali-esque shapes. As intended, the paper contents within were reduced to ash.

Sirens wailed as fire trucks raced to the scene.

Minutes later half a dozen firefighters escorted squinting residents out of the building. As bad as things looked when they arrived, all they had come across so far was dense smoke. But no fire. The trapped tenants had been wise enough to open their windows for fresh air and miraculously no one seemed to be hurt.

No one noticed as a lone fireman exited a fourth-floor apartment with a woman slung over his shoulder. The fireman called out to the people ahead of him. "Make a hole. Watch your backs." A path was cleared for him and the fireman carried the woman down into a stairwell. Jerry and Alice were making a swift escape from the men who were trying to kill them.

Passing them on the way up the stairs were Jonas and his suited apes. Jonas's nose bandage had been reduced in acreage and now only consisted of a small strip that partially covered his stitches. Jonas had no clue that he had just trotted past his prey. Alice wasn't sure she recognized Jonas with the subtler bandage. "Was that who I thought it was?" Jerry assured her that it was.

But Alice was more confused than ever. "Has this happened to you before?"

"Never. But I've been practicing."

Being paranoid was one thing. Performing a challenging escape as Jerry had was something else altogether. "Who are you?"

"Just a guy trying to put out a fire."

Then they were out the door and on the street. Jerry dumped his fireman's rig in an alley. When the coast was clear, they walked away as casually as they could to Alice's car, which was parked safely, as Jerry had insisted, a mile away.

Upstairs, in the smoldering ruins of Jerry's apartment, a fire captain explained an unusual discovery to a fascinated Jonas. "See that aluminum-looking stuff?" He pointed at the silvery material that resembled particle board lining the walls, floors, and ceiling. "Guy designed it so he could turn the place into an incinerator. Leaves the rest of the building untouched."

Jonas's reaction was a combination of frustration and pride. Angry as Jonas was to have lost this round, Jerry's escape plan was worthy of his admiration.

A CIA agent rushed in from downstairs. "Dr. Jonas, there's something else you should see." Jonas followed his subordinate through smoky hallways and into the empty apartment directly beneath Jerry's.

Several other CIA men illuminated Jerry's painted mural of the ecstatic woman on horseback with flashlights. The woman was unmistakably Alice Sutton.

Jonas gave the matter a few seconds thought and then began snarling orders. "In one hour I want to know what she eats, where she sleeps, the name of her kindergarten teacher. *Everything*."

Alice and Jerry raced up the West Side Highway and arrived at her apartment within ten minutes. Alice was relieved to be home while Jerry entered the living room and looked around suspiciously. If they had tracked him down in the Village there was no reason to think they couldn't find him here. Of course, there was no reason for Jonas to be aware that Jerry and Alice were traveling together. Still, that didn't mean the good doctor hadn't figured it out somehow. Jonas was like that. Sometimes it seemed that he could read people's minds.

Jerry froze. Where did that memory come from? Was it even a real memory? Or was it something else? He hadn't even known Jonas's name until Alice had told him. But it sounded vaguely familiar. It was too confusing. Besides, he was waging a battle to save Alice's life and his own. Jerry didn't have the luxury of wasting time thinking about things that sat just beyond the reach of his memory.

Alice seemed to have gotten over the shock of the evening's earlier assault. She seemed in a remarkably good state of mind. She was happy to be home among familiar objects. "See? Home safe and sound." Jerry wasn't buying this line. "It only looks safe. You can't stay here."

"I have to. I know where everything is." Jerry wasn't listening. He was handing out orders. "Check into a hotel. Anonymously. Cash deposit. No credit cards."

"They're after you, Jerry. Not me. Before you go . . ."

Not a chance. Alice wouldn't survive the night by herself. "I'm staying with you. I'll sleep on the couch." Now it was Alice's turn to protest. "*You're going*. But first I have to ask you something."

"Right. Ask me to stay. I'll sleep in the bathtub. Maybe on the kitchen table. Clear a bookshelf if you want. I don't need a lot of room." Alice interrupted him politely. "Jerry! Shut up!"

He did as he was told.

Alice took a deep breath and laid down the law. "I don't believe anything I've heard today. At the same time, I think you're confused but I don't think you're lying. And we can make progress *if* you answer one question. To my satisfaction." Jerry promised to try.

Alice was troubled by the picture of her on horseback. Jerry blushed and stammered but he answered as honestly as he could. "I didn't mean for you to see it. It's like looking in someone's diary and taking it out of context. Know what I mean?"

She didn't. There was more to it than an invasion of his privacy. He had also invaded hers. "It made me feel like you could see inside me. And I don't know how that's possible."

Jerry needed some specifics. "So what's the question?"

The question was direct. "How is it possible?" How had Jerry known her so well that he had perfectly captured the joy she felt when riding her horse Johnny Dancer?

He couldn't say. Instead he looked around for a way out of the conversation. But he was trapped. In the apartment. With Alice. By the question. Jerry noticed a doorway leading to a sitting room. "Could I, um, could I look at something?" Without waiting for an answer he walked into the room where Alice kept her treadmill.

He had seen this room before, but from the other side of the window. How many hours had Jerry watched Alice punish herself on this exercise equipment? He stepped onto the treadmill tentatively. Whether his caution was caused by reverence for a part of Alice's life or because he naturally distrusted modern machinery, he couldn't say. Instead he stood still and stared out the window at the spot where he normally parked his cab and watched. He was looking for some kind of explanation to an unspoken question.

Alice followed him into the tiny room. "I want an answer, Jerry." He turned to tell her that he didn't have an answer when he noticed a framed photograph positioned behind the treadmill. The picture showed Alice in riding habit, standing with her horse and a distinguished-looking older man.

Jerry wasn't sure who he was, but there was something about the man in the picture that troubled him. Although he couldn't be sure, Jerry thought he recognized him. Forcing himself to focus, Jerry recalled a fragment of memory. "Hey . . . this is the judge who got murdered."

Alice's normal confidence sagged and deflated. The tone in her voice was suddenly flat. Drained. Sad beyond comprehension. "How do you know that?"

"He was in the paper."

Alice was overwhelmed by a pain that was always fresh. Always raw. "He was my father." The nightmare of his murder had consumed Alice's life. There had been more than one casualty the night Judge Sutton was shot to death at close range.

Jerry saw her wince—physically and emotionally. If he had punched her in the stomach the reaction might have been the same. Jerry could not tolerate seeing Alice in pain. he had to do something. Say something. Anything to try to make her feel better. His attempt was a sincere if hopelessly awkward gesture to share her grief. "I made a file on him."

There were some issues Alice could handle and some she could not. This conversation fell into the second category. It took everything she had not to scream at Jerry. Somehow she restrained herself and was merely sarcastic instead of devastating. "You think NASA did it? Is my father's murder going into your newsletter?"

Jerry could not meet her eyes. Instead he looked away and noticed the positioning of the framed photograph in relation to the exercise equipment. Suddenly everything became clear to him. "He's why you punish yourself." Alice didn't want to hear any more. But Jerry couldn't shut up. "You run with your back to the picture. Like you were trying to get away. Once in a while you sing along with music, but mostly you punish yourself."

"Music?" What was he talking about? How did Jerry possibly know that she listened to the radio while working out? Then it all came together for Alice. She understood. Her fury was only matched by the sick feeling in her stomach. "You watch me, don't you?"

Jerry had blown it.

Alice went to the window and glared down at the street. She imagined him staring in from the sidewalk—doing whatever it was that voyeurs did when they spied on people. Jerry pulled her back into the center of the room. "Never go to a window like that. There could be . . ."

Alice threw his hand off her shoulder and went ballistic. "Where do you stand? In the alley? Do you sit in a car? Is it every night?" He wasn't just crazy—he was dangerous. A Peeping Tom. A stalker. How had he talked his way into her apartment? What other methods did Jerry have for observing her? What else did he watch her do?

Knowing he couldn't win this particular argument, Jerry tried to steer the conversation toward a more productive direction. So he watched her. So now Alice knew. Big deal. There was a reason that he watched her and a reason why she was running away from the pain of her father's murder. He just didn't know what it was. But surely it was worth investigating. Jerry grabbed the picture of Alice with her father and pointed to the horse. "Johnny Dancer, right? You don't ride him anymore, do you? Not since your dad died."

Alice ripped the frame out of his hands as if he were contaminating the memory of her father. Her anger was subsiding, however, and now all she wanted was to be left alone with her memories. "Get out of here, Jerry. *Please*."

Her request induced a state of near panic in him. He lurched back into the living room and looked at a wall of books. "Do you have a copy of that book I can borrow? *Catcher*? I don't usually go this long without one."

Alice needed Jerry and his insanity out of her life. Instantly. Never to return. "I'll give you one hundred bucks if you leave right now. Buy all the copies you want."

He was the first person Alice had run into who didn't take the money and run. He didn't want her cash. "I got money." Jerry pulled a thick wad of bills out of his pocket. "For a rainy day, you know?" Alice wanted to scream. "Look out your window, Jerry. It's pouring."

But he didn't go anywhere. He stood in the living room with a hurt puppy dog look. Jerry tried to explain that his intentions had been honorable. That didn't cut it with Alice. She wanted him gone. She needed peace and quiet. Right now. She desperately needed a good night's rest to work things through in her mind. "Okay, I'm going to give you twenty-four more hours. Just give me the next eight hours off."

Jerry couldn't allow that. As they spoke, Jonas and his killers were on their trail. They had to leave Alice's home. They had to vanish and hope to live to fight another day. "Forget about that! Pack a few things. *Let's go.*"

Alice thought she had been more than reasonable but he wasn't going away. He was still there. Still mouthing off about Jonas. Alice gave up trying to be nice. "Go to hell. I know you're crazy, but go to hell."

Jerry's eyes filled with tears.

Alice was astonished. Here he was, ruining her life, and now she was the one feeling guilty. It didn't seem possible but Alice's angry words hurt him more deeply than all the physical abuse that had been heaped on him over the last few days.

Jonas had tried to drown him. Jonas had injected him with hallucinogenic drugs. Jonas had stabbed him with a wheelchair spoke. Jonas had sent in a squad of elite killers to murder him—but it was Alice's displeasure that sent him reeling.

It was a heavy burden to bear.

But Alice wasn't going to back down. She didn't

say another word. After a moment passed, Jerry nodded and left the room quietly. Alice never moved, never acknowledged his departure. She listened as the door to the apartment shut behind him.

Finally, Jerry had gone away.

Alice was furious, scared, guilty, and frustrated. She looked over to the treadmill and vented. "You go to hell too!"

Chapter 8

The rainstorm that pelted Manhattan lessened and a few people braved the brisk night air. Distant thunder echoed as new storms drifted in from the Atlantic, making their way across Brooklyn and toward Manhattan. The street outside Alice's apartment was flooded with ankle-deep puddles. As residents tried to dodge them, they looked fearfully at the sky, hoping the respite would last long enough for them to get wherever they were going. Even though it was a busy neighborhood and normally full of life the area had a desolate feel to it. The early-autumn storm had stripped the leaves from a few spindly trees lining the sidewalks and there could be no mistaking the message—trouble was brewing.

In purely meteorological terms, of course, this meant nothing more than the howling winds of a New York winter. But to a man sitting in a large American sedan, it suggested the approach of something more sinister.

Jerry Fletcher was not the only person secretly watching Alice Sutton.

Russ Lowry didn't completely understand the connection between Jerry and Alice, although he had some pretty good ideas. What he found most surprising was the patience that Alice had displayed for a man who was clearly unbalanced. Lowry had asked around and knew her reputation. Yet she had met with Jerry numerous times in her office. To what end? It wasn't as if Jerry were bringing her any information for an investigation. The only reason he could think of was that Alice felt sorry for Jerry and was trying to humor him. Lowry couldn't think of another Justice Department official who demonstrated the same concrete evidence of possessing a heart as Alice.

In an odd way, Lowry was pleased. There were times when the responsibilities of his job coincided with his personal interests. Even though it was a chilly, wet autumn night, Lowry was not unhappy to be keeping an eye on Alice. It wasn't the cold that made him shiver, however. It was, instead, the thought of Alice somehow being dragged into the swamps of Jerry Fletcher's problems.

Sitting behind Lowry in the backseat was Agent Nick Murphy. The two men were well acquainted with the joys of stakeouts and got through their watch in a contradictory mood that combined boredom with a state of constantly being on the alert. Tonight, however, Murphy had made a crucial error in planning. Unofficial agency rules decreed that agents not drink lots of coffee before a stakeout in bad weather. Over the last two hours, Murphy suffered the consequences of ignoring this dictum. He was wide awake, suffering, and in need of relief. But the torrential rain kept him inside the car, debating how much longer he could hold out till his bladder burst.

With the break in the weather, Murphy decided to end his agony. "I'm gonna take a piss in the alley before it starts to pour again." Lowry nodded but kept his eyes firmly on the entrance to Alice's apartment house. Murphy tucked his 9mm machine pistol into his shoulder harness and zipped his jacket shut to keep his weapon out of sight. Then he slipped out of the sedan to make his way to the promised land of the alley.

Lowry was thinking about Alice when Murphy returned to the car. In the back of his mind Lowry was surprised by the remarkable speed with which his partner had finished his business. There was nothing like agency training for the optimum performance in the field. "How's your bladder?"

The barrel of Murphy's 9mm was pressed firmly against the side of Lowry's head. A voice he didn't recognize answered in a friendly tone that didn't square with the hostility of the action. "My bladder? Not bad." The hammer clicked back as it was cocked. "How's yours?"

It wasn't the response Lowry had expected. His eyes darted to the rearview mirror and he recognized Jerry Fletcher as his assailant. Gun or no gun, Lowry was a cool customer. If he was scared he didn't betray his fear. Instead, his tone of voice was even. He was all business, for this was the sort of situation he was paid to deal with. "Lot of folks are looking for you." Jerry offered a congratulatory smile. "Then you must be the smart one."

Hidden by the car seat, Lowry began to slide his hand toward his gun, which sat only a few inches away. Jerry saw exactly what Lowry was doing and his congenial tone never wavered. "Hands on the steering wheel." For someone who was normally volatile, Jerry was acting as calmly as the professional sitting in the front seat. It was almost as if there were two Jerrys. The excitable head case and another person trained in the stealthy arts.

Surprised that Jerry had caught him, Lowry still

didn't bother to comply with Jerry's request. He left his hand where it was and hoped that Jerry's active mind would move on to something else.

No such luck. Jerry nudged Lowry's head with the 9mm. It wasn't a brutal gesture, just painful enough to let the federal agent know that Jerry wasn't kidding around. Lowry got the picture and did as he was told. In turn Jerry thanked him politely for cooperating. Considering that one man was holding a gun to the head of another man, it was a surprisingly civilized confrontation. Lowry wanted to know where Murphy was. Jerry was impressed.

"I like that. A gun to your head and you ask about your partner. He's okay. May have a headache for a few days. Are you here with honorable intentions?" Lowry didn't understand the question. Jerry tried to explain. "You should think of me as Alice Sutton's guardian angel."

So that's what he was. Lowry laughed ruefully. "That's ironic. Because we're here to protect her from you."

Jerry tried to size Lowry up. He might just be telling the truth. "You're here because you figured I might show up."

"It seemed like a possibility." Lowry was no longer certain of anything. How could it be that he was getting a good gut feeling about a known crackpot who was holding a gun to his head? Lowry asked a question he would never have posed to a bona fide criminal. "What about your intentions? Are they honorable?"

"I'm not a violent man, Mr. Lowry. Not by nature, anyhow. But if you hurt Alice in any way, I'll kill you. Does that seem honorable?"

Lowry was certain Jerry would be as good as his

word. But no one needed to get hurt. All Lowry wanted to do right now was get Jerry to lower the gun and talk. Not only was maintaining dialogue a part of standard procedure in standoffs, but there was a lot he wanted to learn about Jerry Fletcher.

Jerry had other plans, however, and slammed the gun barrel into the back of Lowry's head.

The federal agent didn't know what hit him. One minute he was trying to engage Jerry in conversation and the next it felt like an elephant was kicking him. Lowry slumped forward against the steering wheel.

Jerry hesitated to see if Lowry stirred. He didn't. Jerry began to step out of the car and then paused. "Are you pretending?" It seemed an unlikely question. Lowry had toppled forward like a dead man. Still, Jerry knew better than to trust what he saw. Placing the gun near Lowry's ear, he pulled back the hammer.

"Are you pretending?" Jerry didn't have to wait long for a response. Lowry didn't move, didn't open his eyes. He did however answer Jerry's question. Yes, He was pretending. Faking unconsciousness, or worse, was part of agency training. How did Jerry know to ask?

Jerry appreciated Lowry's candor and felt all the lousier for what he had to do. Lowry would know it was coming, so Jerry didn't delay. He whacked the federal agent a little harder than he had before and Lowry sunk deeper across the seat with a deflating groan.

This time, he wasn't faking.

Before Lowry's cheek hit the seat, Jerry had one foot outside of the car and on the pavement. Then he saw something that forced him back into the car.

Alice stepped out the front door of her building,

dressed in running gear. Jerry crouched down to stay out of her line of sight as she took off down the street. Shit. What a night to step off the treadmill and onto the sidewalk. What was she thinking?

He had to do something fast. All Jerry wanted to do was disappear into the lost recesses of the city, but he couldn't leave Alice vulnerable like this. After dragging Lowry over to the passenger side, Jerry climbed into the front seat, started the car, and rolled after her.

Alice might have left the treadmill behind but she still maintained her punishing routine. Running with the attitude of a driven athlete, she splashed off the sidewalk and into the middle of Sixty-fourth Street.

When Jerry left the apartment, Alice needed to work out. She knew, however, that she couldn't get back on the treadmill. Even though she was sure Jerry wouldn't watch her from the street anymore, she was finished with that machine. All she wanted to do was get away from Jerry Fletcher and the madness of the last twenty-four hours. Alice wasn't sure exactly how she could accomplish this, for she had seen things today that would haunt her in years to come.

As an attorney working for the Department of Justice, Alice knew all about the conspiracy theories put forward by various antigovernment organizations and self-appointed watchdogs. There were plots galore. Pick an aspect of modern American life and there was an accompanying conspiracy that was behind it. When Alice was a small child the world had been awash in Communist conspiracies. *They* were taking over the world. Nowadays, since the end of the Cold War, and absent a foreign threat, some people turned their anxieties against their own government. According to their view of the world, the federal government and its bureaucracies were determined to restrict their liberty and take over the smallest details of their lives.

Alice always had been amazed by these ideas. The federal government could barely pass a budget or ensure that thousands of American children didn't go hungry at night. How did these antigovernment activists think Washington could take control of their lives? Even if the intent was there, which Alice knew was ridiculous, there was no way the logistics could ever have worked. Alice had dismissed the theorists long ago as people with too much free time and not enough grounding in reality.

But what had she seen today? Alice ran a little harder. Who were the assault troops who had shot their way into Jerry Fletcher's apartment? There was no question the soldiers came from a government agency. Even the richest drug lords couldn't have fielded such firepower.

The muscles in her legs begged for respite. No chance.

Alice had been caught in the middle of a sophisticated military operation in an anonymous cabby's Greenwich Village apartment. How was it possible? The structures upon which she had organized her life crumbled when confronted by this new reality. While the murder of her father had nearly destroyed her life, this new discovery had the potential to ruin the world she lived in. What if "up" no longer was the opposite of "down"? What if "right" no longer meant the opposite of "wrong"? If secret government shock troops were attacking ordinary citizens, whose side was she working for? It was too horrible to contemplate.

She ran even faster. Now her lungs joined in the chorus screaming for mercy. But Alice didn't slow down. Maybe if she sprinted quickly enough she could escape the horrors of her past and leave the insanity of the present behind.

Jerry followed at an expertly discreet distance. His controlled driving reflected the patience of an intensively trained professional instead of the impulsive actions of a seething New York cab driver. Three-quarters of a block behind, Jerry had a clear view of Alice and everything around her. If someone jumped out of the shadows, Jerry was ready to hit the gas, drive up on the curb, and start shooting before Alice came to any harm.

As contained as his driving was, Jerry couldn't shut up. There were too many ideas whirling around in his brain and he had to talk. It wasn't as if he expected any feedback. Lowry was in no condition to listen and offer advice. But Jerry had to keep chattering. When you saw as many conspiracies in the world as Jerry did, you were obliged to share the information.

Besides. He was worried. He loved Alice and he thought she was being careless about her safety. He jabbered on like an anxious father on his daughter's first date. "She shouldn't be outside at night. What's she doing?" Jerry looked more closely at Lowry. Was he pretending again? "I know you're awake."

All Lowry did was moan. Jerry was pleased that he didn't have to hit the FBI agent again.

His good mood didn't last long, however. As Alice jogged across a wide avenue, she slipped through a gap in a wall and disappeared into the forested oasis of Central Park.

Jerry hit the brakes and Lowry slammed forward into the dashboard as the car skidded to a sudden halt. Jerry backed up and turned the car into a road that crossed through the park but didn't actually go into it. For a few moments he was able to keep an eye on Alice but then she ran deeper into the woods, vanishing altogether from sight.

Unable to find a way to drive into the park, Jerry had to do something and fast. He hit the brakes. A taxi swerved around him, horn blaring and driver swearing. Lowry was flung for a second time against the dashboard. Tomorrow he would feel as though he had spent ten rounds in the ring with an enraged Mike Tyson. But Jerry didn't care. He had more important things to worry about. Abandoning the car and the unconscious federal agent in the middle of the street, Jerry took off on foot to pursue Alice on the shadowy trails.

It was no easy task.

If Jerry seemed to possess a certain professional knack for tracking—knowing how to remain unnoticed, able to read the clues left by the pursued—he was having a hell of a hard time keeping up with Alice. It wasn't that he didn't know what to do. The problem was that he simply couldn't maintain her tireless pace. Before long, Jerry was gasping for air and stripping off his battered leather jacket to lighten the load.

It didn't help. The distance between them was growing. It took every ounce of Jerry's energy just to keep Alice in sight. It was a losing battle but he would not give up. She was vulnerable on her own. And while it occurred to Jerry that Alice could apparently outrun anybody foolish enough to chase her on foot, she wouldn't stand a chance against someone in a car.

Ten minutes later, she ran out of the park and turned south down Fifth Avenue. She was breathing quickly but regularly. Swift efficient breaths that fed her muscles with the oxygen they needed to perform.

Just as her trainer had taught her. Even while pushing herself to the limit, Alice was organized and in control. Her effort was intense but nothing she couldn't handle.

Jerry on the other hand reached the border of the park and collapsed against a stone wall. He couldn't get enough air. Each breath wrenched his body as though it would be his last. Jerry felt a growing sense of panic. He had to watch over Alice but he simply could not move.

Alice grew smaller and smaller as she charged toward Central Park South. Finally, Jerry recovered enough to stagger toward a parked taxi. It was his only chance before Alice disappeared into the night. Waving a hand to hail the cab, Jerry was stunned when the driver flipped down his door locks and sped away. Jerry couldn't believe it. He had been betrayed by one of his own. He shouted earnestly after the cab, "But I'm one of you!"

But the chase was over and he knew it. Jerry looked down Fifth Avenue. Alice was gone. Beaten, Jerry surveyed the area. He wanted to make sure that no one had slipped a tail on him while he was following Alice. The coast was clear. As he looked around, however, Jerry caught his own reflection in the window of a hotel bar and stopped to examine himself more closely. His blank expression suggested that he didn't necessarily recognize the face staring back at him. Then his eyes grew wide with curiosity and his brow furled. It was as though Jerry were seeing his own face for the first time in his life.

Jerry was lost and his condition was getting worse, not better. He peered into his own eyes, desperate for answers to questions that were forming in his mind. "If I'm not one of you, then who am I?"

Chapter 9

It was late by the time Jerry reached the Barnes & Noble bookstore in Manhattan's Chelsea district. His journey south of some forty-five blocks was lengthened by the indirect route he had traveled. Concerned as always that someone might be following him, Jerry traced an elaborate path that involved much doubling back, and spontaneous feints in the wrong direction.

Adding time to what should have been an hour's walk, Jerry also stopped by half a dozen bookstores on his way. Several were closed. Those that were open were temporarily out of the title he was looking for. It seemed odd and Jerry entertained a few paranoid fantasies. Maybe "they" were out to get him by preventing him from reading the book that he relied upon so heavily. But then again the book he was looking for was immensely well regarded and popular. Even someone as deeply suspicious as Jerry Fletcher couldn't believe "they"—whoever they were—would go to such lengths.

The Barnes & Noble was busy as Jerry barged through the doors on Sixth Avenue. The bookstore/coffee shop was a new social center in the neighborhood and the aisles were crowded with people who were browsing each other more carefully than the shelves.

A few heads turned as Jerry rushed nervously through the store. He didn't meet a single glance or return anyone's smile. He was looking for the classics section and was having trouble finding it. Calendars. Cookbooks. Cults. No classics. Why the hell would they hide an entire section? Jerry was getting desperate. Had Jonas's people preceded him? Would they really bother to abduct the classics section? Wouldn't anybody notice? It seemed like a scratch but then again no one was paying attention to the books anyway. Jerry stopped midthought. There they were. Classics. In the rear of the store.

Jerry read off titles aloud as he approached his goal. *Moby Dick. Pilgrim's Progress. Of Mice and Men.* His eyes moved wildly over the shelves as his panic grew. Where was it? Jerry bumped into a young woman who thought he was trying to get her attention, but he kept moving, frantically muttering the titles of great literature as he went.

Just as he was beginning to really worry and sweat was beginning to break out on his forehead, Jerry found what he was looking for. *The Catcher in the Rye.* A new edition in a cheaply bland white cover to be sure, but a quick glance inside confirmed all its pages were intact. Jerry grabbed it off the shelf and began to relax. Not only would he have his fix of Holden Caulfield tonight, but a rapidly developing web of new paranoia evaporated before it ever had a chance to become firmly established in his mind.

Jerry sauntered up to the cash register, handed the book to a clerk, and realized he was grinning a little too triumphantly. There was no way the clerk could understand what had happened to Jerry during the last twenty-four hours, so he offered only a minimal explanation. "Been a long day." The clerk nodded wearily, picked up his scanner, and ran it along the bar code on the back of the book.

Jerry never noticed before how beautiful the sound of an electronic beep could be. Tonight he did. *Catcher in the Rye* was on the shelf where it belonged, which proved that circumstances might not be as dire as he had imagined only a few minutes earlier.

Somewhere in one of the five boroughs of New York City an alarm was triggered in a windowless high-tech surveillance room. Three bleary-eyed technicians who were nearing the end of their shifts sat up with a start and began examining their computer screens. The junior man on the crew spotted something and shouted to his compatriots, "Somebody bought one!" A second technician called up a city grid map onto his monitor and watched as the alarm system honed in on its target. "Barnes & Noble. Sixth Avenue." The commander of the watch flipped on his radio microphone and began to issue orders. "CLEET code 115. Location is 11-546 Sixth. Barnes & Noble. Keep collateral damage to a minimum."

The paranoid vision that Jerry Fletcher had only just dismissed from his mind was about to prove itself to be all-too terrifyingly real.

The clerk placed *Catcher in the Rye* into a plastic bag decorated with an illustration of Stephen King and handed it over the counter. Jerry tossed the bag into the trash, opened the book and began reading as he strode out the door. He was a junkie and needed his fix. As he read the opening lines, everything that seemed wrong in the world seemed better, if only for the moment. If a man as wired as Jerry Fletcher could ever be considered calm or centered, it was during the moments when he was reading Salinger's prose. It wasn't something he could explain. It was just how it was.

Jerry appeared to be entirely absorbed in his book as he strolled down the busy sidewalk. While this might be a hazardous enterprise for most pedestrians, Jerry was, as always, alert to his surroundings. It might look like he wasn't paying attention, but at some level Jerry invariably was on the lookout. It was an odd, urban ballet and passersby were amazed as the avid reader in their midst swerved and bobbed at just the right time.

Then something triggered Jerry's internal radar and he went on high alert.

A rapidly strengthening breeze appeared from nowhere and forced the pages of the book from Jerry's fingers. Trash began to swirl around his feet. Jerry looked down Sixth Avenue and saw nothing out of the ordinary. It occurred to him that the sudden draft of wind was extraordinarily localized. Jerry looked up and saw a sight that confirmed all of his worst fears.

Sweeping down from above was a jet black helicopter. Without running lights, it was visible only as a mass darker than the rest of the night sky. Equipped with sound dampers, the chopper descended, with the muffled "whomp, whomp" of its propeller barely noticeable above the street traffic noise. Silky black cords dropped out of the helicopter and a moment later four commandos slid down to the pavement.

Traffic on Sixth Avenue came to a standstill.

But within moments the drivers who came to a sudden halt weren't sure of what they had just seen.

Most were uncertain whether or not they had seen anything at all.

For as soon as the commandos hit the ground, the dark helicopter rose silently into the air and vanished. The commandos themselves were dressed in plainclothes and almost instantly melted into the crowds.

Jerry saw them, however, and took a good look. Although dressed like civilians, the commandos wore discreet communications headsets and underneath their jackets he caught a glimpse of high-powered automatic weaponry. Taped to their wrists were small photographs of Jerry to help them make a positive identification. Jerry watched as the commandos made their way toward him, checking their wrists and looking at the faces of the people who crossed their paths. They knew he was in the area, they just didn't know where.

Jerry was not interested in making their assignment any easier. Turning tail, he headed uptown. Every nerve in his body told him to run. The prolonged state of anxiety that had been building within him for longer than he could remember seemed primed to detonate into action. His whole being yearned for escape. Jerry wanted to charge up the sidewalk, knocking over whoever stood in his way, and bolt from the threat he had dreaded for so long.

But something deep within Jerry restrained his panic and kept him under control. He didn't know where the knowledge or composure came from but it was there nevertheless. And, amazingly, it was more powerful than the hysteria that stormed through his body. Jerry knew to move discreetly along and not draw attention to himself.

Alert to new dangers, Jerry spotted the second silent helicopter as it swept down and deposited four

more commandos half a block ahead of him. Now his
path was blocked as plainclothes troopers closed in
on him from the north and south.

Jerry froze. He didn't know what to do. Where was
that voice of experience when he needed it? Something caught his eye. A commando on the other side
of the street spotted him. The man stared at Jerry and
then checked his wrist.

Suddenly he knew what he had to do. There was a
movie theater to his left which was showing a revival
of Hitchcock's *The 39 Steps*. He ducked inside and
charged past a surprised usher.

But he hadn't escaped. Not at all.

Five hundred feet above the theater a third helicopter hovered noiselessly and served as the mission
command center for the capture of Jerry Fletcher.
Jonas sat on the flight deck and orchestrated the attack while trying to predict the movements of his
quarry. At the moment he was listening to a report
from one of the commandos on the street. "Target has
entered the theater." Jonas wasn't impressed by
Jerry's strategy. It had been done before. "Oswald
tried the same tactic, if I recall."

Jerry pushed his way past the ticket takers in the
lobby and ran for the darkness of the theater. One of
the employees shouted after him and was about to
give chase when the other nudged his shoulder and
pointed to the four men already in pursuit. Both kids
decided to let the authorities deal with the gate
crasher.

On screen, British actors Robert Donat and
Madeleine Carroll bantered whimsically while handcuffed to each other, trying to elude the clutches of a
mysterious espionage ring. Even though the picture's
stars were in danger, they traveled confidently, cer-

tain that in the England of 1935, decency would prevail.

Jerry had no such guarantees today. On the contrary, if he could be certain of anything, it would be the absolute brutality of his captors if they ever got a hold of him.

The theater was nearly full as Jerry tried to lose himself in the crowd. Anxious to find a seat in the middle of the audience, and far from the aisles, Jerry took the only thing available to him—near the screen and woefully exposed. Looking over his shoulder, Jerry watched as four of the commandos appeared and began to discreetly check faces in the audience as they moved toward the front.

For a moment he tried to relax and look as though he had been in his seat since the lights dimmed and the previews rolled. He was just another film aficionado checking out the early work of a British master. Jerry considered putting an arm around the shoulders of the young woman sitting next to him. He even thought about kissing her. He dismissed the ideas quickly. In the likely event that she got upset and started shouting, he would be caught out cold and wouldn't have a chance.

The closer the commandos came, the more convinced Jerry was that he had to make a run for it. He didn't want to. All he wanted to do was to magically transform into a normal person like everyone else in the theater. A person who paid seven dollars to be entertained by stories of international intrigue instead of someone who was stuck in the middle of one. He wished he could be just another New York cabby whose worst problems were indigestion from greasy spoon chili and traffic jams. More than anything, Jerry wanted the plainclothes commandos and the bald sadist named Jonas to stop chasing him so he could spend time with Alice. He didn't want to lead her out of burning buildings anymore and he didn't want to have to tell her about insidious plots carried out by shadowy organizations. All he wanted was to take her out for a Saturday night movie and dinner. Whatever it was that regular people did when they were in love. Relationships were tough enough without professional assassins interfering every day and trying to kill you.

All this flashed through Jerry's head in an instant and then he returned his attention to the problem at hand. He was in a tough spot and none of the few options were appealing. He calculated a few odds and realized that no matter what he did the chances were he would soon be a dead man.

The commandos were getting closer. Seconds counted. When they reached the halfway point in the audience, Jerry made his move. For all the elaborate escape plans Jerry had worked up in his head since before he could remember, there wasn't anything especially clever about what he did. He stood up and walked as casually as he could toward the emergency exit. Maybe, just maybe, he'd look like a guy who didn't like the movie. As the only person standing up in a theater filled with hundreds of people he stuck out like a sore thumb. But luck was running with him. The commandos were so focused on their task of scanning the faces of people directly next to them, they never noticed Jerry get out of his seat.

Jerry was going to get out of the theater alive. It was more than he could have hoped for.

Then the emergency exit door opened and a plain-clothes commando stepped inside. There was nothing Jerry could do to avoid being seen. Like a deer caught in the headlights of an oncoming pickup truck, Jerry's life expectancy was now reduced to seconds. As he backed up a side aisle toward the lobby and away from his pursuers, the commando radioed urgently to his associates. "He's in the south theater."

Then he gave chase. Jerry began to run and he scoped out the route to the concession stand as two commandos cut off his escape path. There was only one thing left for Jerry to do. He shouted at the top of his lungs, "BOMB! There's a bomb in here!"

After the Mad Bomber in the fifties and the World Trade Center terrorism a few years back, New Yorkers knew precisely how to deal with an impending explosion. Instant panic. The crowd jumped to its feet in one collective motion and bolted for the exits.

Jerry grinned. Instant cover.

People who faced modified combat on a daily basis just to get onto the subway had no compunction about shoving their way to the emergency exits when confronted with a bomb threat. The commandos swore into their headsets as Jerry disappeared amid the pandemonium.

The window of opportunity was going to be short. In a few moments the commandos' surprise would subside and they would stake out the exits to screen every person passing through. Jerry lost himself in a surge toward the street and was swept past a commando who never even knew he was there.

Jerry hid behind the bulk of some of the larger moviegoers as they charged for the alley. Ahead of them a commando tried to get a good look at every fleeing member of the audience. He hadn't yet noticed Jerry but the moment of truth was rapidly approaching. Jerry turned his head away from the commando until he was within an arm's distance.

Then he lunged at the commando and swung the man facefirst into the side of the theater.

The commando was still on his feet, however. He drew his machine pistol from his jacket and would have opened fire if Jerry hadn't slammed him twice more into the brick wall. The commando dropped to the ground and was down for the count. Jerry looked behind to see if anyone was following and made eye contact with a terrified woman. Jerry needed her to keep her mouth shut. "I didn't like his looks. Did you?" The woman shook her head in agreement, too stunned to shout for the police. Jerry took advantage of her silence and escaped down the alley.

The theater management had called the police, however, and moments later several squad cars pulled up. Ambulances, fire trucks, and the news media were not far behind.

Jonas's eight commandos relayed this news to the command helicopter and were given orders to disperse. Pulling off their communications headsets, the secret soldiers looked as normal as anyone else in the crowd. As silently as they had arrived, the commandos dissolved into the horde of frightened moviegoers.

It was as if they had never been there. No one had seen them. No one had heard them. It was as if the commandos had only existed in Jerry Fletcher's mind.

Chapter 10

A lice Sutton slept like a dead person. Completely exhausted by the events of the previous forty-eight hours, Alice fell into a deep sleep as soon as she lay down on her bed. Normally a woman who followed a specific routine every night before turning in, Alice simply didn't have the energy left to go through "the ritual" by the time she got home.

After several hours of blissful oblivion, however, Alice's numbed mind recovered enough to begin reviewing the insanity which had entered her life. Although still sleeping, Alice began to experience memories of what she had gone through. At the same time she became dimly aware of her surroundings. Feeling a palpable sense of danger, her body put itself into a semiconscious state of alert. Maybe it was triggered by a nightmare. Maybe it was prompted by a noise she heard.

Alice fidgeted and rolled over into a new position.

At some level she was aware of a new sound in her room, like soft voices. Whispering voices. Voices talking with a certain urgency. Voices talking about Alice. Voices talking in a low, cabalistic, conspiratorial manner.

A shadow passed near a window. Alice sat up suddenly in bed and the voices stopped. But what about the shadow? Had she been awake when she had seen it or was it part of a fitful dream? She wasn't sure. The sense of uncertainty was disturbing in itself. Alice was a woman of definite opinions. She did not normally acknowledge a hazy border between reality and imagination. Alice knew what was real and what was not.

But since meeting Jerry Fletcher her confident vision of the world had begun to change. A world that Alice had thought she understood in concrete terms of black and white, suddenly offered grays. It was deeply unsettling.

Sitting up in bed, she listened intently for the sound of approaching danger, growing angry with herself when she heard nothing. She felt like an idiot for being frightened in her own bedroom. Alice couldn't remember feeling like this since she was a teenager growing up on her father's rural farm in Connecticut. How could Alice Sutton, twenty-eight years old, graduate of Stanford University and Yale Law School, attorney for the Department of Justice, be frightened like a child?

Flinging herself back onto her pillow, she closed her eyes, and immediately thought she heard something in her living room. She sat up again and cocked her head to listen more carefully. Had she heard the click of a door latch catching? A footstep in the kitchen? More than a little spooked, Alice left the lights off, crept out of bed, and made her way to the living room.

From the doorway she saw nothing but long dark shadows. Lights from a passing car reflected into the apartment. It was all deeply disconcerting. Alice loved the living room and its view of the park. After her father's murder Alice had moved a few favorite pieces of his furniture into the apartment. She found the presence of his possessions comforting. It made her feel closer to him. Her modest apartment was, for the first time, truly her home.

And yet tonight it all looked entirely different. Alice saw everything from a new perspective and it was not a pleasant feeling. The shadow thrown by her father's bookcase was no longer just a shadow but something threatening. Maybe there was a man lurking behind it.

Alice reached for a switch and turned on the lights. To her relief the room was empty.

But she wasn't done yet. The source of the sound that awakened her could still be skulking around the apartment. Alice slunk past her father's Art Deco coffee table, hugged the wall, and stuck her head into a sitting room. She flipped on the lights. Nothing. The room was empty. No lurking assassins. No government operatives. No attractive if deranged conspiracy theorists spying on her from behind the curtains.

The coast was clear in the bathroom as well. Or was it? The shower curtain seemed unusually bunched together near the drain. Had Alice been so tired that evening she hadn't bothered to draw the curtain evenly as she did every night? Or had someone taken refuge in the tub, waiting to attack her later on? Alice wanted to go to bed. She did not want to give in to her unreasonable anxiety. Alice thought of herself as stronger than her fear and knew that if she drew back the shower curtain she would always remember this moment of weakness. Still, Alice also knew that if she didn't see for herself that the shower was empty, the uncertainty would come back to haunt her when she went back to bed.

Alice pulled the plastic curtain back slowly. There was nothing there. The tub was empty.

As she walked back toward her bedroom, the only thing that surprised Alice was that she wasn't mad at herself after all. On the contrary, Alice grabbed an empty beer bottle from the kitchen and returned to the living room and balanced it upside down on the front doorknob. She stared at the bottle for a second and shook her head. Alice wasn't sure if she wanted to run away and hide or just start laughing. It was the strangest sensation. Alice realized she was adopting the habits of someone she considered to be mildly insane. "I'm turning into Jerry."

The next morning a tired Alice trudged up the steps to her office at the Department of Justice. The world looked better to her in the bright light of day and the fearful thoughts of the night had receded in her mind. As she went to work the only concern prominent in her mind was a strong desire for a couple of grandes from Starbucks. Without a massive infusion of caffeine, the day promised to be a long bleary affair.

It wasn't that Alice had forgotten Jerry Fletcher and Jonas. She planned to speak with her boss immediately and initiate an investigation. It was just that she no longer felt directly threatened by whatever it was that had frightened her last night. As she returned to her office, her confidence reasserted itself. Alice began to feel in control again and no longer saw herself as a target.

Alice was wrong.

The morning sunrise might scare off demons that frighten children but the same could not be said for the secret agencies that were monitoring her activities. As she entered the Justice Department Building, two surveillance agents sat in a black Chevy Suburban and followed her progress. Hidden behind mirrored glass, the two operatives assumed they were well camouflaged and unnoticed.

They were wrong.

Someone was watching the watchers.

Jerry Fletcher stood in the window of an empty coffee shop and peered at the surveillance truck through a small pair of binoculars. After a night spent watching Alice's apartment, Jerry knew that the Justice Department Building would be staked out in the morning. He was aware that if Jonas's people couldn't find him, they would follow Alice and hope she would lead them his way.

Jerry had an altogether different agenda.

Normally Wilson would have invited Alice to sit down. Not today. He didn't know exactly what kind of mess she had involved herself in and he really didn't want to know the details. All he was sure of was that he had been given orders in no uncertain terms and that he was going to make damn sure that Alice did as she was told.

While Alice and Wilson might not have been the best of friends, they had a respectful working relationship. On her way to work, Alice drew up a rough plan for an investigation into Jerry Fletcher's allegations. It sounded too absurd to be true. Who would believe that NASA was trying to kill the President? And yet she had seen the assault on his apartment with her own eyes. Almost certainly Jerry was reaching the wrong conclusions regarding NASA. But just because his analysis of the situation was incorrect didn't mean he hadn't stumbled across something important. She didn't know what beehive Jerry had stuck his nose into but she meant to find out.

Wilson wasn't in a listening mood. "I've been given a cease and desist on all matters relating to Jerry Fletcher. We're not to discuss him with the press, the NYPD, anyone. Building police are to arrest him on sight and we're to report any attempt he makes to contact you."

Alice was dumbfounded. "This doesn't make sense." Wilson was only a few years away from retirement. It made perfect sense to him. He was sure he could help Alice see the logic. "It makes perfect sense. Fieldwork is not our specialty."

"I don't like it. Something's wrong."

"Dr. Jonas thought you might be inclined not to cooperate. Why is that?"

It was all very confusing to Alice. How could Wilson challenge her like this? Wilson counted on her and trusted her. She was the best person on his staff and she knew he knew it. Now suddenly Jonas was questioning her loyalty and effectiveness. Alice had her own questions about the mysterious psychiatrist. "We don't know who Jonas is. We don't know who we're cooperating with."

Wilson knew. While not a man to be easily cowed, Wilson was aware that there were times to duck and get out of the line of fire. "I've had a lot of credentials flashed in my face, Alice. What I saw yesterday, I know not to ask questions. We're out. Shut off. Terminated. *Understood?*"

What could Alice say to that? She said what Wilson expected to hear. "I understand."

But she didn't. Not for a second. And Alice Sutton was not the type of person to walk away just because she had been threatened. Alice hadn't yet begun to ask questions.

But for the moment all she could do was pretend to agree and she walked out of Wilson's office without another word.

Alice strode down the corridor lost in thought. Her job was difficult enough. Encountering resistance from her superiors didn't help. There was a lot to do, but for the first time in her life she wasn't sure how to begin.

In the hallway outside her office, a group of men lay in wait for her. Alice grimaced when she saw them and immediately recognized their misguided intentions. She would deal with them.

Three first-year Justice Department attorneys straightened their neckties and flashed their best grins. They knew the stories about Alice—all she did was work, hadn't taken a vacation in years, didn't laugh at jokes, hadn't dated since her father's death, but none of them thought Alice could resist their own particular brand of Justice Department charm.

They were wrong.

The most confident of the crew stepped toward Alice as she surged down the hallway. "Alice, settle a bet for us."

Alice was not charmed and snapped back, "What do I look like to you? Switzerland?" Without breaking pace she stormed by her suitors as they pressed their backs against the wall to give her enough room to pass. The young attorneys watched her wistfully and consoled each other on their collective defeat.

Breezing past her secretary Jill, Alice didn't bother with "hello" or "how are you?" She did, however, offer a quick if guarded smile. "Any messages?"

Nope. No messages.

Alice was surprised but continued on into her office. After straightening out her already organized desk, Alice checked in again with Jill. "You're sure? No messages?"

"Not a thing."

Alice sighed, opened her briefcase, and pulled out a copy of Jerry's *Conspiracy Theory* newsletter. As always, Alice was startled by the audacity of the current cover story regarding NASA. She put the paper down and pulled out a copy of Jerry's subscriber list. With only five names to its credit, it wouldn't take long for Alice to verify a few things.

She hit the power switch on her computer and got down to work. What Wilson didn't know wouldn't hurt him.

Sometime later, Jerry Fletcher continued his surveillance of the stakeout team watching Alice. Crowds filled the sidewalks as the massive office buildings released their employees for lunch.

When Jerry estimated the crowd was at its peak, he put a baseball cap on his head and stepped into the throng. He walked directly toward the black Suburban and enjoyed a quiet laugh. "They can't see the tree for the forest."

As Jerry moved toward Jonas's team; he carried a homemade rigging of uncertain purpose in his left hand. It was made up of a coil of high-strength wire cable with a short piece of steel rebar attached to either end. Jerry held the equipment as inconspicuously as possible and was pleased by the thought that anyone who noticed it would assume it was some sort of heavy duty fishing gear. It wouldn't be an entirely incorrect guess. For as Jerry saw it, he was about to go fishing for sharks.

Passing the van, Jerry looked in the front windows and saw there was no one sitting there. Jonas's agents were hiding out of sight in the storage section. When he reached the rear of the van, Jerry bent down as though to tie his shoes.

The hunters were farsighted and it would cost them.

Inside the van, two surveillance agents were entirely unaware that their prey stood only several inches away from their feet. Instead they focused their attention on a reel-to-reel tape recorder as it switched itself on in response to the placement of a telephone call.

Somewhere far away a phone rang and a Midwestern woman's voice could be heard answering. The surveillance agents listened carefully when Alice began to speak. It had been made very clear to them that anything Alice Sutton said was highly confidential and relevant to national security. Jonas was also explicit in warning them that if they screwed up this assignment their next mission would be undesirable, to say the least. Something about monitoring farting camels in Iraq. The two sound experts listened to Alice and made entries into their log. "I'd like to speak to Mr. Ketcham."

There was a pause followed by a wary response. "This is Mrs. Ketcham."

Alice sat in her office, stared at her copy of *Conspiracy Theory*, and pretended to be a sales representative. "Hi, Mrs. Ketcham. Your husband subscribes to our newsletter. I'd like to ask him if he'd like to renew his subscription."

Alice waited impatiently as Mrs. Ketcham seemed unable to reply. Silence echoed through the phone line. What was wrong with her? It wasn't that difficult a question. Subscribe, don't subscribe, or put Mr. Ketcham on the line. Those were the choices. Pick one but do so quickly because Alice was busy enough without waiting for some flat-accented Hoosier to make up her mind.

But Alice was wrong. Mrs. Ketcham's hesitation was well founded. In fact when she spoke, her answer would change the course of Alice Sutton's investigation. And maybe even the direction of the rest of her life.

"My husband's dead. He was killed last night in a car accident."

The surveillance agents monitoring Alice's conversation listened intently. All the while they were entirely unaware that the man they were looking for was kneeling behind their observation post.

After making sure that no one was paying attention to him, Jerry looped his steel cable around the rear axle of the van and secured it with one of the rebars. Then Jerry stood up and walked toward a nearby hot dog cart, nonchalantly paying out the steel cable as he went. After ordering a deluxe dog with the works, Jerry knelt down again to fix his other shoe even though it was perfectly tied. While the *chef du cuisine* topped a frankfurt with onions, mustard, and relish, Jerry eyed the hot dog cart's axle and got to work.

Alice looked at the list of subscribers to *Conspiracy Theory*. Four names, including that of the late Bernie Ketcham, had lines drawn through them. It looked as though Jerry's startup publication needed some help in the circulation department. There was only one name left for Alice to track down: a Henry Finch in Milwaukee.

Before she could dial Wisconsin, however, Jill was at the door holding a small bouquet of seven sun-flowers. "They just came for you."

Alice was puzzled. Who would send her flowers?

Jill and the rest of the Justice Department staff were equally surprised and fascinated. Alice's secret love life became the instant subject of speculation.

Alice opened the card and the mystery was only partially resolved. "Go out front. Take the westbound bus."

Obviously her "admirer" was Jerry. But what was going on? Justice Department phone lines were se-cure. Or maybe Jerry didn't think that was the case anymore. And what was with the sunflowers? Did they have special significance? Were they symbolic of light, or of plants that grew toward the sun? Alice wanted answers. Either way, she was determined to do exactly as Jerry asked.

Alice stood up, grabbed her cell phone, and left in-structions with Jill. "I'm expecting a call from the post office in Milwaukee. Transfer it to me when it comes."

The surveillance operatives swung into action as Alice left the Justice Department building and walked to the local bus stop. One man made his way into the front of the Suburban and climbed into the driver's seat. The other flipped a switch on his communica-tions system and reported back to headquarters, "Subject is on the move."

When Alice boarded her bus the Suburban started its engine and prepared to follow. Whatever Alice was doing, it was not what they had expected.

Several feet, and one length of steel cable behind them, a hot dog vendor prepared his specialty for a pair of tourists. He always got a kick from out-of-towners and assembled his creation with an extra dose of boisterous New York flair. Two dogs lay on a small counter as the vendor energetically poured condiments on top. His customers were suitably impressed.

And then the tourists were completely puzzled when the hot dog cart shot away down the avenue like a bat out of hell, leaving the vendor with only a stupid look on his face and squirting mustard onto the pavement. Was this part of the show?

The vendor, who like most New Yorkers thought he had seen everything, was floored. What the hell had happened? Hot dog carts didn't have engines. How could a cart, most especially his cart, take off on its own like an Indy 500 racing machine?

Dumbfounded pedestrians, the vendor, and the tourists watched as the hot dog cart sped down the avenue, bouncing along behind a black Suburban, fishtailing as it went, and slamming into a number of parked cars.

It took a while for the driver of the surveillance vehicle to notice the crashing noises coming from behind him. It sounded as though a creature were reaching down from the heavens and smashing cars with a celestial hammer. Curious, the driver looked into his side mirror and realized that somehow he was dragging a hot dog cart behind the car. So much for keeping a low profile. The driver slammed on his brakes and the Suburban came to a screeching halt. But the cart's momentum wasn't slowed in the least and it sped forward until it smashed into the rear of the car.

The second surveillance agent flung open the rear door and tried to disengage the cart from the Suburban, but found a steel cable hopelessly wrapped around his axle. The driver hit his horn with frustration. "We're losing her!" There was no choice. The second agent gave up and jumped back into the vehicle. It was one thing to drag a hot dog cart around Manhattan—it was entirely a more serious matter to lose sight of Alice Sutton and engage the wrath of their commander, Dr. Jonas.

The driver put the pedal to the metal and the Suburban took off after Alice Sutton's bus at full speed. The bouncing wiener wagon followed in hot pursuit, leaving a trail of sausages and condiments in its wake. When a light in an approaching intersection turned red, the driver had no choice but to keep going. The cross traffic, including a squad car of New York's finest, hit their brakes and squealed to a halt.

But the police car had trouble stopping in time and skid a few extra feet, driving over the steel cable that connected the surveillance car to the cart. It hooked the high-speed hot dog cart like a Navy jet making a carrier landing and yanked it to a grinding stop.

Simultaneously, the driver of the Suburban hit the gas and his vehicle shuddered horribly. But the surveillance car didn't respond. Nothing happened. They didn't accelerate forward. Instead, the back of the vehicle hit the pavement and sparks exploded upon contact.

The driver couldn't maneuver without his rear wheels and he barely managed to keep the vehicle on the road. When the Suburban finally came to a halt, he got out from behind the steering wheel and saw the root of the problem. His rear axle had been ripped out of the chassis when the hot dog cart was snared by the police car. It sat forlornly on the avenue and reminded the driver of a skeleton from a freshly filleted fish.

The chase was over. While the two surveillance operatives weren't concerned about dealing with the police, well aware that the agency would clean up the mess, they dreaded their next meeting with Jonas. Both men began to worry seriously about the flatulent Iraqi camels that were so prominent in agency lore.

Chapter 11

Two blocks to the west of the wrecked surveillance van, Alice's bus pulled over to take on new passengers. Jerry stepped aboard and walked to the rear to join her. Alice was worried when she saw him. There was something odd about the way he approached. Odder than usual, anyway. Jerry wasn't making eye contact. He seemed to be peering through the rear window of the bus at some unknown object. But when he joined her, Jerry was in a cordial state of mind. "Did you see that?"

Alice hadn't. She had no idea what he was talking about.

Jerry wanted to laugh but was also half serious. "Typical. No one ever sees what I see." Still, his plan had worked perfectly. As the bus turned uptown, Alice and Jerry left Jonas's agents far behind. For the moment they were free and clear.

Alice didn't give him a chance to start talking. She had questions that needed answering immediately. "Jerry, where did you get your five subscribers?"

"I put an ad on a computer bulletin board. I logged on at the library so I couldn't be traced."

It was easy to read the expression on Alice's face. She was alarmed. Alice held up the *Conspiracy Theory* subscription list, "They're dead. Four out of five anyhow. All in the last twenty-four hours. One car accident, two heart attacks, and a stroke. The only one I haven't reached is Henry Finch."

For someone who was used to seeing plots everywhere, even Jerry was stunned. This news was big. Too big to fully comprehend. It took a few moments before he was able to reply. All of his subscribers dead within twenty-four hours? The lethal reach of the conspirators was even wider than he previously had realized. "Henry Finch. Henry Finch." Why had Henry Finch survived? How much longer could he last? For all of his thoroughness in distributing the newsletter from different mailboxes around the city, Jerry had still screwed up. He hadn't recognized the skill of his opponents and his subscribers' deaths were all his fault. "I should have realized. They monitor everything. It was only a matter of time."

The time for vague speculation was over. Alice needed specifics. Hard facts. "Elaborate on 'they,' okay?"

Had their circumstances been less dire, Jerry might have enjoyed a moment of triumph. Alice was no longer scoffing or treating him like a lunatic. She was getting down to business and was ready to listen. "There are all kinds of groups, all kinds of initials. But they're all part of two opposing factions."

To illustrate the predicament Jerry held up a single fist, "One: families that have held wealth for centuries. They want one thing. Stability." Jerry held up a second fist. "Group two: Eisenhower's military industrial complex. They want instability."

"And you think group one is at war with group two."

Exactly. To make the point clearer, Jerry smashed his two fists together and nodded sagely. "Latest casualty? One of the richest men in America. Ernest Harriman. Murdered."

Wait a minute. That didn't sound right. Alice was confused all over again. "Harriman? Murdered?" That wasn't the story she had read. Not at all. The old uneasy feeling about Jerry's fragile hold on sanity crept back into Alice's mind.

But Jerry didn't notice her dubious expression. He was as certain of the facts. "Murdered. Right here in Manhattan."

"It said in the paper he drowned in a swimming pool. Accidentally. In Newport." For the better part of a century, Newport, Rhode Island had been the playground for the nation's weathiest families. But Jerry didn't budge from his position. "Nobody dies in Newport. They couldn't even kill Sunny Von Bulow there. Harriman drowned, but it wasn't in Newport."

There was no time left to humor him. Alice needed concrete answers and she needed them now. "Where then?"

The block-long subway station below Times Square was a world away from the rarified atmosphere of Newport's Gold Coast. Despite the new mayor's efforts to clean up the city and improve the quality of life, the subway still offered a glimpse of the underworld to everyday straphangers. While taking the train was generally a safe and remarkably fast way to get around town, Alice winced as Jerry led her down the worn steps toward the station platform. The fetid smell was overpowering. Alice rode the Number One train almost daily and she couldn't remember the last time a subway was as offensive as it was today. Looking past the hustling crowds, Alice noticed a filmy layer of scum on the white tiles that lined the station.

She hadn't seen a station in this poor a condition since the late eighties. There was something peculiar about the whole situation and Alice wanted to know why Jerry had dragged her here in the first place.

He answered Alice by repeating her last question from the bus and offering an explanation. "Where was Harriman killed? Right here. In the Seventh Avenue subway station."

His response was preposterous and Alice began to doubt her own sanity. Why was she listening to him? Why was she letting him drag her around the city on this wild-goose chase?

"A billionaire waiting for the subway? Why not drown him in his limo instead. I mean, come on."

But Jerry wasn't laughing. He was calm. "Do you watch the news? Read the paper? A few days ago this whole place was underwater." Alice had read about it. It had little enough to do with sinister conspiracies. "A water main broke." Jerry began to get a little worked up. It was so obvious. How could she not see the truth? "Do you know what building is right over this spot? Harriman Tower. Their subbasement was flooded! He didn't die in a pool! Call the coroner in Rhode Island! Ask if the water in his lungs was chlorinated!"

"Okay, I will."

Jerry had expected more of a fight from her. Alice had taken the wind right out of his sail. "You will?" No official had ever offered to help him before.

"If that's what you want. Yes." Alice wasn't sure why she agreed. It was almost as if Jerry's story was so ludicrous that he couldn't possibly have made it up. But there was something else at work here and she found it even more bothersome. She wanted to help him. Not because she feared a terrible conspiracy and not because she pitied him. For some reason, Alice wanted to help vanquish the demons that haunted Jerry Fletcher.

Jerry was moved by Alice's offer of help. After meeting with resistance from everyone he had approached for so long, Jerry was at a loss for words. "I don't know what to say."

Then something that had been building within Jerry for a long time demanded attention. Never a person with much impulse control, Jerry blurted out, "I love you."

They were both surprised. Alice could only choke out a disbelieving, "What?"

It had been a long time since Jerry had expressed an intimate feeling to a woman. And now that he had, Jerry worried that his confession would scare Alice away.

Alice's shock was altogether different. She was only now, after six months of knowing him, grudgingly willing to admit that Jerry wasn't a complete madman. Now this. It was a less welcome development than the wild plot about Ernest Harriman's murder in a flooded subway station.

Jerry knew he had to keep talking. Whatever he said it would either distract Alice from his confession or maybe, if he was lucky, Jerry could find the right words to keep her from being frightened off. "I . . . It's like, I resolve to call you up a thousand times a day. To ask you if you'll marry me in some old-fashioned way." Jerry shrugged as though his extraordinary feeling for her were a natural reaction to someone as remarkable as she was. "Everything you do is magic."

Alice almost believed him. That was the problem with crazy people. Jerry was as sincere as a person could be, but that didn't mean he knew what he was talking about. Alice wasn't buying his explanation. "Those are song lyrics, Jerry."

"I know that. I'm just—I'm nervous." Here was a guy who had survived a deadly assault by a team of elite commandos and she was making him nervous. Alice wondered what it all meant. Jerry kept on going. "I reached out and grabbed the first thing out there. I know they're song lyrics. And I know how I feel."

It was an impossible situation. Ridiculous even. Alice decided to stop him before he got hurt any further. "Don't do this to yourself, Jerry. You're confused."

The moment he had dreamt about for so long was slipping away and Jerry knew it. He had to make Alice understand. "Yesterday you were wondering about the wall. How it was possible."

"Now's not really the time to get into this, Jerry."

He took his last shot. He didn't know how else to express what he was feeling. "It's Geronimo. Love. It lets you see things. It gives you insight. I've loved you since the first time I saw you."

Alice knew all too well that he saw things. He also had "insight" into matters that others couldn't see. But the thing he was talking about wasn't love. It was insanity. Alice tried to bring him back to reality as gently as she could. "You don't love me, Jerry."

As gentle as Alice tried to be, she still managed to devastate him. Given the choice, Jerry would have preferred another torture session in Jonas's water tank to having his love denied. It was one thing to be drowning and unable to breathe. It was worse to feel your heart being ripped into pieces. The pain from Jonas's torture made Jerry want to fight for life. Conversely, the misery created by Alice's dismissal of his affection made Jerry want to die. There wasn't much

Jerry could say. "I thought you . . . why . . . love ruins everything, doesn't it?"

He turned and began to push his way through the crowd.

"Jerry? Come back." Alice couldn't let him leave like that. Just because he was mistaken about his feelings didn't mean they couldn't work together. She felt as though she had pulled the crutches away from a guy with a broken leg. Alice started after him but the station platform was too crowded and he was quickly lost in the swarm of commuters.

A train pulled in and the straphangers boarded. Alice spotted Jerry just as the doors closed and the car lurched into motion. She followed the moving train as best she could and rapped on the window to get Jerry's attention. He must have heard her or at least noticed that the other passengers were wondering what she was up to. But Jerry would not look in Alice's direction. Instead, he stared at the floor, looking impossibly sad and lost.

As the train picked up speed, Alice had to stop. She watched Jerry disappear and knew that she had made a mistake even though she had done nothing wrong.

All he wanted to do was look at her. In those wonderful moments when Jerry was near Alice he knew that life was worth living. Despite the sorry state of his existence. Despite the plotting of organizations that sought to silence him. He could deal with all of it if only he could share his life with her. But Alice didn't love him and he was overwhelmed by a grief he had never experienced before.

She was there, on the other side of the subway glass, running after him, but Jerry couldn't raise his head. It was better never to see her again, for at that moment Jerry knew that to do so would kill him.

But when the rapping on the window stopped, Jerry felt a profound sense of loss. How could he go on knowing that Alice was never very far away, knowing that she was living her life but didn't want any part of him? Jerry realized that he was willing to die right then and there if he could only see Alice's face one more time.

Just as the train left the station and entered the tunnel, Jerry went to the window and searched the platform for a last glance of Alice.

He saw her staring in his direction, watching sadly as the subway car sped away. Alice was as beautiful and graceful as ever, but suddenly more vulnerable. In an instant Jerry knew he had made a terrible mistake. How could he abandon her? He dragged her into this mess with Jonas and the NASA conspiracy and now she would need his help. His pain didn't matter. All that counted was for Alice to be safe. Jerry knew what he had to do.

But he wasn't going to get the chance to do it.

The train entered the tunnel and suddenly everything around the subway car was pitch black. Absolute darkness except for a thin row of white lights that flashed past Jerry like a strobe. He was instantly mesmerized. Even though he knew he should look away, Jerry couldn't do it. In a last-ditch effort, Jerry blinked his eyes shut. For an instant he was safe and Jerry thought he would escape from whatever dangers the strobe posed. Then he began to hear the sound of conspiratorial voices whispering all around him. Whatever effect the strobing lights had on Jerry, they already had done their damage.

He opened his eyes and looked around the subway

car wildly. The voices were still there but he couldn't see anyone talking. Where were the voices coming from?

Jerry was desperate to see something normal. A kind face or maybe a transit cop. Someone or something that would help him keep a grasp on reality. An old lady turned and met his gaze. Thank God. She looked like somebody's grandmother. But the gentle smile she gave Jerry quickly transformed into something less benevolent. The old lady was leering at him. Jerry looked away and was stunned to meet the glare of other passengers—ordinary straphangers except for the peculiar and threatening way in which way they were glowering at him.

And then Jerry wasn't on the subway car anymore. He was somewhere even worse.

A man stood in front of Jerry with his back toward him. Jerry recognized him from the photograph in Alice's apartment. It was Alice's father—Judge Sutton. Jerry's perspective moved closer to the judge as though he were approaching surreptitiously. The whispering voices grew louder in his mind and he saw his own hand raise a pistol toward the back of Judge Sutton's head. Suddenly the voices began to scream and Judge Sutton turned to meet his assassin.

The taillights of the train disappeared into the darkness. Alice stood at the edge of the platform and swore to herself. This was not how she wanted things to turn out. Now Jerry was gone and she had no idea how she could ever find him again.

Her cell phone began to chime and Alice was only too happy to answer it. It was her secretary, calling as instructed. "Alice. We got a call from the post office in

Milwaukee. The mail for Henry Finch is being forwarded. Right here to Manhattan."

"Where to?"

"The International Fund for Mergers and Acquisitions."

Alice felt a chill run down her spine when Jill told her the location of the IFMA's headquarters. Maybe Jerry Fletcher's worst nightmares were about to come true after all.

Alice caught the next train for downtown. On the way she tried to analyze various explanations for the latest news and concluded that coincidence was almost certainly out of the question. Half an hour later Alice entered the lobby of the lower Manhattan Federal Building and examined the directory of tenants just as Jerry had done only a few days earlier. The Central Intelligence Agency occupied the eighteenth through the twenty-second floors. The International Fund for Mergers and Acquisitions was located on the twenty-fourth floor. Jerry had told her that he had been abducted, drugged, and tortured immediately after visiting the lobby. He had claimed it had something to do with the CIA. Alice wasn't so sure and her pulse began to race. Whoever the IFMA was, Alice didn't think they'd be happy to see her.

The elevator stopped on the twenty-fourth floor and she walked through the smoked glass doors of the International Fund for Mergers and Acquisitions. If it was the nest of vipers that Alice had anticipated, the IFMA certainly did a thorough job of disguising itself as a bland organization. A group of conservatively dressed bureaucrats passed by. Alice listened to their discussion, hoping to hear something relevant to Jerry's conspiracy theory and the four dead subscribers. Nothing doing. All Alice could pick up were snippets of dull economic forecasts. Interest rates and trade deficits. She could have stayed home and heard the same information on National Public Radio.

Alice was more curious than ever to connect the dots. What did a man who was supposed to live in Wisconsin, Jerry Fletcher, and a NASA plot to kill the President have to do with each other? She stepped up to the receptionist. "I'm here to see Henry Finch."

The receptionist put down her magazine and looked at Alice blankly. "Who?"

"*Henry Finch.*" Her heart raced. It would be a disaster to run into a dead end now. She needed answers immediately and didn't have time to do more research.

The receptionist looked at Alice more carefully, sizing her up. "Is he expecting you?"

Alice restrained a smile. Henry Finch existed and he wasn't very far away. Whoever he was, he could be the first solid lead in a chain of clues that had emerged from Jerry's hazy mind. Alice enjoyed a quick rush of victory and then was slightly intimidated. Suddenly, Alice wasn't so sure she wanted to go on. To confront Henry Finch and take a further step into the labyrinth could mean that Alice's life might change forever. At the very least her job could be jeopardized if Wilson learned she was pursuing a private investigation on behalf of Jerry Fletcher. The worst-case scenario might be something altogether more dangerous.

Giving up, however, was never really an option. She was her father's daughter and Alice knew all too well that he never shied away from the truth because of personal risk. His courage had cost him his life and Alice would never betray that legacy. Flashing her official credentials to the wary receptionist, Alice offered her steeliest drop-dead attitude. "I'm Ms. Sutton with the Justice Department. Could you tell Mr. Finch I need to see him at once."

That seemed to do the trick. Minutes later, Alice was being led by a secretary through a cubicle maze. Dozens of administrative assistants went about their business as if they worked for an ordinary financial institution. Maybe they did. Alice would know soon enough.

She was shown into an impressive office with a view of the Empire State Building. A door leading into a private bathroom was ajar and Alice could hear the sound of someone washing his hands. The secretary smiled politely. "He'll be right with you" As she waited, Alice grew apprehensive again. Was she really doing this? What on earth made her think that the entry into a vast international conspiracy lay in the office of an anonymous economic functionary? What was she going to say to Henry Finch? How furious would he be to have been ambushed by a Justice Department attorney? Who were his friends? Who would he complain to?

Whoever Henry Finch was, he now had clean hands, for Alice could hear the water faucet being turned off. She would know soon enough what this was all about.

A moment later Jonas stepped out of the bathroom.

Both he and Alice were truly startled. Neither expected the other. But both being consummate professionals, they recovered quickly and got down to business. Jonas returned to his normal attitude of slightly threatening bemusement. "I am impressed. How's Jerry this morning."

Alice was trying to figure out why Jonas kept popping up everywhere she turned. It was clear that his sphere of influence as a CIA psychiatrist was much wider than that of an everyday therapist. What was his interest in Jerry Fletcher? More to the point, what was his interest in her? Alice wasn't in the mood for Jonas's menacing charm. "He's fine. Now who are you and what the hell is going on here?"

"Those are bigger questions than you think. Please sit down."

Alice had no intention of doing what he suggested. If Jonas had asked her to remain standing she would have taken a seat. He in turn watched her closely, his thoughts impossible to discern. Jonas offered an explanation in an amiable tone which made Alice's skin crawl. "For reasons which will soon be regrettably clear, I'm going to tell you a secret. And with it you'll know who I am. Years ago I worked for the CIA in the M.K. ULTRA program. Are you familiar with it?"

Alice knew all about ULTRA. Or at least as much as the public was allowed to know.

In the fifties, at the height of the Cold War, the American military brass had begun a program to create the ultimate warrior. Aware that the Soviets had great success in the field of mind control, the Pentagon feared the prospect of divisions of Communist zombies crossing the borders into Western Europe. ULTRA was the American response. If the Soviets could turn a soldier into a mindless killing machine, so could we.

It soon became clear, however, that the ethical price that had to be paid to control a man's mind was too high for even the Communists to pay. The methods were brutal, obscene, and not at all suitable for large-scale programs. The American military had quickly discontinued its research.

Mind control soon became the province of the Intelligence community. Seeing that creating divisions of human killing machines were an unrealistic proposition, the CIA began a program to create the ultimate assassin. An individual man, trained properly, could do enormous damage to the enemy.

And in fact there was historical precedent for their experimentation. The word "assassin" itself derived from an Arabic phrase "hashishyun." Centuries earlier, men were drugged with hashish before being sent to murder an enemy. It was an impressive technique. In their anesthetized state the killers had no fear for their own well-being and carried out their missions with devastating effectiveness.

The CIA program merely applied the latest technological and pharmaceutical developments to an ancient tradition.

Yes. Alice knew something about ULTRA. "It was mind control. Manchurian Candidate kind of stuff, right?"

The Manchurian Candidate was a 1962 movie with Frank Sinatra about an ULTRA-like intelligence program.

The normally unflappable Jonas seemed offended by the suggestion. "A vulgar generalization, but yes. Take an ordinary man and turn him into an assassin. That was our goal. M.K. ULTRA was terminated in 1973. But not the research." Jonas paused and then dropped his bombshell. "I continued the research. Shall I go on?"

Alice was stunned but maintained a steady composure. "The truth will set you free."

There weren't many people Jonas could brag about the good old days to. He was fairly confident that when Alice learned more about Jerry's past, she would switch her allegiance. "It involved hallucinogenic research, the use of electroshock to produce vegetative states, terminal experiments in sensory deprivation."

"Terminal?" Alice's composed bearing took a hit. She couldn't have heard him correctly. Surely he didn't mean terminal.

But he did. That was exactly what Jonas meant. "As in 'resulting in death.' Yes."

This was astonishing information. Alice flinched visibly. At first she could not bring herself to accept what he said. It didn't seem possible that the U.S. Government would be involved in such a program. Jonas went on as her mind reeled. "You understand I was a minor missionary, a heretic really. Besides, now I'm trying to pay my penance."

Now Alice understood. "These things you're talking about. You did them to Jerry?" Jonas didn't deny it. The pieces of the puzzle were coming together in Alice's mind. Jerry wasn't just a crank or someone in need of a good psychiatrist. Jerry was the victim of an appalling government policy. His mind had literally been destroyed by the man sitting across from her. Her heart went out to him. Alice only hoped that she could find Jerry in time to save him from further damage.

Jonas was untroubled by his confession. He wanted Alice to understand precisely what had happened. "M.K. ULTRA was science. Unfortunately it all ended the moment John Hinckley shot Ronald Reagan." Jonas was enjoying himself now and was thrilled by Alice's obvious shock. Jonas had always taken pleasure from tearing down another person's psychological "armor" and sense of self—whether it was through torture or by simply telling the truth. This conversation was no different. She was responding beautifully. In fact, Jonas was having a very good time. He did, however, want to clear up any confusion about the attempt on President Reagan's life. "It wasn't us. The science had been stolen. Pandora's Box opened. My subjects were taken from me and used by the private sector. Jerry was one of them."

Jonas had confessed. Incredulous, Alice could only repeat the latest information. "He was one of your subjects."

"It is imperative I learn who stole the technology. I will do what is necessary to stimulate Jerry into telling me what he knows."

"Stimulate? Technology?" Alice was as horrified by Jonas's impersonal language as she was about what she had just learned. He wasn't even referring to Jerry as a human being.

"Alice. Jerry is dangerous. Jerry has killed."

She didn't want to hear any more. All she could do was try to hold herself together. It wasn't easy. She walked away from Jonas and stood by the window. She had to look outside and see the city. Something normal. Something to remind her that the world that she knew still existed. But how could it? Everything was different now. With the revelation of the truth, Jerry's nightmarish version of reality replaced her own. The skyline she loved might still be there, but the world as she knew it was forever altered.

Alice hated Jonas. For everything he had told her. For everything he had done to Jerry, and God only knew how many other innocent victims.

"Alice. To find out who conditioned Jerry, I need to

find Jerry. And I don't think I can do that without you."

Jonas's smug tone of voice changed. He was asking for help. Jonas pulled a worn wallet-sized photograph from a file on his desk. "Do you recognize this?"

Alice didn't want to look but curiosity overwhelmed her. The photo was a smaller version of the framed picture of Alice, her father, and Johnny Dancer. How did Jonas happen to have it in his possession? What new level of hell was he dragging her toward? "Where'd you get it?"

Jonas offered a sympathetic smile and spoke kindly. "You do recognize it then?"

She did. Of course she recognized it. "It's my father's copy. He kept it in his wallet. Where did you get it?"

Jonas got out of his chair and took a step toward her. Alice sensed that she was about to hear something that would alter her perspective all over again. She felt as though she were caught in a rapidly spinning revolving door. Jonas just finished telling her terrible, despicable secrets and yet his tone was now somehow paternal. "Tell me what you know about your father's death." He handed her the photograph.

"He was a federal judge. He denied a man in prison an appeal for a new trial. Ezekial Walters . . ." Jonas interrupted, "Walters had nothing do with your father's death." Alice was increasingly uneasy. "You sound so sure." Jonas said nothing more but simply observed as Alice examined the picture. Alice swallowed hard to try and hold back her tears. "When they found him, he was holding his wallet. The only thing missing was this photo. *Where did you find it?*"

Jonas held up a ring with an oddly shaped key that

had been confiscated from Jerry Fletcher's hospital room by the CIA. "The picture was in Jerry's safe-deposit box."

Alice tried to comprehend what he was suggesting. It was too terrible to contemplate. As the information settled in, Jonas began to paint the rest of the picture. "When do you think Jerry first took notice of you? What is it the two of you have in common?"

"I was mugged. He saved me." Her words sounded hollow. Alice was trying to convince herself that their meeting had been accidental. Merely chance. Nothing more.

"He may have saved you, Alice, but he wasn't there by coincidence. You're a lawyer; think like one."

She didn't want to think like a lawyer. Not anymore. Not on this subject. The chain of evidence added up to an unthinkable conclusion. Jonas, however, was not about to let her dodge the unavoidable. "Your father was assassinated."

Alice wanted to run but she couldn't move. The breath left her body and tears started down her cheeks. There was no place to hide from the next progression of logic. Jerry had murdered her father. Jonas carried on. He was unstoppable. "And the sonuvabitch has been obsessed with you ever since."

Alice knew it was true. It was the only explanation for everything that had gone on. As she accepted the fact, she needed to sit down or she would fall. Jonas took her by the shoulders, steadied her, and led her to a chair. He couldn't have been more compassionate. "I'm sorry. I truly am."

Jerry hadn't been trying to save Alice from some unknown assassin. He had been the killer all along.

Chapter 12

Jerry stood seventy-five stories above the pavement of lower Manhattan and checked things out.

It had been amazingly easy to slip into the law offices of Berger, Cowden, Goldman & Young during lunchtime. Dressed in a vaguely institutional uniform and carrying a bucket of soapy water and squeegee, Jerry was the image of a maintenance man. Nobody bothered to ask him for identification as he proceeded from the lobby to a partner's office high above the city.

To make things look on the level, in case somebody did happen to wander back from lunch, Jerry washed half a window before getting down to the serious work at hand. Using a discreet but highly powered telescope, Jerry monitored activity outside the Department of Justice.

The building was staked out but Jerry wasn't exactly sure by whom. Two separate black sedans waited patiently to follow Alice if she left her office. Jerry didn't know for a fact that the operatives waiting for Alice belonged to Jonas, but he assumed so.

Jerry swung the telescope around and peered at the surrounding rooftops. The buildings immediately adjacent to the Department of Justice seemed to be clear.

Well, maybe not entirely clear after all. Two plain-clothed commandos stepped into view on a roof across the street. Wearing headphones, they scanned the Justice Department building with heavy duty parabolic microphones.

Jerry was grimly pleased. There was no question in his mind. These were Jonas's elite assault troops. While they were dangerous opponents, he was pleased to know exactly who he was dealing with. It was also gratifying in a perverse way to know that someone was finally taking him seriously. Jerry had a strategy in mind and it depended on Jonas coming after him with everything he had in his arsenal.

He looked at his watch. What was taking so long? He had been specific about timing. While there was some leeway built into the scheme, his design could collapse if certain things didn't happen near enough to schedule.

Something caught his eye on the sidewalk. A delivery man ran up the Justice Department steps carrying a pizza. Good. The kid from Pizza Parlor was the first act in his gambit. Everything was humming along. Jerry collapsed his telescope and headed out the door.

"Hey! You!"

A big voice sounded and a firm hand grabbed Jerry's shoulder. Jerry balled a fist, ready for action.

But there was no real threat present. Just a young lawyer who didn't think much of Jerry's cleaning skills and wanted to keep the partners happy. "You call that a clean window?"

Alice, Jonas, and a number of aides sat with Wilson in his office. For law enforcement officials on the trail of a dangerous assassin, they didn't seem to be doing much of anything. The ball was in Jerry's court and they knew he was up to something. Exactly what, they couldn't say, but their troops were deployed all around the area, ready to swing into action. Until Jerry made contact all they could do was wait.

When Wilson's secretary barged into the office, Alice jumped out of her seat. She had been involved in numerous investigations during her career and was normally known for her steady nerves. But today was different. Catching Jerry was not like going after just any other criminal. Her grudge was personal. Jerry had murdered her father. Alice was not going to let him get away with it.

Wilson's secretary had a steaming, flat box in her hands. "Ms. Sutton's pizza, sir."

"A pizza?" No one ordered any food. What kind of joke was this? "I didn't order . . . a pizza."

Simultaneously Jonas and Alice realized who had placed the call to Pizza Parlor. Alice trailed off in midsentence while Jonas grabbed the box and placed it on a table in front of her. Alice exchanged a look with Wilson and opened the box.

Pepperoni pizza and a note.

Alice began to read, "Go to the northeast corner. Bring the pizza. I have something important to tell you." Alice hesitated as she read the next section. "There's a poem." She read the note again but didn't understand his cryptic words. Maybe the others would. "Roses are red, violets are blue. If the Pope goes to Washington, I would too."

"What the hell does that mean?"

Everyone looked at each other in bewilderment. Wilson began to shout orders. "Somebody find out if the Pope's scheduled to visit Washington!" Several men and women scrambled out of the room to figure out the Pope's current itinerary.

Alice gave the note to Jonas. He reviewed it carefully and reached a conclusion. "Jerry has something important to tell you." Jonas put down the communiqué and asked Alice officially to join his team. He needed help that only she could provide. "I've done everything to make him talk. Would you engage him? You'll be perfectly safe."

Wilson's objection surprised Alice. "No way. The risk is too great." She appreciated the fact that Wilson was looking out for her. But Alice couldn't turn down Jonas's request. She would do whatever it took to nail Jerry Fletcher. If she died in the process, well, that was a risk she was willing to take. Alice was not going to run away from the pain of her father's murder any longer. She was ready to confront it head-on.

"It's okay. I'm game."

Jonas handed the pizza box to one of his associates. "I want this box wired for sound and rigged with a beacon!"

Alice hit the street, carrying the pizza box, and walked over to the northeast corner as instructed. Moments later, a yellow cab pulled up beside her. Jerry was behind the wheel. "Where to, lady?"

It took a superhuman effort for Alice to repress her wrath. How could he be so goddamn glib? Alice wanted to give the order to her backups to open fire. The idea that she had to spend any time at all with Jerry Fletcher did not appeal to her in the least. Alice knew, however, that if she wanted to get the people who had planned her father's murder, the men who had sent Jerry on his deadly mission, she would have to play along. Where did she want to go? "You tell me, Jerry."

Alice got into the cab, slammed the door, and Jerry pulled away from the curb.

Two sedans followed at a discreet distance, just as Jerry knew they would.

Several blocks away, the black helicopter with its plain-clothed commandos on board lifted off to pursue the yellow cab from a position high in the sky.

Just as Jerry had expected.

Simultaneously, Jonas, Wilson and their subordinates rushed into a waiting black Chevy Suburban parked behind the Justice Department Building. The driver flipped on a monitor displaying a city grid and watched a flashing dot moving toward the East River.

Wilson gave an order and the driver swung into action. The pursuit of Jerry Fletcher was going to be a highly organized operation. Jonas put on a headset and directed the affair from the front seat of the Suburban.

As Jerry drove toward the river he couldn't spot any sign of the helicopter or pursuit on the ground. Jonas's team was good. That was okay with him. Jerry liked a challenge.

While the pilot maneuvered the chopper through the urban canyons, the copilot acted as spotter for the hunt. He shared his information with the chase team over the radio. "Rolling east. Fender number 6x24."

Sedan Number 1 confirmed they had Jerry in sight. "We're on him. Seventy-five yards back."

The tension in the cab was palpable. At least it was obvious to Alice. Instinctively, she sat as far away from Jerry as possible and leaned against the passenger side door. Alice didn't say much and kept an eye on Jerry as he turned uptown. Alice began to worry.

Where was he taking her? Even more troubling was Jerry's attitude. He seemed to be having a good time. Didn't he understand that none of this was a joke?

Jerry, however, was oblivious to her indignation and delighted to be back in Alice's company. He flipped open the box and grabbed himself a slice of pizza. "It's good, have some." Alice couldn't answer. She wasn't hungry. Same old Jerry. How could she ever have been deceived by him? Unaware of Alice's barely disguised antagonism, Jerry dove right into conversation. "How'd they like that thing about the Pope? I made it up. Threw it in there to get 'em going."

The manic charm that Jerry had once possessed was gone for Alice. His act wasn't cute anymore. It was infuriating. It was bad enough she had to ride with him but Alice didn't know how she was going to keep her cool if he didn't shut up. Alice took a nervous look in the side mirror to see if she could spot her backup.

Jerry misunderstood. "You look great."

"Thanks." Alice's voice was flat, devoid of emotion. She didn't want his compliments. She hated herself for having once felt warmth for him. Alice tried to convince herself that her feelings had been nothing more than pity. But deep down she knew that wasn't exactly true.

Alice despised herself and Jerry all the more for it.

If Jerry noticed her irritation at all he totally misread it. Just being near Alice again energized him. The words poured out of his mouth with a teenager's love-struck enthusiasm. "Are you okay? I wish I hadn't told you what I did. But I can't help the way I feel. You don't hold that against me, do you?"

Alice was as cold as her reputation made her out to

be. "No. That wouldn't be fair. What did you want to tell me, Jerry?"

"I'm not sure you'll believe me."

Inside the Chevy Suburban, the pursuit cars, and the helicopter, everyone listened to their conversation. Wilson and his Justice Department subordinates were fascinated. Once no more than an irritant to them, Jerry had grown in stature. It wasn't every day they got to tail a rogue assassin from the legendary ULTRA program. Even for jaded officials who had seen almost everything, this was, well, almost glamorous—a piece of history.

Jonas was not caught up in their excitement. He had a job to do and was focused entirely on the business ahead of them. Jerry Fletcher had to be stopped before he did any more harm. Jonas hoped to keep matters quiet, but if something went wrong he didn't care who was in the line of fire. He was going to bring his man down.

Jerry's cab swerved to miss a jaywalker and Alice's heart began to race. Her nerves were taut enough knowing that Jonas and his commandos might attack at any moment. Her goal was to keep Jerry as calm as possible and draw out any information that might be useful in putting together a case against him and his handlers. He was worried that she wouldn't believe him. Alice tried to put his fears to rest. "Jerry. All that's important is the truth."

He looked at her and knew he had to come clean. It was as though Jerry couldn't hide anything from Alice. He didn't know why. It was just the way it was. Jerry steeled himself. Confessions were never easy. "I think I know who really killed . . ."

He paused. Alice involuntarily leaned toward him. This was it. He was about to tell her. Her father's murder would no longer be a mystery. Alice could stop punishing herself and try to pick up the pieces of her life. In the pursuit vehicles Jonas, Wilson, and the others held their collective breaths.

"I know who killed President McKinley."

President William McKinley had been assassinated in 1901.

Jonas wanted to kill someone. They had been so close. Was Jerry really that confused? Or was he playing with Alice?

Alice was wondering the same thing. "You brought me out here to tell me that?"

"No." Jerry signaled left but turned against two lanes of traffic and made a right. Horns blared and chase cars swerved to keep their target in sight. Now they were headed up First Avenue. Alice couldn't figure out where they were going. Jerry tried to decipher what was going on in his brain. "I feel what I want to say, but I can't think it." Alice didn't understand. Jerry offered another explanation. It was crucial that she understand. "It's like when you can remember the words of a song, but only when you're singing along with it. No music and you're helpless."

In the pursuit vehicle Wilson was nervous. Jerry Fletcher sounded less and less rational. Wilson didn't want Alice exposed to this serious a threat any longer than absolutely necessary. "Let's take him." Jonas refused. They needed to be patient.

Jerry checked his rearview mirror, looking for a tail. Alice feigned ignorance. "Is something wrong?" She was a better attorney than she was an actress. But Jerry didn't care. He was well aware they had company. He was just making sure that Jonas's men could keep up with him. They all had a role to play in his master plan. In the meantime there were more important matters to discuss with Alice. "Nothing's wrong. Don't worry about it. Look, I want to take you where the music's playing."

"Where's that?"

Jerry put the accelerator to the floor and the cab lunged forward. Apparently he was going to show her where the music was.

The chase cars followed as the cab charged toward an intersection. Jerry's timing was perfect. A traffic light turned yellow but he would make it through. He swore as the car ahead of him stopped. Out-of-towners no doubt. No self-respecting New Yorker would stop for a yellow light. Jerry had no choice. Weaving around the stopped car, Jerry sped up as he entered the intersection and squeezed through only inches ahead of the cross traffic.

The lead chase car pulled into the oncoming lane to follow but was forced back by a garbage truck barreling directly toward them. Traffic stopped for the light. They were stuck. The driver shouted into his headset, "He made us!"

High above First Avenue Jonas's airborne commandos watched the whole business unfold from their helicopter. No problem. "We've got him. He's headed for the bridge."

The second chase car made a hard left to avoid the red light that had caught their colleagues. The strategy was to drive parallel to the target car and catch up with him on the Queensboro Bridge. The driver let the command car know that they were in pursuit. "We're on him!"

As the Suburban sped around a corner, Jonas monitored the blip of Jerry's cab on his tracking grid. "Jonas to ground units. The helicopter has him. Hang back and let him think he lost you."

As the second chase car followed orders, Jerry turned the cab onto a ramp leading up to the mammoth Queensboro Bridge, which spanned the East River. Jerry drove onto the lower section of the double-decker bridge. Alice was confused. "The music's playing in Queens?"

"Not today." Jerry's cheerful tone was gone. He was concentrating. Something was about to happen.

The helicopter pilot realized that something was up but it was too late to remedy the situation. The cab disappeared from view as it continued along the lower section of the bridge, which was hidden by the upper highway. The spotter in the chopper radioed down to Jonas, "On the bridge. Lower level." Then the helicopter turned to the east to wait for Jerry on the other side.

But for the moment, Jerry had taken the airborne surveillance out of the picture. He new that until he and Alice reached Queens, the cab was free and clear from their pursuers.

Jerry was not, however, about to relax. Just because he had shaken off the bad guys temporarily didn't mean they still weren't after them. As the cab reached the halfway point across the bridge, Jerry stepped on his brakes and spun the wheel without warning.

One moment Alice was trying to figure out how Queens figured into the picture—maybe it was one of the airports, maybe Jerry was headed for Long Island—the next instant she was screaming as the taxi pulled a three-sixty and skidded down the pavement the wrong way. Jerry fought the spinout and maneuvered the cab so that it came to a halt with its doors facing the traffic coming behind it. The taxi sat across the road and blocked all the traffic heading away from Manhattan.

Brakes squealed, tires burned, and cars rear-ended the automobiles ahead of them. When the chain reaction was finished, horns began to blare and a chorus of furious New Yorkers vented their anger.

Jerry paid no attention and jumped out of the cab, shouting for Alice to follow. Alice was beyond fear. She had no idea what he was up to. Had Jerry spotted the tail? Was he anticipating an assault? Had his paranoia finally taken him over the edge—was he seeing an approaching enemy no one else could see? Alice grabbed the pizza box and did as she was told. She was counting on Jerry to be too busy to notice she was carrying it. If he did, he might be suspicious. Or at least more suspicious than he normally was. But Alice was willing to take that risk. She didn't want to lose contact with Jonas and Wilson. The idea of being alone with Jerry frightened Alice terribly. He was, after all, a killing machine.

Jerry led her toward the center guardrail. Alice was dubious. "Now what?" He was cool and collected as though they were taking a walk in Central Park, not standing in the middle of one of the busiest roadways in the city. "This way."

Jerry climbed over the median strip and lowered himself onto the Manhattan-bound traffic lanes. He held out his hand to help Alice make the leap. She hesitated, jumped, lost her balance, and dropped the pizza box. Jerry caught her but the pizza hit the pavement. As Alice tried to pick it up, Jerry pulled her along, apparently unaware of the pizza's real function. "Forget it! I'll buy you another one!"

Jerry held out a cautionary hand to the slowly moving traffic and started across the highway with Alice in tow. Reaching the breakdown lane, Jerry approached an abandoned 1978 Monte Carlo with its front end up on a jack. Jerry gestured with mock gallantry toward the huge rust bucket. "After you." Alice didn't understand. Jerry tried to reassure her. "It's okay. I'm the one who left it here."

That didn't make anything clearer. On the contrary it was much more confusing. Why would he lead them to a broken-down car in the middle of the Queensboro Bridge? Then Alice understood. All of it had been carefully planned. Jerry had just executed a perfect evasion procedure. He had lost the aerial surveillance and had prevented the ground teams from following. The Monte Carlo had been parked here earlier in the day, waiting for their arrival. The car didn't look like it could be driven, but Alice knew that it would. They would soon be on their way. Free from surveillance tails and with the loss of the wired pizza box completely out of contact with Wilson or Jonas.

Alice was on her own. "Where are we going, Jerry?"

"Connecticut."

"What's in Connecticut?"

"The music. I think." Jerry guided her into the front seat. He got in next to her, sat behind the steering wheel, started the car, and froze. The engine idled as he stared out the front window as though transfixed by something wondrous. Alice followed his gaze, but the only thing she could see were three red-and-white smoke stacks from a Con Edison plant that sat on the eastern shore of Manhattan not far from the United Nations.

Before Alice could ask what he was looking at, Jerry snapped out of it and flipped the transmission into "drive." The rear wheels dug in, the car pitched forward, spat out the jack, and the front end hit the asphalt. Jerry pulled into the traffic and they were off to find his music.

Hovering over the Queens-end of the bridge, the airborne surveillance team watched the exit ramps with increasing curiosity. The spotter gave the pilot instructions. "Drop down." The helicopter dove and Jonas's men realized that no traffic was coming off the bridge. The spotter called out over the radio. "Something's wrong."

The men in the second chase car were stuck in traffic at the beginning of the bridge. They had no idea what was going on. But stop-and-go traffic was hardly surprising. It happened every day. While they didn't especially enjoy being stuck, they took comfort in the fact that Jerry and Alice would be caught in the same jam. It might be a pain in the ass but they weren't going to lose their target. They weren't unduly troubled by the helicopter's message until the next one crackled in over the radio. "We're going in." That was all the men in the second chase car needed to hear. Surveillance teams only "went in" when there was serious trouble. They jumped out of their car and began running through the stalled traffic, searching for Jerry's cab.

They would find the taxi soon enough but Jerry and Alice were nowhere to be seen.

As the ground units looked around in bewilderment and the chopper flew low, trying to peer in at the lower level traffic, Jerry's Monte Carlo sped off the bridge in the opposite direction, heading back into Manhattan.

Jerry made his getaway as cleanly and professionally as he had been trained to do. Jonas and his men never had a chance.

For all of their sophisticated effort, Alice Sutton

was out of contact and in a real jam. She was stuck in a car with the man who had murdered her father and who represented the intelligence community's greatest experiment run amok—a soulless, unstoppable killing machine named Jerry Fletcher.

Chapter 13

It didn't take long to reach the border and cross into Connecticut. As evening fell, Jerry kept the Monte Carlo at sixty-five and the enormous engine roared as they left a major highway and made their way along the quieter back roads. Connecticut was really two states in one. Its major cities—New Haven, Waterbury, and Hartford—embraced all the usual problems of urban areas. Poverty, crime, and hopelessness were as rampant there as in any section of New York or Los Angeles. But the Connecticut that most people thought of was the sort of area where Jerry was now headed. This Connecticut was the backyard of the wealthy and powerful. It consisted of charming towns, massive estates, farms, beautiful shorelines, and huge areas of undeveloped land.

Alice knew the area like the back of her hand, for she had grown up in Connecticut. Her sense of discomfort grew as Jerry drove down familiar roads. It was funny, she thought. She should have felt more at ease driving through her home turf. But the implication inherent in Jerry's choice of direction made her furious. Alice kept as much distance between herself and Jerry as she possibly could. Where exactly was Jerry going? Alice wasn't sure she wanted to wait around to find out.

Jerry hadn't said a word since leaving Manhattan. The radio was tuned to a soft rock station and Alice thought she was going to scream. Jerry, no doubt, loved the gooey ballads and Alice grew nervous when he began to move his lips in a distracted sort of way. It was bad enough to be his hostage. Alice didn't think she could stand it if Jerry started to serenade her. It took a while before he was vocalizing loudly enough for Alice to hear what was coming out of his mouth. It wasn't a love song, however, and after Alice was certain of what she heard she began to wish he was wooing her with a little Barry Manilow after all.

"Ted Bundy. David Berkowitz. Richard Speck."

Jerry didn't seem to expect a response from Alice. The names just hung there between them—a testament to the madness and cruelty of human beings.

Alice reviewed the sick history as best she could.

College graduate and one-time law student Ted Bundy had traded on his good looks to lure women into his grasp and had left a trail of murder victims across America. He died in Florida's electric chair.

David Berkowitz was the infamous "Son of Sam" serial killer. His twisted specialty was to hunt down young couples who were making out in cars and shoot them. Currently, Berkowitz was locked up in an asylum, almost certain never again to walk as a free man.

Richard Speck had murdered a dormitory roomful of student nurses in Chicago during the sixties. Alice didn't remember much more than that and didn't know whether or not he was still alive. She hoped not.

She was curious and frightened but tried not to respond. She didn't want to validate Jerry's mantra by acknowledging it. But it was impossible to ignore the names of three vicious killers while in the presence of a fourth. Did Bundy, Berkowitz, and Speck have any special meaning to Jerry? Were they role models? Against her better judgment, Alice found herself asking, "What about them?"

"How come serial killers have two names, but lone gunman assassins have three. John *Wilkes* Booth. Mark *David* Chapman. Lee *Harvey* Oswald." Clearly Jerry had given the matter a lot of thought during the ride from New York.

Alice looked for a flaw in his logic. "John Hinckley. The guy who shot Reagan. He only had two names." Jerry didn't miss a beat. He knew what he was talking about. "Reagan didn't die. If he had died, everybody would know what Johnny's middle name was."

Jerry offered Alice an incongruously warm smile. He was impressed with his hypothesis. Alice wasn't. She looked the other way. Granted, Jerry's mind had been messed with in a way that minds shouldn't be. But his fascination with assassins and killers was troubling, especially now that she was all alone with him.

Rebuffed, Jerry turned his attention back to the road. Alice watched him carefully. Somehow she had to make contact with either Jonas or Wilson without him noticing. It didn't matter which. It just had to be done. Quickly. Since she dropped the bugged pizza box on the Queensboro Bridge, Alice had been out of contact with anyone who could help her. That was a frightening thought. Not sure that her plan would work, she wanted to make an attempt to improvise a homing beacon.

When she was certain that Jerry was focused completely on driving, Alice carefully slipped her small cell phone out of her pants pocket. Holding it between her body and the car door, out of Jerry's line of sight, Alice flipped the phone open, powered it up, and hit a speed dial key. She glanced down at the readout to make sure everything was working properly. The display flashed "WILSON" and Alice covered the tiny speaker with her thumb.

Back in Manhattan, Wilson, Jonas, and their respective departments were preparing to work late into the night. They had no idea where Jerry had taken Alice but they were determined to figure it out and bring him in. No one was going home until Alice Sutton was safe.

Jonas listened to Wilson and approved of his noble motivation. Jonas's secret ambition was less complex, however. Rescuing Alice would require intricate planning and coordination. All Jonas wanted to do was kill Jerry Fletcher. It was much easier to bring someone back dead than alive. It was just a matter of firepower. The simplicity and elegance of what Jonas needed to accomplish practically guaranteed success.

A phone began to ring outside the door to Wilson's office. Wilson's secretary answered it. When she didn't hear anyone on the other end of the line, she paused and then hung up. Wrong number.

On some level, Jonas registered the phone call and its brevity in the back of his mind, despite the fact that he was simultaneously lecturing his troops on the strengths of a pursuit strategy. Like a powerful computer, his mind operated on multiple tasks at once. No one else in the room had even been aware that the phone had rung.

Night had overtaken the Monte Carlo as Jerry drove north. Shielding his view with her body, Alice watched with frustration as the lights blinked out on her cell phone. In the dark, she worried that Jerry would be more likely to notice a reflection from the orange cell phone display but knew she had to try again. Alice hit redial and hoped Jerry would keep his attention on the road.

"Mr. Wilson's office. Hello? *Hello?* Is anyone there?" Wilson's secretary was about to hang up on the crank caller a second time. Now she was getting mad. It was bad enough that she had to cancel her dinner plans. What's more, she had to admit that while she didn't particularly like hard-edged Alice Sutton, she certainly didn't wish her any harm. The people who worked in Wilson's department could be real pains in the ass, there was no doubt about it. But when one of them was in trouble, everyone pulled together.

All the more reason to be angry. What sort of jerk would tie up the phone lines during a crisis, when they needed to be kept open for important calls. The secretary raised the phone high above its cradle and prepared to smash it down with such force that the crank caller would never forget the impact.

But when her arm began to make its descent it stopped in midair against her will. Jonas loomed above her and held her wrist. Grabbing the phone out of her hand, he put it to his ear and listened. No voices. Nothing but road noise and the crackle of a distant cellular phone connection. Jonas knew victory was within his grasp. "*It's her.* The line's open. Get a trace on it. Now."

Everyone got up from where they were plotting strategy and swung into action.

Alice kept an eye on the cell phone light. It didn't blink out this time. The connection was holding.

Someone in Wilson's office understood what she was doing. Alice was not necessarily going to die that night. Now she had a fighting chance. Alice had paged the cavalry.

As unobtrusively as she could, Alice placed the live phone behind her seat and left it resting on the rear floor.

When she finished this task Alice had a chance to pay more attention to where they were going. As Jerry turned off the main highway onto Bumps River Road, Alice knew that trouble was only a few miles ahead. She needed answers. "Where are we going!" Jerry concentrated on driving with a strange intensity. It was as though he had no idea where he was going, even though he had been there many times before. *"Where?"*

Jerry pulled over to the side of the road and pointed to the woods. "Somewhere in there. It's somewhere in there."

On the other side of a stone wall, illuminated by the full moon stood a barn that had seen better days. Fifty yards further along stood the large, rambling Colonial home where Alice had been raised.

Alice watched Jerry vigilantly. He wasn't pretending. Jerry really didn't know where he was, he just knew this was where he had to take her.

Alice filled everybody in. "We're at my father's house." She hoped to hell Wilson and Jonas could hear her. Jerry seemed mildly surprised by the news and stepped out of the car. "Come on." Alice cast a last glance at the cell phone in the backseat. It was her best shot at being rescued.

Alice was pretty sure that help was now on its way. All she had to do was stay alive long enough for Wilson and Jonas to arrive. But what was the best way to do that? Should she run and hide in the nearby woods? Alice was trained in self-defense. Maybe she should try to disable Jerry? As satisfying as it would be to get her licks in, Alice was aware she was no match for an ULTRA-trained killer. For the time being, Alice did as she was told, stepped onto a dark path, and made her way toward the barn. Jerry followed only a few steps behind.

"I got another one!" Jerry's mood shifted yet again and careened from serious to incongruously cheerful. Alice was more annoyed and afraid than ever. He sounded like a little boy on a picnic. Jerry rattled on. "James Earl Ray. Three names. Lone gunman."

Alice's mouth went dry and she began to sweat, the cold autumnal night notwithstanding. She was nervous as hell. Whatever hold Jerry had on reality was succumbing to the pressure. Alice scrutinized the property surrounding her, desperate to spot somebody or something that might be of help.

There was nothing. Alice's mind raced as she tried to find a way to distract her father's killer. She expanded upon Jerry's theory about the names of infamous killers. "Of course then there's Sirhan Sirhan. I still haven't figured that one out yet."

As they approached the barn, Jerry knew they had to go inside. He reached for the large door. As though warning the intruders, the large doors groaned as Jerry pulled them open. He was delighted that Alice seemed to understand his ideas and tried a joke. "Maybe it's really Sirhan Sirhan Sirhan." he was a killer not a comic, and then suddenly the time for humor came to an end.

As they stood on the threshold of the dark barn, it was suddenly very quiet and Alice was more afraid than she ever had been before in her life. Jerry shut the doors behind them and they stood silently for a moment while their eyes adjusted to the dark.

Alice was no longer sure what was going on. How could she escape from him now? What was running through Jerry's mind? When was the last time he had seen this view? What exactly had he been doing here on that night? Scared as she was, Alice wasn't going to shy away from the memory of her father's murder. Jerry might kill her for confronting him with the truth but Alice wasn't going to pretend anymore. He had taken away from her the only truly important person in her life. Jerry loved her? Oh, really? Well, she loathed him and now the time had come for him to kiss his psychopathic romantic fantasy life good-bye.

"What's your middle name, Jerry?"

Jerry cocked his head at a funny angle as though he didn't quite grasp the question. Alice wanted to shout at him. Three names. Killers always have a middle name. Wasn't that his theory? So, what was Jerry's third name?

But likable, vulnerable Jerry was back. "What do you mean, Alice?" He didn't understand the change of tone in her voice. Why was she angry? What was wrong? Jerry took a worried step toward her.

And Alice took two petrified steps back. She was no match for him in a physical contest. She looked around for a long-forgotten tool, something she could swing easily or use as a club. But there was nothing available. Things looked grim and Alice figured she was about to meet the same fate as her father. If this was truly the end, Alice wanted Jerry to understand that she knew the truth and hated him for it. That would be the best way to hurt Jerry Fletcher. "Did you kill him, Jerry?"

"Alexander Hamilton? Before my time." Secretary

of the Treasury Alexander Hamilton had been killed by Vice President Aaron Burr during a duel in 1804.

Was Jerry lost again in his bewildering world of light and darkness, or was he toying with Alice before murdering her? Alice couldn't tell. She didn't care anymore. All she wanted to do was wound him as best she could. "Did you kill my father?"

"No."

He didn't? How could he explain the evidence taken from his safe-deposit box? Jerry took another step toward her.

"Maybe."

Maybe? A person would know if he shot another person in the back of the head. It wasn't the sort of thing someone forgot.

"I don't think so."

"You don't think so?" Alice didn't buy it. Still, he was a great performer and almost convincing. Alice thought to herself that Jerry would have made a fine actor if hadn't chosen to be an assassin instead.

All Alice could do was ask more questions. As an experienced Justice Department attorney she had met with her share of sociopathic personalities before— people who could do terrible things but carry themselves as innocently as newborns. Alice knew the evidence pointed in Jerry's direction, despite his counterfeit confusion. "Why'd you have my father's picture in your safe-deposit box?"

Jerry searched for an answer. "He . . . gave it to me."

Yeah. Right. Before you shoot me in the back of the head, how'd you like a nice family portrait? Meet my pretty daughter. She's not seeing anyone right now. The two of you should meet.

It was insane. Why would her father give him a photograph? "Where? Where did he give it to you?"

Jerry pointed to the center of the barn. "Right over there."

"That's where he died. Did you kill my father, Jerry? Answer me."

Jerry began to walk away and talk distractedly. His head was somewhere else entirely. "You were at a horse show that day. It was the last time you rode, wasn't it?"

How did he know? Alice *had* ridden Johnny Dancer on the day her father had been killed. She had won the semifinals of the Regional Competition in Litchfield and couldn't wait for the next round. But her world had crumbled upon her return to Manhattan. Wilson was sitting in the lobby of her apartment building. He told her the horrible news. Her father had been shot earlier in the evening.

Alice hadn't seen Johnny Dancer since that night.

But how did Jerry know all this? Had he been pursuing her even then?

Jerry walked away from her, toward the spot where Judge Sutton had died. "I think you blame yourself. I think . . ."

Alice ran after Jerry, grabbed his arm, and spun him around. Alice wasn't aware of it but for the first time since that horrible night she was expressing her emotions instead of repressing them. Her grief, anger, fear, and frustration erupted after being hidden inside for far too long. "Did he beg for his life? Did he see you coming? You pointed a gun at him and you killed him! Didn't you? Didn't you?"

Jerry was assaulted by images from his past and the pain caused by Alice's contempt for him. "It's on the tip of my tongue . . ."

And then he knew. It all came back to him as surely

as if someone were opening the floodgates of a dam under intense pressure.

It was unforgivable. But Jerry remembered all too clearly that he *had* gone to kill Judge Sutton. "I went to, to court to do it. At the Ezekial Walters hearing. I had a gun, but I couldn't shoot. Because you were there. You, Alice. That's when I met you."

Alice wasn't afraid anymore. Instead, she detonated into an unrestrained rage. "Love at first sight. Is that what you call it? You watch me, Jerry. You steal from me."

Jerry was unable to move, paralyzed by guilt from a crime he could not remember. But Alice would have none of it. "My father died right in here. Like an animal! In a barn. Did you do it?! Did you kill my father?!"

He stared at the ground but said nothing.

"Answer me!!"

More silence. And then Alice let him have it. She hit him in the chest and then the face. Over and over again. She wanted to wound him as he had injured her. Her assault was relentless and Jerry's face was quickly bloodied. Alice attacked him with a ferocity she wished she could have called upon to defend her father all those many nights ago. But she hadn't been there for him and Judge Sutton had died alone, at the hands of the man standing before her.

The assault hurt. But Jerry was more bothered by Alice's anguish than his own. If he was guilty he'd be happy to accept the punishment. But he just didn't know. The only thing he could be sure of was that Alice was lost in her misery and she needed his help. As tears started to stream down his face, Jerry finally grabbed her wrists and tried to calm her down. "Stop it!"

As if wakened from a spell, Alice broke off her on-slaught. She needed an answer, and her voice was caught between a plea and a demand. "I have to know what happened. You tell me."

Maybe it was the vehemence of Alice's outburst. Maybe it was the shock of seeing her raw pain. Maybe it was the effect of standing in a place where he had been long ago, where something terrible had hap-pened. But Jerry began to remember the details of that tragic night. "After the courthouse, I knew they'd send someone else. So I watched him. Kept him safe."

Could it be true? Jerry had been sent to kill the judge. But having fallen in love with Alice on the day of the hit, had he changed sides and become the judge's secret defender?

Alice couldn't ignore the sincerity in Jerry's voice. What's more, his account corresponded with what she knew about her father's last days. "My dad felt there was someone after him. He started carrying a gun."

"I know. He stuck it in my face when I introduced myself."

Alice was stunned. Jerry knew her father? Could the chain of evidence have been so wrong? Alice re-lied on logic to make her way through the world. It was her source of strength and the only thing in her life that she knew was reliable. And yet suddenly everything was upside down again.

It was all coming back to Jerry. The terrifying glimpses of memory that had tormented him for so long were not as uniformly horrible as he had feared. There were good memories too. Memories of friend-ship, time spent with a truly admirable man, and the redemption that came with defending someone who had been intended as a victim. "We became friends.

He made really good coffee. He tried to help me . . . remember my past." But it had all come to an end on the day when Jerry had left the judge to watch Alice perform at the horse show. "Then one of Jonas's guys showed up to finish the job. When I got here, your dad was dying."

Alice tried to make sense of everything she was hearing, for she knew it was all absolutely true. "What does Jonas have to do with Ezekial Walters?"

"Walters was the fall guy on the bank bombing. Jonas builds fall guys. Guys who do it and can't remember why. Some of them are guys with middle names. That's what I think I was supposed to be."

Jonas created Jerry to be a fall guy who couldn't remember his crimes. Alice, however, had restored his memory. Jonas had a lot of weapons in his arsenal but they were no match for the attention of a good woman.

But what was the connection between Judge Sutton and Ezekial Walters? It was on the tip of his tongue but Jerry couldn't quite grasp it. He looked apologetically at Alice. She had to know. Her pain could not be alleviated until she knew. Jerry couldn't let her suffer. The need to save her stimulated his memory. "Your father was going to reopen the Ezekial Walters case. he didn't believe the official story."

"Why not . . . ? *Why not, Jerry?*" The answer to that question would be the key to everything else.

"Because, because he believed me."

Jerry kneeled at the spot where Judge Sutton had been murdered. "Even when he was dying. Your father worried about you. He took your picture from his wallet. He called you his baby."

Jerry looked up and stared into Alice's eyes. "I told

him I'd keep you safe. I took the picture and I've been watching you, stealing from you, ever since."

That was it. The flip side of the mystery. Jerry hadn't been stalking Alice. On the contrary, he had been watching over her, keeping her safe. He was her slightly mad, wounded knight, fulfilling her beloved father's dying wish.

Alice wasn't angry anymore and knelt down beside him. "I believe you."

"You do?" No one had believed anything Jerry had said for a very long time.

The truth that would set them free was in the details. "My father made great coffee."

After all they had been through there was nothing more that could be said. With Alice's darkest fears proven to be unfounded and Jerry's nightmarish loss of memory cured, there was nothing left for them but a wordless expression of affection for each other. The embrace of two fractured people—a lost soul and a lonely soul—eased their pain and made them whole again.

If only briefly.

As Jerry clung to Alice, she suddenly pulled away. "You've got to get out of here. My cell phone's on. Back in the car."

"They'll trace it."

"I'm sorry."

He wasn't angry. He understood, "It's okay. You . . . you thought I was bad."

Before Alice could reply, the doors to the barn burst open as a battering ram punched them off their ancient hinges. Jonas's plain-clothed commandos charged inside. Armed with 9mm machine pistols, they directed strong flashlights at the startled couple.

Jerry grabbed Alice's hand and pulled her toward a side entrance.

They didn't get far.

As they ran out of the barn, an amplified voice thundered out orders. "Hands above your heads!"

An intense beam of light descended upon them from a helicopter. The Nightsun, a piece of military hardware, was so powerful that it felt as though Jerry and Alice were being crushed into the dirt. They couldn't move and they couldn't stand up. Their escape had failed.

Jerry knew he was near the end, but one question remained in his mind. He needed an answer. He was certain this would be his last chance to speak to Alice. "You switched the charts, didn't you?"

"Jerry, not now with this."

"Now's all I got. Did you switch the charts?"

The amplified voice was yelling at them again. "Hands above your head! Step away from him, Ms. Sutton!" Jonas's plainclothes commandos approached with their weapons drawn and their faces washed out by the overwhelming Nightsuns. They were expressionless, featureless troopers, petrifying in their anonymity and barely human.

Jerry was out of time. Desperately, he begged Alice for an answer. "Tell me. Please."

"Yes. I switched the charts."

Considering the circumstances, the victory was small enough. But at least Jerry now knew for certain that he hadn't been crazy. It hadn't all been in his head. And there was only one thing left for Alice to do. "Get out of here, Alice." She didn't understand. Alice had every intention of supervising the arrest and making sure that Jerry got the treatment he needed. And once that was accomplished she had every intention of leading a Justice Department investigation into Jonas's criminal behavior.

"Go." Jerry's voice was urgent but Alice didn't understand. Why did he want her to run? Who was she supposed to be running away from?

"Step away, Miss Sutton!"

Four commandos grabbed Jerry, cuffed him, and dragged him toward the waiting helicopter. They never said a word. No explanation of his Miranda rights. Nothing. They didn't even acknowledge Alice, who was sure she outranked them.

Alice took a step after them. "Wait a minute." A commando shoved her away from the hovering helicopter. Jerry dipped to the side and drove an angry shoulder into the commando's back. The man hit the ground and lay there stunned. As the others wrestled with Jerry, he fought long enough to look back over his shoulder to Alice. He wasn't trying to save himself. He was worried about her. "Run!"

The commandos beat him into submission as the helicopter touched down only yards away. A door was flung open and Wilson stepped off. The commandos hustled Jerry past him and onto the chopper as he moved to assist Alice. "Alice, are you all right?"

She stared, happy to see her boss but certain that something out of the ordinary was about to happen.

The helicopter engine revved and Wilson turned with a confused look on his face. The chopper lifted off, leaving him and Alice on the ground. What the hell was going on?

Then both Alice and Wilson saw a sight that chilled their blood. Jonas stood in the doorway of the ascending helicopter and seemed to be waving goodbye to them.

As the chopper rose into the sky, three of Jonas's

commandos were revealed standing behind it. They were being left to mop things up. Their 9mm automatics were aimed directly at Wilson and Alice. It didn't make sense.

But it didn't have to. Nothing that had anything to do with Jonas was what it seemed. Alice understood this as the lead commando opened fire and cut Wilson in half.

Alice didn't hang around to ask questions. She bolted for the house. The commandos fired after her and were amazed they had missed. Alice was faster and used the darkness better than anyone they had ever seen.

On board the helicopter, Jerry was still struggling with his captors. Jammed into a corner, he pressed himself against the window glass and stared down at the estate, watching as Alice evaded the killers.

Jonas was delighted to have Jerry in his custody. "You've embarrassed me, Jerry. You've made certain people take notice of me who shouldn't."

Jerry wasn't listening. It took all of his rapidly dwindling energy to resist the commandos and keep an eye on Alice. Her legs churned powerfully, increasing the distance between herself and the commandos. Her great athleticism and the anger that fueled her speed combined to improve her chances with every step as she neared sanctuary.

Watching Jerry's futile struggle made Jonas want to smile. He was a cordial man when the entertaining prospect of bloodletting was imminent. "We've arranged for you to take the blame. Everyone knows how you've been harassing the poor girl."

"Alice!!" Jerry shouted even though she couldn't possibly hear him. It was a cry of love and fear. It was encouragement to run just a little faster and make her escape. It was an acknowledgment of their solidarity against a common enemy. Every vein in his neck and face popped with the exertion. Jerry's face was bright red with fury and effort, his blue eyes focused on the woman he loved with such intensity that they would have rivaled the Nightsuns if only their energy could have been harnessed.

"You shouldn't watch, Jerry. It's a moment without hope." Jonas was enjoying himself immensely. As the commandos choked him, Jerry spat out his words with an absolute confidence that made a mockery of Jonas's observation. "You've never seen her run."

Jerry held his position against the window long enough to see Alice disappear into the trees. Unable to help, he pounded his forehead against the glass in frustration. Jerry saw Jonas smile. He lunged toward him, dragging several commandos along for the ride.

Jonas kicked Jerry in the head and incapacitated him. It was a dispassionate move and completely effective. He could have just as easily been stepping on a bug. The battle was over and Jonas had won. Still, he shook his head with exasperation. As usual the people who worked for him were not up to their task. Did he have to do everything? As his winded subordinates cuffed the unconscious man, Jonas moved to the cockpit of the helicopter and began to consider his next move.

Alice didn't have the luxury to plan ahead. She was outnumbered and outgunned. Her only chance was to take advantage of her knowledge of the estate's layout. As a commando closed in on her from behind, Alice rounded a corner and spotted something she recognized. It was an innocuous enough object but it just might save her life.

Just ahead of her lay a ground-level well that was covered with rotted wooden planks. For ages her father had planned to fix the well cover so that no one would fall through. Anybody unlucky enough to take the plunge would almost certainly meet a quick end. Uncharacteristically, he hadn't lived up to his word. But that was good. For tonight Judge Sutton's rare display of carelessness might make the difference between her living and dying.

Alice ran for the well at full speed, coaxing everything from her legs that she had trained so hard to build. Reaching the well cover, she darted to one side, skirting its edge and making her way safely across.

Just a few steps behind her, the commando wasn't so lucky. Running right across the center of the rotted planks, he fell through to a watery death.

Alice kept going at full speed toward a corral where her father had kept their horses. Quickly enough another commando fell into step just behind her. Weaponless, Alice knew her only chance was to somehow surprise him. But how could she surprise the commando if he could see everything she was doing? She simply didn't have the opportunity to improvise a weapon or hide.

The solution was the gate to the horse corral.

If she could lure her pursuer into the fenced-in area at just the right time, she might have a chance.

Alice could hear the commando huffing, puffing, and falling slightly behind. He was running out of steam. That wouldn't do. He had to be right on her tail for her scheme to work. It went against every instinct in her body but Alice slowed down and let the man pick up a few steps on her.

Her hastily improvised strategy worked perfectly. The commando was encouraged when Alice cut back her pace. He lunged for her just as she crossed the threshold into the pen. Her timing was impeccable. Just as she could feel her attacker's fingertips on her shoulders, Alice spun around and swung the metal gate leading into the corral back into his teeth with all her strength.

Two down. One to go.

Although technically the odds had improved, Alice was about to reach the end of her great escape. The one surviving commando was about to put an end to the whole business.

Just before the second commando was taken out of the competition, number three stopped where he was and aimed his weapon while steadying it on a fence post. Alice ran right into the greenish murk of his night vision crosshairs. The commando was confident of a kill. He was pleased and knew Jonas would be too. It was the sort of thing that could make a man's career.

As he pulled the trigger, however, his view of the target was obliterated by a large green shape.

The second commando, whose teeth had been dashed against the unforgiving metal of the corral gate, rose shakily to his feet just in time to take the bullet meant for Alice. Now his toothless grin was the least of his worries. The man was dead before the shards of his skull and the goop of his brain splattered over the dirt.

Alice heard the silenced "whoop" from the last commando's gun. She was pretty sure she wasn't dead and that inspired her to pick up her pace even more. Alice knew that as fast as she was, she couldn't outrace a bullet. She had to get out of the open air where she was an easy target. The playing field had to be leveled. If the last killer was using an automatic weapon, her best chance would be inside the house, where close quarters would make it difficult for the commando to maneuver.

Alice bolted up the steps to her father's house, grabbed a deck chair from the patio, and flung it through a picture window. As she vanished inside the dark house, the last commando charged up the steps to the patio and followed.

While he had the advantage of firepower, she at least knew her way around the house in the pitch dark. Slipping out of the living room and into a hallway as her attacker tripped over a footrest and sprawled across the floor, she heard him fall. She ducked back into the room, grabbed something from near the fireplace and made her way as stealthily as she could back down the hall.

The commando got to his feet and listened. This is what he was trained for. There was no doubt in his mind but that he could accomplish the mission. The woman didn't have a chance. Whoever she was, she was about to vanish from the face of the earth.

The silence made Alice nervous. Where was the commando? Why wasn't he coming after her. Was he hurt? Could she make a getaway? Alice started to move around a corner and stopped herself when the wooden floor beneath her feet creaked. It was like stepping onto a land mine. If she moved now the noisy plank would certainly give away her position. Surprise was her best ally. But then again, there were all kinds of surprises. Alice moved down the hallway, knowing that the man who was trying to kill her could hear the creaking floorboards. She would have to move quickly and there was no room for error.

The commando loped across the living room and stood at the threshold of the hallway. This was too easy. Like shooting ducks on a pond. He'd be drinking beer with his buddies before the sun rose.

A shock wave blasted down the corridor as a soprano screamed. The volume was shattering. A hundred chorus members bellowed verses from *La Boheme* at the top of their lungs. It was deafening. The commando couldn't believe a sound system could be that loud. Pictures on the walls began to vibrate. An empty vase sitting on a hall table toppled over. The commando tried to focus on his mission but the thunderous noise of the music was disorienting. There was no way he could hear his prey any longer. There was only one thing to do. Kill the music before the woman.

He moved swiftly down the hallway toward a room that held the sound equipment. The closer to the source he got, the worse it became. The volume was tangible. Glass in a hanging light fixture quivered.

He took aim at the sound system. He never made it into the room. As he stepped into the doorway, Alice leapt out of the shadows and swung at his head with a fireplace poker.

She looked down at her would-be assassin and felt nothing. The son of a bitch got what he deserved. It was bad enough they had tried to kill her, but they had already murdered Wilson. God only knew what they were doing to Jerry at this very moment.

They would have to pay.

There was work to be done. Jonas and his whole rogue organization had to be dealt with. Jerry needed to be saved. But who could she call for help? The Justice Department was contaminated by its contact with Jonas. Which of her colleagues was really working for him? She couldn't be sure nor could she take the risk of being wrong. Who could Alice trust?

She had an idea. It was as good a bet as any. Alice picked up a phone and dialed a number. Moments later an operator answered, "Federal Bureau of Investigation." Alice was amazed at how calm she was. "I need to speak with an Agent Lowry."

Russell Lowry. The fed from Jerry's hospital room. The guy she caught tailing her when she left the hospital with Jerry hidden on the floor of the car. The operator was perfunctory. "The office is closed for the evening. It this an emergency?"

Alice started to get nervous. Had she made a mistake? What did she really know about Lowry? She hesitated, realizing that now she was thinking like Jerry. And maybe that wasn't such a bad thing. His "paranoia" had kept them alive through a wide variety of dangerous confrontations. In the end, however, even a person as tortured as Jerry was compelled to take a chance and trust someone. No one would make it in this world entirely on his own and Russ Lowry seemed as decent and grounded a guy as she had met in a long time.

Nevertheless she began to sweat. Let's establish some basics about old Russ right from the start. "Do you *have* an Agent Lowry in your New York office?"

"Yes."

Yes. A straight answer. Incredible. No ambiguities. No hidden meanings lurking in shadows. What a great thing to hear. Alice was home free. Or as close as someone in her position could be. "Then this is a goddamn emergency."

The man sat in his Kips Bay apartment on the East Side of Manhattan and read the newspaper after a long day's work. A phone on the table next to him began to ring. He picked it up quickly before it disturbed his sleeping wife. "Lowry."

"Agent Lowry, It's Lynn Mathews at the Bureau. I hate to disturb you at home, but I have an Alice Sutton on the phone from the Justice Department. She says it's an emergency."

Lowry scratched his thinning white hair. At sixty, nearing mandatory retirement, he was surprised to receive a late-night phone call. They usually went to younger agents. Quiet evenings were the privilege of seniority. Compounding the mystery, Agent Lowry didn't know an Alice Sutton. "Never heard the name." He considered his options. What the hell. He had nothing better to do. "Put her through."

In a windowless surveillance room at a secret location somewhere in Manhattan, the handsome young man Alice knew as Agent Lowry waited with a phone in his hands as technicians monitored the call. Together they listened to the FBI operator talking to Alice. "Go ahead, Miss Sutton." Alice's voice was strong but the relief she felt in making contact with the FBI was also evident "Agent Lowry?"

A technician nodded to the fake Agent Lowry and switched him into the conversation. "Alice, what can I do for you?"

In his Kips Bay apartment, the real Agent Lowry listened to the dial tone. "Hello? *Hello?*" He hung up the phone, puzzled and disappointed. His pulse had begun to race when he received the mysterious call and it had been a long time since he had enjoyed an adrenaline rush. For a few moments he had been excited by the prospect of getting back into the saddle again. On the other hand, he could see the advantage of staying inside his cozy building on a raw night and getting to bed on time. Lowry flipped on HBO and forgot all about Alice Sutton—whoever she was.

The elevator doors opened on the twenty-fourth floor of the downtown Federal Building. A building security guard led Alice, the man she knew as Agent Lowry, and six "FBI" agents down a hallway. They stopped in front of the entrance to the International Fund for Mergers and Acquisitions. As the guard fumbled with the lock, Lowry and his agents drew their guns and tensed up. When the door opened they burst inside ready for action.

But there was no one to shoot—no one to arrest. Just an empty floor of undecorated, unfurnished offices. No receptionist. No financial types discussing business. No work stations for the administrative assistants. No office with Henry Finch's name on the door. No Jonas.

A few scattered building materials—tarps, paint, and ladders—were placed indiscriminately around the vacant space. But that was it.

Alice was stunned.

The security guard showed his irritation at having been disturbed for such nonsense. "I told you. Been empty for a year."

Chapter 14

Jerry was back in the one place he prayed never to return to. He would rather have been killed back at Judge Sutton's estate.

The moldy tiles. The filthy windows. The chained doors. The freezing cells. Institutional hell. An asylum that was as insane as the maniacs it was built to house.

Yet Jerry could have dealt with all of it if it hadn't been for the torture of the hydrotherapy tank.

Held under water. Lungs searing. Throat choking. Limbs flailing. Lights burning down from above. Jonas's distorted face smirking down at him.

Only when Jerry's struggling ebbed did Jonas allow the goons to lift his head above the surface. Jerry gasped for breath but it didn't come immediately. His body was shutting down from the terrible abuse. He was dying, and Jonas was prolonging the process for his own entertainment.

Deprived of oxygen, the synapses in Jerry's brain fired off randomly and he babbled incoherently. "Monkey finger . . . shot Coca-Cola . . . Monkey shoot cola . . ."

A few minutes later Jerry's mind was functioning again and he knew what was happening to him. He wished he hadn't returned to consciousness. Jonas cupped Jerry's chin gently in his hands and turned his head so that their eyes met. "You've damaged my work, Jerry. You've touched upon it in your newsletter and so your subscribers are dead. You told Alice Sutton. She's dead as well."

Hearing the news of Alice's death, Jerry just wanted it all to end. "Then you can't hurt me anymore." If Jonas was going to kill him he might as well get on with it.

Jonas disagreed. "I'll be the judge of that." There was still important information that Jerry might provide. He placed the heel of his palm against Jerry's forehead, pausing before sending him back to hell. "Call it my own paranoia, but who else knows what we know?"

Jerry didn't say a word. He was frightened by the prospect of being forced underwater again but welcomed the oblivion that he hoped would soon overwhelm him.

Alice was dead. Worse, she had died because of him. That news was the most vicious torture Jonas could have devised. As he submerged, all fear left him. He deserved what was coming to him.

Alice, Lowry, the FBI agents, and security guard piled into the elevator on the twenty-fourth floor. Alice didn't know what was going on but she needed a private conversation with Lowry. "Can I talk to you a second?" Lowry told his men to go on, he'd follow in a few minutes.

When the elevator door closed, Alice looked almost helpless. "Do you believe me?"

"Yeah, I do."

"I want to believe in you too."

Lowry didn't understand. "What do you mean?"

Alice pulled a gun she had taken from one of Jonas's dead commandos and stuck it in Lowry's face. Suddenly she wasn't so helpless. She wanted answers. "Who's the deputy director of the FBI?" Lowry got mad. "You think we have time to fool around like this? Come on." Alice cocked back the hammer of her weapon. In case Lowry didn't know it by now, she was no pushover. "The deputy director."

He didn't know. Instead he shrugged. His cover was blown. "What gave me away?" If he lived through this episode it would be useful to know for future reference.

"Nothing. I was just making sure." Alice hadn't known anything definitely. She hadn't even been particularly suspicious of Lowry, in fact she liked him. She was certain, however, that Jerry wouldn't have accepted anything, or anybody, at face value. Jerry taught her to always read the shadows, and that lesson might have just saved her life. "So who are you?:"

Lowry said nothing and shook his head.

Now Alice was getting mad, "I'm going to find Jerry. *Who are you?* One of them?" She was ready to pull the trigger. That was abundantly clear to Lowry. It was time to defuse the situation. "It really doesn't matter who I am. Think CIA and an exponentiate. I'm a government employee and I've been watching Jerry for a while."

"And Jonas?"

"He's why I watch Jerry. Jerry's the bait for Jonas."

"He's shown himself." Alice was seething. How many people did Jonas get to kill before Lowry and whichever watchdog intelligence service he belonged to reined him in? "Why don't you arrest him or kill him or do whatever it is you do?"

It wasn't that easy. "Jonas builds assassins for a living. Several of whom may be in place already. We have to know who they are and who Jonas works for." The explanation that Lowry offered wasn't all that different from the one Alice had heard from Jonas. Jonas had provided Alice with textbook disinformation. He stuck close to the facts while altering a few fundamental points—such as who were the good guys and who were not.

"Jonas had my father killed, didn't he?"

"We think so."

"And where do you think Jerry is?" Lowry had no idea, but he wanted to know what Alice's plans were.

"I'm going to find him. Because he'd find me." It was all too clear that if she didn't look for Jerry, no one else would. The competing government agencies would have been happy to let him vanish. To them he was just another victim of a renegade program run amok. The unfortunate case of Jerry Fletcher was an embarrassment to the system and better forgotten.

Lowry wanted to help. The resources his agency could provide would be invaluable. But Alice declined his offer. The only person Alice fully trusted anymore was a person she had considered insane only hours earlier in the day.

Lowry pressed the issue. "At least let me give you a number. You can call me if you need me."

As he reached into his pocket, Alice cold-cocked him with the barrel of the 9mm. She wasn't taking any chances. As Lowry crumpled, his business card fluttered to the ground. So he hadn't been reaching for a weapon after all. Too bad. She hoped his headache wasn't serious. Alice scooped up the card and ran to make her escape down the emergency stairway.

Lowry hit the ground in a semiconscious state. Remembering that Jerry had knocked him out in much the same way, he figured the two were meant for each other. Before he passed out Lowry made a mental note to demand a raise.

He didn't get paid enough to take all this abuse.

Chapter 15

Her entrance into Jerry's old apartment building was hardly subtle. Uncertain about what she would find, Alice crept through the abandoned building with a gun in one hand and a flashlight in the other. She was ready for anything that came her way.

Alice stopped at a door covered with yellow police tape that declared the apartment to be an "arson investigation site." The room was sealed with a series of two-by-four wooden planks. Wrenching a pair of them off, Alice entered the apartment.

It was as empty as the last time she had been there. Other than the mattress placed underneath the trapdoor to Jerry's real living quarters upstairs, it was barren.

Alice wasn't sure what she was searching for but she knew exactly where to look. Shining the flashlight against the Wonderwall, Alice examined the astonishing collage, desperate for a clue. Somewhere among all the headlines, the photographs, and the images of destruction and betrayal, somewhere hidden in this visual diary of a society gone mad was a clue to what had happened to Jerry. Alice didn't have a logical reason for believing in the importance of the wall, she simply relied on a recently discovered sense of instinct.

Maybe the clue was in the photograph of her jumping the rails with Johnny Dancer. The picture made her uncomfortable because Alice didn't know how to feel about it. She hated Jerry for having spied on her. Yet she was also grateful that he had captured this moment of joy. Alice couldn't remember ever having felt so happy, but the proof was on the wall. In a strange way the picture served as a lighthouse to the lost ship at sea that she had become. It showed Alice how to find her way back to the person she once had been.

How could she not be grateful to someone for such a gift?

Something else about the Wonderwall moved her. While Alice was not especially interested in interpretive art, she couldn't miss Jerry's intention in the way he juxtaposed a huge, ecstatic image of herself against the myriad tragedies of modern life. Alice understood that to Jerry she represented the hope and redemption for a world crippled by its own savagery. Alice was humbled by the power of his love for her.

Yet if there was a message on the Wonderwall regarding what had happened to Jerry, Alice couldn't figure it out. The more she stared at it the more frustrated she became. To be so close to the truth but not to be able to help him infuriated her.

Alice continued to examine the images without success. Just as she was about to give up, her flashlight illuminated an image in a corner near the floor. It took a moment for her to understand what she was looking at and then she perceived it for what it was.

It was one of Jerry's most skillfully rendered drawings.

She found herself staring at a frightening image of a room. Drawn with colored pencils, the picture was as chilling a sight as Alice had ever seen. In the foreground sat a sinister-looking chair with straps, hooks, and other restraining apparatus meant to keep a victim sitting still. Littered on the floor around the chair were macabre syringes—some with distended needles, some with puddles of a menacing liquid beneath.

The middle portion of the picture featured a shaft of blinding light that bore down on the chair. It reminded Alice of the Nightsun equipment from the assault at her father's estate. It was an oppressive image and conveyed a sense of searing pain.

A brilliant glow hovered around the scene and washed out any features in the immediate vicinity of the chair. Alice studied the picture closely, desperate for a clue that Jerry might have left behind. An elaborately designed mirror drawn on a wall of the room caught her attention. Was there a figure reflected in its glass? Was it a face? Was it Jonas? She couldn't be sure.

Alice's heart sank further when she spotted a tiny title printed at the base of the picture: "In My Room." Alice was overwhelmed by a sense of sadness she hadn't known since her father's murder. What had Jerry been put through? How had he survived? No wonder his mind was confused. No wonder he saw hidden agendas in every face, conspiracies in every shadow.

Alice was more determined than ever to rescue him. She didn't know exactly how she was going to do it. But if she had to die trying, that was exactly what she was going to do.

Something grabbed her attention as she noticed a window drawn into the background of the room.

There was something in the window—a sight that looked vaguely familiar.

The view looked out upon three red-and-white striped bars.

Alice looked more closely. No. Not bars. Instead they were something she had seen with Jerry less than twenty-four hours earlier.

Alice ran from the apartment. She knew time was running out for Jerry, and she finally had an idea how to help him.

The Blazer slowed as it drove over the Queensboro Bridge near where Jerry had "abandoned" his Monte Carlo. The view of Manhattan and Queens was stunning. But Alice wasn't interested in the skyline. Instead her eyes locked on the three red-and-white smoke stacks of the Con Edison power plant that sat on the Manhattan shoreline.

The red-and-white stacks matched the view from the window drawn on the Wonderwall. Wherever Jerry's "room" was—he could see the Con Edison stacks in the distance. She was getting warmer.

The next step was to figure out which building had the view that Jerry had drawn. Alice ruled out anything in Queens. The distance across the East River was too great—the smokestacks would have been much smaller from the outer borough.

Alice considered a number of buildings in Manhattan but dismissed them. The angle was wrong. No. It was becoming clear. The room where Jerry had been tortured had to be located on Roosevelt Island—several square miles of land stuck in the middle of the East River. Formerly known as Welfare Island, it boasted an assortment of abandoned buildings, an underutilized psychiatric hospital, and at the far end upscale housing with a great panorama of Manhattan.

Alice tried to visualize the perspectives from different hospital buildings on the southern end of Roosevelt Island. But try as she might, she couldn't match the view from the Wonderwall to any of the illuminated windows. It didn't make sense. The only structure that seemed to duplicate the position pictured on the Wonderwall was located in a dark, empty, seemingly abandoned wing of an outlying hospital building. How was that possible? More to the point, if Jerry had once been held prisoner in this annex, there was no logical reason to think he was there now. It didn't look as though anyone had been inside the building for years.

It didn't add up but Alice knew in her heart that it was true. If she was wrong the consequences would be grave. Jerry was in serious trouble and she knew the clock was ticking. Alice prayed that Jerry could hold on just a little bit longer and she floored the accelerator.

Alice swung into the hospital driveway but didn't stop. She kept going. Even though it was not late at night, the main entrance was protected by a security guard. She would have to find another way in.

Driving to the rear of the complex, Alice found her way into the building along the same path Jerry had used for his escape not that many days previously. The loading bay through which food, laundry, and medical supplies were shipped into the hospital was unguarded.

Alice parked nearby and fell into step behind a delivery man carting goods on a hand truck.

Alice found herself inside an institutional kitchen

and immediately ducked behind a massive dish-
washer while she tried to figure out where to go. The
kitchen itself was fairly quiet. A middle-aged woman
checked in the food delivery against an invoice and
seemed totally involved in her work. She wouldn't be
any trouble.

But before Alice moved along she found herself
staring at something just a few feet in front of her. An
apron hung on a hook with the name of the hospital
stenciled on its front. The stained garment was
draped in such a way that Alice couldn't read the
print. What should have read "Property of the Germaine O. Nicols Mental Hospital" looked to her as if
it said "Ger O. Nicols Mental Hospital."

There was something familiar about the name but
Alice wasn't sure what it was. She stepped over to the
apron and folded it a little differently.

And then it all made sense. The puzzle had come
together.

"Ger-O-Ni-M-O." Alice took a deep breath and almost shouted out loud. Instead she enjoyed a silent
victory. "Geronimo!" The same word Jerry had
scratched onto the hospital nightstand the night Alice
had switched his chart. The same word he used to describe love. If she had any doubts that this was the
right place, they were immediately dispelled.

Alice slipped out of the kitchen, waited for a nurse
to round a corner, and then padded quickly down a
corridor.

A door was open. Alice looked inside. Three middle-aged men lay on their backs sound asleep. Even
though they were unconscious, it was clear to Alice
they were tormented. Sleep provided no relief. Alice
shuddered and crept past a nurses' station while the
woman on duty watched the late news.

Another door was ajar. A black-and-white television played softly. Alice slipped in and found three women patients. Two slept in beds while a third sat on the floor, rocking back and forth quietly chanting to herself.

Alice had seen some awful sights that day. But the groaning inmates on this ward were even more horrific than the bodies at her father's estate. She had to find Jerry—and fast.

As Alice watched the chanting woman she gradually became aware of a news report on the television. The network had interrupted regular coverage and an anchorman was reading the story. "The President had left the area only moments earlier and is currently safe in Germany. Again the quake in southern Turkey measured 7.3 on the Richter scale. Thousands are feared missing or dead . . ."

The room began to spin as the implications of what Alice just heard sunk in. It couldn't be. It was too incredible to even contemplate. The plot to kill the President by triggering an earthquake in Turkey from the orbiting space shuttle was the front page story of Jerry's latest issue of *Conspiracy Theory*. It was the article that had set the whole madness of the last several days into motion. Was such a thing possible or was this the most bizarre of coincidences?

A sick feeling grew in her stomach. Alice had learned something since Jerry had come into her life. She no longer believed in coincidence. The assassination attempt had happened just as he had predicted. Was it the work of Jonas? That was the only answer. It also explained why Jerry's subscribers—all of whom had received a copy of his *Conspiracy Theory* newsletter—were dead.

Jerry needed her. Right now. Ten minutes ago. As

she bolted through the hallways of the decrepit mental hospital Alice prayed she wasn't too late.

It was a nightmare. Alice ran through the empty hallways accompanied by the groans and screaming of the incarcerated patients. She had no idea where to go, she just knew she had to keep moving. She would know when she got there.

Alice climbed a flight of stairs and entered another ward. As she started down the corridor, she ran right into a hulking orderly. The man was gigantic and didn't look happy. He glared at Alice with his hands on his hips. "Can I help you?"

The best way to deal with a low-level authority figure was to pull rank. Alice gave it a shot and flashed her Justice Department identification. The man didn't respond. He simply stood there squarely, not hostile, not polite, just unimpressed. Alice pulled out her wallet and offered him her standard issue—a crisp one-hundred-dollar bill. Bribery could work wonders too.

Alice got down to business. "I need to see any new patients you've gotten in the last twelve hours." She noticed his attention was on the 9mm in her hand. Alice softened, realizing the man was more than likely terrified. "You can say I threatened to shoot you." The guard relaxed. "Sounds like you got it covered. Come on."

Jonas had once said something to him about a place without hope. Now Jerry understood what he meant. All he wanted at this point was to die, but Jonas wasn't even going to allow him that liberty. The torture session in the hydrotherapy tank had been endless. Pain, grief, and suffocation were all that existed in

Jerry's universe. He lay on the cold, filthy floor of the hydrotherapy room, balled up in a fetal position.

He was closer than he had ever been before to getting his final wish. If he lived long enough, he might make it to the next appointment with Jonas and the hydrotherapy tank, but he certainly couldn't survive another session of torture.

Jimmy Williams was trying his best. After fifteen years working the night shift at the hospital he thought he had seen it all. But the polite and beautiful young woman with the nasty-looking firearm was something new. He led Alice to a second-floor ward and let her peer through a tiny window in a door. "In here. White guy in his thirties." The patient had his back to them and Alice indicated that she wanted to see the man's face. Jimmy unlocked the door and they entered.

From behind Alice couldn't be sure. She leaned down and touched the man's shoulder as gently as she could, hoping not to frighten him. The man's head shot up to meet hers and grinned lasciviously. It wasn't Jerry. The straitjacketed madman struggled wildly as Alice shook her head with pity before leaving the room.

They started down another hallway, but were rapidly running out of patients and options. The orderly was sincere in his efforts but there wasn't much more he could do. Alice began to feel desperate. Jerry wasn't far away. But a close call wouldn't be much good to anyone. Alice knew that sooner or later whoever was keeping Jerry here against his will would discover she was here.

And that would mean the end of everything for both of them.

* * *

It wasn't a conscious decision. He had already slipped beyond the stage of awareness and active thinking. As Jerry lay with his head against the freezing cement floor some merciful portion of his brain decided to take him to a kinder place. There was no point being where he was. Instead, Jerry returned to a happy, even joyful memory.

Jerry watched Alice in his mind as she ran on her treadmill and sang along with the radio. He was pretty far gone, but Jerry wanted to sing too. His voice was weak but he did his best to participate in the duet. "You're just too good to be true. Too good to be true. Can't take my eyes off of you. You're like heaven to touch. Oh, baby, I need you so much."

"You okay?" Jimmy didn't know exactly what the problem was but it was clear that the young woman with the gun and the credentials was mixed up in some kind of pretty major difficulty.

Alice leaned against the railing on the wall, thinking she had reached the end of the road. She and the orderly had checked every patient who fitted Jerry's description. There was no one left. Still, she wouldn't allow herself to give up. There could be no surrender, for to do so would condemn Jerry to die. All she could do now was hope for a miracle.

Jimmy followed Alice as she started down a hallway they had already checked out. He tried to be helpful. "We got some new patients last week. You want to see them?"

Nice of him to offer but what was the point? Last week Jerry had been on the streets, fighting his lonely battle to keep Alice safe.

Alice waved off the orderly's suggestion and

stopped at the end of the hallway. Dawn began to break and she peered outside through the heavy mesh that protected the windows.

She had made a terrible mistake.

Alice had let Jerry down. He was outside in the city somewhere, not in here at all. Jerry was on his own and hunted by Jonas and his killers. How much time had she wasted? Could she have saved him if she hadn't been sidetracked by the picture of the red-and-white smokestacks?

"Look, I gotta get back to work." Jimmy was apologetic but began to wonder whether the woman who had just led him on a wild-goose chase actually belonged here—as a patient, not a visitor.

Before he could walk away, however, Alice spun around and grabbed his arms. "Did you hear that?"

He hadn't heard a thing. Audio hallucinations represented a major symptom of disconnection from reality. How many times had Jimmy listened as doctors explained the facts to the confused relatives of patients? He stared back at Alice with pity. The lady was making it all too clear that she could benefit from some treatment. Jimmy would have to get the doctor on duty to check her out before she left.

Jimmy took a step toward Alice, hoping to calm her down. He had a lot of experience in this field and knew his large size and soothing voice could work wonders. The only thing that bothered him was that he never had dealt with someone carrying a gun before. Still, the young woman didn't look dangerous—just frightened.

For all of his experience, he jumped a foot off the ground when Alice suddenly pulled back beyond reach. She looked around the hallway with a fervor bordering on panic. Then she stopped and her attention rested on an air duct. Grabbing a stray laundry cart, she pushed it underneath the duct, climbed up on it, and pressed her ear against the grill.

A tiny, lonely voice echoed through the system. "You're just too good to be true. Can't take my eyes off of you."

Alice wasn't certain. Was it Jerry? She strained to hear. "I need you, baby, and if it's quite all right . . ." Jerry was in such a battered state that Alice might never have recognized his voice. But weakened as he was, Jerry still managed to convey the strength and depth of his feeling for her in his delirious serenade.

It was Jerry. There could be no doubt. He was somewhere in the hospital complex and he was alive. Just.

Jerry still lay on the floor of the hydrotherapy room curled up in a fetal position. If he had been conscious he might have heard Alice's voice bouncing off the walls of the ancient ventilation system. She called his name but he was too far gone to notice.

Like a dying man in the desert, Jerry conjured up a comforting mirage in his head. It seemed he could actually hear Alice singing back to him. If he was going to die this would be the last thought of his life, and that was okay with him. Jerry was overwhelmed by the loveliness of her voice and then he felt a chasm in his soul open up all over again. She was dead.

Jerry was semiconscious again. His eyes opened. Something, he didn't know what, pulled him back from the void. He could hear a woman's voice singing somewhere in the distance.

"Can't take my eyes off of you."

There it was again. His mind began to function a little more clearly and he was pretty sure it wasn't a delusion after all. But how could it be Alice? Jonas had killed her. Jerry sang more loudly. "You're just too good to be true."

"You're like heaven to touch."

She was alive. Jonas had lied to him. Jerry decided to live again too. It took all of his energy to pull himself up into a sitting position and look around the room for the source of Alice's voice.

All of Jimmy's suspicions were confirmed when the lady with the 9mm stood on the laundry cart singing into the air duct. It was sad to watch someone as lovely as she was suffer from such an obvious affliction. Jimmy moved toward her with a pacifying smile on his face. He didn't want to alarm the crazy woman but she needed help.

Alice didn't notice. As Jimmy reached up to take her arm, he suddenly began to fear for his own sanity. Was this kind of thing contagious? Jimmy stared at the grill over the air duct and heart a fragile voice singing back. "I love you, baby. And if it's quite all right . . ."

The crazy woman, who turned out not to be so crazy after all, sang more loudly, as though to encourage her partner. "I need you, baby. Through all the lonely nights."

Jimmy Williams had seen a lot during his career at the Germaine O. Nicols Hospital but never anything as strange and wonderful as this. He felt like singing along too.

Jerry pulled himself up against the soiled walls of the hydrotherapy room and listened to Alice. He began to feel anger. And then he felt something entirely different. It was an infinitely more powerful feeling.

Jonas was wrong. This horrible room, this modern-day torture chamber, was no longer a place without hope.

He stopped singing. "Alice?"

"Where are you?" It was a simple question and her voice promised deliverance.

Love could rescue.

"Here. North wing. First floor."

Jimmy saw Alice look to him for help but he was confused. It didn't make sense. Who would have put a patient in there? It was an abandoned section of the main building and off limits to the staff. "The north wing's closed off . . ." Alice wasn't buying it. He knew she expected him to take her there anyway. "Come on. This way."

Alice took his hand and jumped off the laundry cart. Jimmy led her at a run toward a section of the hospital that he had never once entered during his long employment.

It was easy to see why no one ever set foot in the north wing. The galvanized door that led to the off-limits area looked impenetrable. Furthermore, the heavy locking bracket that was riveted into the steel portal was equally imposing. There was no quiet way to get inside. Anybody who wanted to take the chance had to be willing to make a lot of noise and risk detection.

Alice nodded and Jimmy hammered the lock with a hefty fire extinguisher. It didn't budge. He tried again. Nothing. He smashed the extinguisher against the lock a third time, using all of his weight to emphasize the point. It shattered into pieces that flew across the floor at their feet.

Winded by his effort, Jimmy stood back while Alice

gingerly pushed open the door. She peered inside and shivered. the hallway leading into the north wing was dark and not deserted. Years of dirt and garbage covered the floor. Windows that were meant to bring in fresh air and light were shuttered. The air was stale and damp. If the steel door and heavy duty lock weren't enough to discourage a trespasser, the appearance of the hallway very well might.

Jimmy began to sweat. He still couldn't figure out what a patient might be doing in here. Whatever it was, it couldn't be good and he chose not to follow Alice inside. "This is as far as I go." He had a family to support and wasn't interested in whatever mystery might lurk within the structure of the north wing.

Alice understood. She didn't blame him. Alice didn't especially want to go any further herself. There was one thing he could do for her, however. "Get the police down here." He nodded. Alice wondered if the police would be up to the task of dealing with Jonas. She didn't think so. Alice swiftly weighed the options. Should she call Lowry. How could it hurt? If his agency was pursuing Jonas as he claimed, then Lowry might be able to provide assistance. But if Lowry had been lying to her, it wouldn't matter. Jonas and his troops would know soon enough that she was wandering around their lair. Alice handed Jimmy the card Lowry had given her earlier. "And call this number too."

Jimmy agreed and offered Alice an encouraging smile. As he ran for help, Alice made her way down the ominous corridor.

He needed to create a diversion. Alice was coming and Jonas's commandos had to be distracted. The adrenaline pumping through Jerry's body helped clear his mind and he began to formulate a plan.

Jerry was in no shape to do much of anything, however. He tried to stand up but was immediately overwhelmed by dizziness. He fell to his knees and without waiting to recover began crawling past the hydrotherapy tank toward a sink built into a wall.

As Jerry dragged himself along the floor, Alice made her way through the rundown hallways of the north wing. There was no way to know exactly where Jerry was. It would just have to be trial and error.

Alice stopped dead in her tracks. Did she hear footsteps coming in her direction? Someone was moving toward her at a near run. Alice ducked into a vacant room and let the man pass. Dressed in plainclothes, the man was one of Jonas's commandos and carried a lethal 9mm in his hands.

Alice's heart was pounding.

When the commando disappeared down the hallway, Alice ran from her hiding place and took off in the opposite direction.

Inside the hydrotherapy room, Jerry hauled himself through shards of broken glass and did his best to stay focused. His head was still spinning and the strength of his body was ebbing. The journey across ten feet of the torture chamber was endless. It seemed to him that he wasn't going to make it in time. He feared that one of Jonas's men would catch him during their normal rounds or he could simply collapse, leaving Alice on her own against a ruthless enemy.

His anxiety kept him going. Jerry was not going to let Alice down again.

When he finally reached the large set tub built into the wall, he was struggling to draw breath into his lungs. But there was no time to spare. He had to keep going. He had to grit it out. Jerry forced his back against a cold wall and braced his feet against the set tub. Calling upon every last drop of energy left in his body, Jerry began to yank on the input pipe leading into the bottom of the set tub. Nothing doing. He pulled hard. Sweat burst from his pores and the veins in his neck and face appeared near to bursting. The pipe groaned and creaked under the strain. Jerry wasn't sure he could do it. Was everything going to end in this futile effort? His anger built. Jerry focused on Jonas and the hydrotherapy torture. The pipe didn't give. Then Jerry thought of how Jonas would treat Alice if he was given the chance.

The pipe snapped. Water geysered across the room and its intense pressure caught Jerry in the face, leaving him sputtering for air.

A commando responded to the unexpected noise and peered through a small window into the room. The prisoner had ripped a sink from the wall. There was water everywhere. The guard was furious and wanted answers. "What the hell are you doing?"

He unlocked the door to the hydrotherapy room and was determined to teach the prisoner a lesson he would never forget.

The guard entered and kept his 9mm machine pistol trained on the soggy captive. Spray from the broken pipe hit him in the face. As the guard wiped his eyes, Jerry lunged at him.

He didn't have a chance. The guard was too well trained and clubbed Jerry down with the butt of his gun. As Jerry writhed on the floor, the guard gestured toward the broken pipe. "Where the hell did you think this was going to get you?"

As if to reply, Jerry stopped thrashing around and smiled up at his perplexed captor.

Alice appeared in the doorway behind the commando.

Inspired, Jerry pulled himself to his feet. Where had he thought breaking the pipe would get him? "Right where we are now."

The guard lifted his gun to wallop Jerry one more time. He froze, however, when he felt Alice press the muzzle of her 9mm into the back of his neck.

"Drop it." Alice's voice was steady. In control. The guard did as he was told. "Turn around." As he obeyed, Jerry grabbed a piece of pipe, swung for the bleachers, and struck Jonas's man in the back of the head. The guard collapsed. Jerry went down too. The exertion had been too much for him and he sprawled across the floor. Alice rushed to his side. "Are you okay, Jerry?"

"I am now." He certainly was. In fact he was more than okay. Jerry Fletcher was as deliriously happy as a half-dead man could be.

Two cars pulled up to the main entrance of the Germaine O. Nicols Mental Hospital. Agent Lowry jumped out of one and Flip Tanner climbed out of the other. Jerry wouldn't have recognized the newsstand operator from Times Square, for he was no longer wheelchair-bound. In fact, Flip moved with a grace and athleticism of a man in top physical condition.

It was a funny thing. While Jerry's mind had been muddled by endless conspiracy theories and he mistrusted almost everyone he met, the one person he had never doubted was his friend Flip Tanner. For all of Jerry's heightened awareness and self-professed expertise, he had never broken Flip's cover.

Whether or not Jerry would ever get a chance to laugh at this irony remained an open question. He and Alice still had to survive the night—and it was unclear whether or not the arrival of Lowry and Tanner would improve or hurt their chances.

The elderly security guard slept in his chair at the main entrance to the hospital. The night shift was his favorite and was a reward for years of service. At nine o'clock the front doors to the lobby were chained shut. The Germaine O. Nicols Hospital was a long-term care facility and never took in emergency cases. There were plenty of other medical centers to handle that business.

The old guard would normally sleep for several hours before retiring to the kitchen to talk with friends over a snack. On some nights, if he was feeling spry, he would go up to the wards and flirt with the nurses.

On this particular night, however, the old guard would not get the chance to enjoy his routine.

The explosive sound of Russ Lowry shouldering open the front door woke the guard from his nap. The old man didn't know what was happening and was too shocked to dial the police. All he knew was that someone was trying to force their way in, which was unusual in hospitals catering to the psychologically challenged. Security in a facility like the Germaine O. Nicols Hospital was usually designed to keep patients in, not to keep people out.

The old guard wasn't too worried, however, for the chain that kept the doors from opening was holding just fine. He picked up the phone and was about to dial the police when he saw something that made him hang the receiver back in its cradle.

While Lowry held the door slightly ajar, Flip Tanner lit a blow torch and began to cut through the chain links. Moments later the chain fell harmlessly to the ground. Lowry and Tanner burst into the lobby and charged past the sputtering old guard without saying a word or harming a hair on his head.

In the north wing of the hospital, Alice helped Jerry to his feet. He was feeling much better but he was still beaten and battered. "Can you walk, Jerry?" He took her hand for support and changed the subject. "Kiss me."

"What?" Alice was prepared to deal with many eventualities but this one startled her.

"Kiss me for luck."

They were in the middle of a life-and-death crisis and Jerry was putting the moves on her? "Jerry, you're crazy."

"Certifiable. Come on. Kiss me. Then we'll go."

Alice could only stare as Jerry closed his eyes and puckered up his lips. All she wanted to do was get out of the north wing as quickly as humanly possible. She knew, however, that Jerry wasn't going to move until they kissed. Alice leaned forward and gave him a per-functory peck on the lips.

She was about to pull away when she took a good look at Jerry's face. The madness over the previous months had kept her from noticing just how good-looking he really was. What was more, when Jerry claimed to love her he did much more than just talk. Jerry had proven his devotion to her in a truly tragic, noble way. Alice kept her mouth where it was. Sens-ing this, Jerry's eyes opened and they held each other's gaze. After all they had been through to-gether, Alice realized that she really *did* want to kiss him. Not just a peck or something polite but a real kiss that would tell him that she returned his affection.

Alice leaned a little more closely to Jerry's lips. Jerry came a bit closer to hers. Now it was time for them to close the gap in a mutual gesture of warmth.

Jerry and Alice were so entirely focused on their feelings for each other, however, that neither heard Jonas as he entered the room. They couldn't miss his menacing voice, however. "Jerry, you continually amaze me."

Jerry and Alice froze. Jonas stood in the doorway, flanked by two of his commandos. Jerry had a lot of reasons to hate Jonas, but the idea that he might never get to kiss Alice because of this most recent interruption really infuriated him.

They were in a tough spot and the future didn't look bright. All Jerry knew was that Jonas would never get to lay a hand on Alice. He didn't know how he could stop Jonas, but Jerry also knew that it would take more than bullets to keep him from protecting the woman he loved.

Jonas gestured for Alice to drop her gun. As she placed it on the ground, gunshots could be heard ricocheting off the walls somewhere in the dingy expanse of the north wing. Jonas grabbed Alice's gun from the floor, aimed it at Jerry's chest, and ordered his men to find out what was happening.

Alice was in a defiant mood. If Jonas was going to defeat them, she wanted him to be aware that she had uncovered the truth. "You had my father murdered, didn't you?" Jonas, as always, was cordially malevolent. "You're a remarkable girl, Alice. I'm sorry it has to end this way."

More gunfire could be heard in the corridors. Jonas looked away quickly to see what was happening. For the first time since Alice had met him, Jonas looked vaguely worried. Whatever the source of the gunfire, it was now substantially closer than it had been before.

Lowry and Tanner were moving swiftly through the rubble-strewn corridors of the north wing. Their weapons drawn, they infiltrated the facility with the expertise of a team that had worked together many times before in the past.

There were several dead men left in their wake as they were confronted by the troops who had just been ordered by Jonas to investigate the shooting. The commandos opened fire. Tanner and Lowry shot back. It was a fierce battle. All four men were highly trained battle-scarred veterans. They were the best of the best—the top men of the nation's military and intelligence services.

And they were all trying to kill each other.

A tense Jonas looked in the direction of the gunfire. It was now disturbingly near.

While he was distracted, Alice leapt at him, knowing it would be her only chance. She didn't think it through and it wasn't necessarily a logical thing to do. A more considered decision would have had her waiting to see who was shooting a path through the corridors. Maybe help was on its way. Maybe it was the police. But Alice knew in her heart that even if rescuers were on their way, Jonas wouldn't let Jerry and her live.

For a brief second she had the advantage. Alice tried to wrench the gun from Jonas's grip and while he was off balance she almost succeeded. But Jonas quickly regained the upper hand. Several vicious punches to the head and torso sent Alice reeling back across the floor, where she collapsed against obsolete therapeutic equipment.

Alice tried to pull herself to her feet but was too dizzy. She slipped on the floor. A cart holding Jonas's syringes and vials of hallucinogens toppled over with her. Glass shattered everywhere. Alice lay on the cold tiles without moving.

Jonas stepped toward her, lifted a gun, and aimed it at her heart. To some degree he was impressed by her fighting spirit. While his injuries were painful they were not serious enough to truly anger him. His decision to kill Alice was not emotional, for the truth was that Jonas never lost enough control to get angry. Instead it was simply business. Alice knew more about him than she should. Jonas couldn't allow her to live.

Before he could open fire, however, Jerry grabbed Jonas's right forearm and his throat. Jonas had allowed himself to be distracted by Alice's attack and was caught off guard. It wasn't that he had forgotten Jerry was in the room, however. Instead, he assumed that Jerry was so enfeebled by the hydrotherapy session that he no longer posed a threat.

Jonas was in for a surprise of his own making.

Despite a broken body and a wounded spirit, Jerry called upon inner resources of strength that were only available to him because of the training Jonas had given him long ago.

Engaged in a death grip, the two men stumbled across the room. Jerry had one objective and that was to push Jonas as far away from Alice as possible. Once she was safe he would figure out what to do next.

The decision was taken away from him, however, as both men fell backward into the hydrotherapy tank.

Whether it was the reimmersion in frigid waters that had nearly killed him so many times before, or an accumulated fury toward Jonas for his treachery, Jerry was powered by a rage that transcended his wounds.

As Jonas fought for breath, Jerry held him under the surface of the water, drowning him. Jonas couldn't die quickly enough as far as Jerry was concerned.

The world was upside down. Jonas was underwater, looking up at the distorted face of Jerry Fletcher. He tried to master his growing sense of panic. He was trained. He was not wounded. He could get through this.

But when his lungs started to beg for oxygen, Jonas's discipline wavered. His face contorted and he suddenly became aware that Jerry might win this round. It seemed inconceivable. Jonas was the master. Jerry the student. Jonas was the keeper. Jerry was the prisoner. Yet Jonas was drowning in a torture chamber he had designed. He was staggered by the situation. His thought process began to seize up. This. Could. Not. Be. *Happening.* Jonas breathed in water and he screamed silently under the surface just as Jerry had a few hours earlier.

As his hands began to clench spasmodically, Jonas gradually became aware that there was something in his fingers. It was cold. Steel. Salvation. Jonas was still holding his 9mm automatic. His body was weakening rapidly but in the last surge of strength Jonas pushed the muzzle toward Jerry's chest and fired twice.

As his consciousness wavered, Jonas could hear the two bullets torpedo up through the water with a high-pitched whine. He didn't know how it was possible, but Jonas realized he must have missed, for

Jerry's frenzy was undiminished. Jonas couldn't pull the trigger again. The energy in his body dwindled. The end was near.

Jonas made a last effort to escape before passing out. To his relief the resistance lessened. Jonas's mouth broke the surface. He breathed in air. Then he was forced down again, but the pressure on his chest wasn't what it was. Jonas got another mouthful of oxygen and then realized he was being rained on by a shower of red. Blood. Jerry's blood.

Jerry hadn't felt the bullets hitting him but he could feel the life draining from his body. He saw the water turning a ruby color. His chest was a dark, soggy crimson. Jerry had vowed earlier that even bullets wouldn't stop him. he was close to fulfilling his task. Just a little more. If he could only keep Jonas underwater a few minutes longer, Alice would be safe. It was increasingly difficult to focus but Jerry tried. Protect Alice. Didn't matter what happened to him. Save Alice.

The sudden lurching pressure on his chest forced Jonas deeper into the freezing waters of the hydrotherapy tank. It occurred to him that this might be the last sensation he would ever feel. Jerry seemed stronger than ever, and Jonas was no longer any match for the great weight that was drowning him.

But suddenly the force wasn't holding him down. Instead it slipped slightly to the side. Jonas realized that Jerry had passed out and fallen on top of him. Jonas tore Jerry's hand away from his throat and forced himself to the surface. Now it was time to deal with Jerry Fletcher and Alice Sutton once and for all.

He never even got to enjoy a first breath.

Five bullets pumped into his chest and Jonas was dead before he fell back into the water.

The cold of the hydrotherapy tank woke Jerry from his stupor and he held out a hand to Alice. She dropped the gun and helped him out of the water. For a moment, Jerry stood on his own two feet and smiled at her. Alice was alive. The threat was gone. He had fulfilled his promise to her father. Then he crumpled to the floor.

Alice was by his side in a flash and could see he was fading all too quickly. She shouted to anybody who might hear her, "Help! Somebody help me!" Alice cradled Jerry's head in her lap and all he seemed to want to do was to look at her. She begged him, "Don't die on me, Jerry. Okay?"

"I can't promise you anything."

Alice began to cry. There was so much she had to tell him. So much she had to thank him for. "You've been my best friend for years and I didn't even know you were out there."

They shared a smile. Jerry was overwhelmed by a sense of bliss. "Geronimo."

"It's this place, isn't it?"

Jerry tried to explain. "Not anymore. Geronimo is love. And love gives you wings. We can fly away from here."

How she wished they could. But Jerry was slipping. This was a hospital. Where were the doctors? Where were the police? "Don't do this to me, Jerry."

"I don't know why I love you. But I know that I do." His tone was almost apologetic. As though he wasn't the one who was dying. As if he were saying he was sorry for putting her through terrible stress.

Alice lowered her head toward his. Her heart was stripped bare. There was only one thing she wanted to say and she hated herself for having taken so long to come to this realization. "I love you too."

"Now she tells me." Jerry sighed with joy and resignation. His eyes shut.

Alice held him tightly until she was aware of footsteps approaching from the hallway. Without lessening her embrace, she turned her head to see who was coming. It was Russ Lowry and Flip Tanner. She pleaded with them, the desolation in her heart apparent in her voice. "Help him. Please."

Minutes later, Alice was caught in a madhouse outside the psychiatric facility. Policemen and federal agents swarmed over the grounds. Alice watched in horror as Jerry was loaded into a Medivac helicopter. The medical technicians stepped back as he was defibrillated and his body jerked wildly as the electricity coursed through his system.

A cop slammed the doors shut and signaled to the pilot. The rotors picked up speed. A small windstorm blew dust everywhere. Alice could not longer see clearly and felt herself being blown around by forces greater than herself.

She didn't care. Alice rushed for the helicopter as it lifted off. "Wait! Wait for me!" Lowry and Flip Tanner charged after her and grabbed Alice before she hurt herself. As the Medivac flew off into the night, she tried to release herself from their grasp but they were too strong for her.

When the realization set in that Jerry was out of reach, Alice stopped. Lowry and Tanner tried to comfort her but she was beyond their help. Overwhelmed by all she had been through, Alice collapsed into Tanner's arms.

The two men kept her from falling and led her away to a waiting car.

It was all over.

The President was alive. Jonas was dead. And Jerry was battling for his life.

Alice would have to settle for that. It was time for the healing process to begin.

Chapter 16

A low winter sun cast a weak light over the gray landscape of a small Connecticut town. The world seemed an empty place—no people, no birds— just barren trees and gravestones.

A chilly gloom pervaded Alice Sutton's coat and emphasized her already melancholy mood.

Alice stood beside the freshly turned earth of a new grave.

Jerry Fletcher had lost his last fight.

Alice was alone and tried to come to terms with the loss of a man she had learned to love only when it was too late. A man who gave his life for hers. A man who suffered not only terrible physical pain but the most serious psychological torment, on her behalf. What had the lonely vigils been like for Jerry when he had watched over her? What had it been like to go home to the miserable warren of files and yellowing newspaper headlines? What had it been like to live with the constant, overpowering sense of imminent danger?

Alice took some small comfort in knowing that Jerry's last moments of awareness were spent with her. She knew that he had been happy. More than happy. As delirious with joy as the photograph he had taken of her on horseback and then pasted onto the Wonderwall.

Alice wondered about what might have been if Jerry had lived. Could her love have rescued him? Would Jerry's mind have healed? A bereavement counselor had told her that Jerry would probably have been a hopeless case. Once a person was that far gone they rarely returned. If that was so, then Alice at least found consolation in knowing Jerry was free from his torment. At some level he was finally at peace.

"You got away, Jerry. They'll never find you now."

She couldn't say anything more. Tears began to overwhelm her, but Alice held them in check. "Get a hold of yourself, baby."

Alice stared at the grave for another moment before turning and walking away. She never looked back.

It was midweek and the stable at the Ox Ridge Hunt Club was quiet. The stillness was broken, however, when a large, beautiful horse began to whinny with excitement. Someone was approaching the magnificent animal and he was as thrilled as a horse could be.

Alice placed a hand on her horse's snout and looked him over. He looked great and Alice was pleased the club had looked after him in her absence. Even the stall was immaculate. She didn't forgive herself for ignoring him but she was happy to see that Johnny Dancer hadn't been neglected. "J.D., I'm back. If you'll have me."

Johnny stomped a hoof while Alice began to gently stroke his neck. She had not seen her horse since shortly after her father's death. It had been far too long and both of them had suffered for want of the other.

Their reunion was interrupted by a rough-looking groom who had been surprised to hear Johnny neigh. The groom hadn't worked at the club for long and had never heard the horse utter a sound before. As far as he knew, Johnny was a silent, sad animal. "Can I help you with something?"

Alice resented the intrusion and snapped at the groom haughtily, "You got a saddle around here? This is my horse."

The groom was surprised. "I've never seen you here before." Alice sighed, reached into her pocket, and pulled out her trademark hundred-dollar bill. Money facilitated everything. A hundred bucks would let this kid know who she was and he would do exactly what she wanted.

The groom had moved closer to the stall, however, and didn't notice the bribe. Instead, he examined a minor cut on the animal's leg. It was healing nicely.

Alice was about to thrust the cash into his hand and then hesitated. She couldn't do it. She knew she had been making a terrible mistake. Alice could no longer go through life buying cooperation whenever she needed it. There was more to dealing with people than purchasing their obedience and affection, even if it was a ruthlessly efficient practice.

Jerry had never been interested in money and he had done more for her than any other person she had ever known. Alice understood in that moment that life was not meant to be spent avoiding people. If life was about anything it was about dealing with them, learning about what they liked and loved and trying to share the short time everyone had together.

The money went back into her pocket. Alice tried another tact. "Could you help me out? Please."

The groom had a poor first impression of Alice. Whoever she was, he hadn't appreciated her arrogant manner. He could see, however, that Alice felt bad about her rudeness. He softened immediately. "I think I can find a saddle for that horse."

Alice rode Johnny Dancer into the riding ring. Both of them were tentative at first, for it had been a long time and each had to get used to the other again.

Soon, Alice and Johnny were reacquainted and cantered around the corral with rapidly growing confidence. Their bond had not diminished. Alice and Johnny belonged together and they were lost in the moment.

Together, they were taking the first steps down the road to recovery and Alice focused her attention on the fence that surrounded the riding area. Clearly, Johnny Dancer wanted to make the jump. All that was necessary was for her to agree. Alice considered her options and then leaned forward and whispered into Johnny's ear, "Geronimo."

Geronimo. Love. Gives you wings. Sets you free.

Rider and horse galloped toward the fence, picking up speed with every step. With a natural ease, Alice and Johnny flew over the barrier and charged across the fields that lay beyond the corral.

They were free and they left the past behind them.

But they were not alone.

Someone was watching.

A black Chevy Suburban drove along a rural road, following Alice and her horse. The car's windows were tinted black and the passengers hidden from view.

If Alice had noticed the Suburban she would have remembered the fleet of cars used by Jonas and his troops. She would have ridden away from the road and tried to escape the deadly tentacles of Jonas's rogue agency.

But she never had the chance.

Sophisticated surveillance equipment captured her within its view and watched as Alice rode her horse in all innocence. Suspecting nothing. Unaware that someone was pursuing. Johnny Dancer was a fine horse but he would not be able to outrun the anonymous Suburban. The car followed as though its occupants were waiting for the perfect moment to make their kill.

If Jerry Fletcher had still been alive, he never would have let Alice put herself in such a vulnerable position. He would have reminded her to always be aware of the surroundings, to always be alert to an approaching threat.

While Jerry was never far from Alice's mind, the sense of dread and vigilance he advocated had lessened. While riding Johnny Dancer, Alice could begin to forget the terror of the last few days and could actually enjoy the moment.

A tinted window in the Suburban was lowered. It would take less than an instant for a single shot to be fired and the last witness to the whole embarrassing affair would be forever silent.

Startlingly intense eyes stared at her from the moving car. They were locked on their target. They didn't blink. Their concentration was complete. "She's okay."

The voice that accompanied the blue eyes was conflicted in more ways than one, for the man to whom the voice belonged was supposed to be "dead," but in truth he was very much alive.

Jerry Fletcher had survived and was thrilled to see Alice looking so well. On the other hand, he was solemn because it would be a long time—if ever—before he could let Alice know that he was actually still alive.

Jerry watched her ride and steeled himself for the difficult mission that awaited him.

Alice galloped through the open fields. For the first time in ages she enjoyed the sunshine and began to remember all the good things in life. She had been trapped in the darkness for too long, until Jerry Fletcher careened into her life and set her free.

As she rode she sang silently to herself.

"You're just too good to be true . . ."

Jerry watched as Alice smiled gloriously. Her head arched backward as she let the sun warm her face. Alice lifted her arms to the sky in a gesture of joy and hope for the future.

Jerry had seen this jubilation in Alice once before. He had captured it on film and had made it a part of his Wonderwall. It was the image of faith and redemption amidst the anarchy and despair of a world at war with itself.

And it would not have been an exaggeration to say that Jerry shared a portion of Alice's elation.

For long ago he had made a promise to Judge Sutton—that he would protect his dying friend's daughter. Jerry had kept his word.

That was all that mattered.

Jerry Fletcher, a man transformed into a killer, a man whose soul had been stolen, had wrenched it back and in the process had restored himself to life.

Jerry said good-bye to Alice and raised his tinted window. As the Suburban picked up speed, Jerry softly crooned the song that had liberated him from his incarceration. He looked straight ahead and began to map out strategies for the work that lay before him. "As long as everyone thinks I'm dead, then whoever Jonas worked for, they'll leave Alice alone. She'll be safe. Right?"

From behind the steering wheel, Russ Lowry grinned into the rearview mirror while Flip Tanner swiveled around in the front seat and offered a reassuring smile. "Uh, huh. You got it."

Jerry was no longer fighting on his own. He had joined a new team and their mission was clear: track down Jonas's superiors and the surviving members of his rogue operation and bring them to justice.

For the moment Jerry would have to love Alice from afar. If he remained "dead," then Jonas's colleagues wouldn't feel threatened and wouldn't pursue people who were close to him. Until the new goal was accomplished it was the only method for Jerry to continue protecting the woman he cherished.

It was an enormously difficult task, but Jerry was confident he would succeed.

He had no choice.

It was time to get to work. "Thanks for letting me see her one last time."

Lowry floored the accelerator and the Suburban raced away from Alice and her horse. "That's our end of the bargain, Jerry."

Jerry Fletcher was ready. After trying for so long to find someone who would listen, he now had an attentive audience. He would tell Lowry and Tanner everything he knew about Jonas, the ULTRA program, and the shadowy organizations that caused havoc in the world. All the information he gathered, and all the information he had forgotten, was beginning to come back to him.

Jerry, Lowry, and Tanner were all satisfied. They had a deal and working together they might make a difference.

It would be a long road and every day he would think of Alice Sutton. He would miss her terribly. Jerry knew that he would reminisce about the short time they had had together, when Alice's radiance had brightened his world and freed him from the shadows that threatened to consume him.

But whatever challenges were in his future, Jerry was ready to begin. The possibility that he might survive to see Alice again was all the motivation he needed. If indeed they were ever reunited, Jerry would never let anything draw them apart again.

She was just too good to be true.